P9-DNC-695

THE
EVERYTHING®
WINE BOOK

The Everything Series:

THE

EVERYTHING® WINE BOOK

Plus everything else you'll ever need to know to impress your friends and intimidate the wine steward

Danny May and Andy Sharpe

Adams Media Corporation
Holbrook, Massachusetts

An Everything® Series Book. The Everything® Series is a
registered trademark of Adams Media Corporation.

Published by Adams Media Corporation
260 Center Street, Holbrook, MA 02343

ISBN: 1-55850-808-2

Printed in the United States of America.

J   I   H   G   F   E

Library of Congress Cataloging-in-Publication Data
May, Danny.
  The everything wine book / Danny May and Andy Sharpe.
      p.   cm. — (The everything series)
      Includes index.
      ISBN 1–55850–808–2
  1. Wine and winemaking. I. Sharpe, Andy.
      II. Title. III. Series.
      TP548.M375   1997
      641.2'2—dc21   97–18140
                                    CIP

Product or brand names used in this book may be trademarks or registered
trademarks. For readability, they may appear in initial capitalization or have been
capitalized in the style used by the name claimant. Any use of these names is editorial
and does not convey endorsement of or other affiliation with the name claimant. The
publisher does not intend to express any judgment as to the validity or legal status of
any such proprietary claims.

ILLUSTRATIONS BY BARRY LITTMANN

This book is available at quantity discounts for bulk purchases.
For information, call 1-800-872-5627 (in Massachusetts, call 781-767-8100).

Visit our home page at http://www.adamsmedia.com

This book is dedicated to the winemakers of the world—the men and women who earn their living growing grapes, doing battle with weather, pests, and economics, in order to put affordable, quality wine on our tables. *Salut!*

D.M. and A.S.

Contents

CHAPTER 6: WINE AROUND THE WORLD

Introduction

The idea for this book came when we couldn't find a good general introductory wine book that truly addresses the monetary realities of wine. This book focuses on the $10-per-bottle-and-under wine experience. The vast majority of wine sold around the world costs less than $10 per bottle. These are the wines that we usually drink.

Learning about wine is, for many people, an important rite of passage into adulthood—an enjoyable experience with many benefits. For instance, your journey through the world of wine will entail a vicarious trip around the globe, perhaps to California, Australia, South Africa, South America, and through most of Europe. In all likelihood you will become familiar with a broad range of styles of wine and find among them your favorites. In fact, you will probably develop very definite ideas about what you find enjoyable—which grape varieties, which geographical regions or countries, and which producers. As your taste in wine becomes more sophisticated, so too will your appreciation of food; the two are not easily separated. Thus your newfound appreciation of good wine will add an extra dimension to the pleasures of the table. The ability to enjoy a good wine is an acquired one—and its own reward. Of course, this journey is not without its pitfalls.

Most wine merchants, large and small, offer a vast array of wines—red, white, and rosé wines from perhaps fifteen different countries. To the wine novice this can be baffling and intimidating, and it has discouraged many people from

learning more about wine. "Wine talk" is another common obstacle. The terminology used to describe wine can be difficult to comprehend, and all too often proves to be very subjective. To many beginners, the wine labels themselves do more harm than good, as far as describing the contents within. Some wines are labeled according to their region of origin; some are labeled by grape variety; and still others are sold under brand names. This confusion can easily lead to a bad experience with a wine purchase. For the novice this often means failing to decode both the label and the pompous description offered by a sales clerk, and bringing home a wine completely different from what was expected. Such a mistake can easily deflate one's enthusiasm for wine. To make matters even worse, wine has become associated with an unfortunate degree of social stuffiness, and a wine snob can be the most annoying snob of all. Because of such people, many wine novices have an unreasonable fear of looking foolish. As you learn about wine, you will soon find that all of these pitfalls are easily avoidable.

It is simple, really—read about wines, taste them, and make a note of what you like and dislike. If you taste without reading, your accumulated knowledge will consist of "I like this" and "I don't like that," without understanding the complex and wonderful reasons why wines taste the way they do. Conversely, if you read without tasting, you may well acquire a thorough working knowledge of the world of wine, but you will lack the most important information of all—what wine actually *tastes* like, the sensual experience that words cannot fully describe.

Buying and tasting wines yourself can be an expensive undertaking. Fortunately, many wine shops offer tastings on weekends. This can be a lot of fun, since you will be among other people with similar interests. Arranging group tastings with like-minded friends is a cost-effective way to sample several different wines of your own choosing. In either case, don't forget to take notes. Also, more and more restaurants and bars offer quality wines by the glass. Although you contribute greatly to the restaurant's profits by ordering wine this way, it still beats buying an entire bottle just to taste it.

There are many wine books

in print, several of which are directed squarely at the beginner. One problem shared by many of these "beginner" books is that they have been written by wine experts who seem to have forgotten that they, too, were once novices and have lost sight of the novice's perspective. The enormous wealth of wine information typically presented in these books is usually lost on someone with very little prior knowledge or experience. More often than not, the supposed "beginner" books are more suitable for someone wishing to establish a wine cellar than for someone who wants to find a good $7 red.

This book was not written by wine experts; rather, it is a unique collaboration of a relative newcomer to wine (Andy) and a knowledgeable wine buff (Danny). While writing *The Everything Wine Book* we realized that what we decided to leave out of the book was as important as what we put in it. There is too much information about wine for any one book, let alone a beginner's book. Therefore, much of this book is written from the perspective of the inquisitive novice who might ask:

- What do I really need to know about wine in order to get started?
- What do I need to know about purchasing wine, both in stores and in restaurants, in order to get the most for my wine dollar?
- How can I maximize my enjoyment of wine?

We also thought it would be useful to give an overview of the history of wine, in order to establish the important role of wine in our culture. Understanding that you are drinking five thousand years' worth of Western civilization will enhance your enjoyment. A grasp of the various processes by which wine is produced will give you a better understanding of the many different styles of wine available. Chapter 4, "Varietal Wines, Grape by Grape" addresses the distinctions among wines produced from different types of grapes. Similarly, Chapter 6, "Wine Around the World," explains the strengths and traditions of the world's leading wine-producing nations. The buying guides are intended to help you get the best wines for your money, and the "Wine with Food" chapter should enable you to succeed at the mysterious food–wine matching game.

Although we discuss wines ranging in price from $3 to $500, the goal of this book is to allow you to enjoy as many types of wine as possible that sell for no more than $10 per bottle. Accordingly, and with the novice in mind, we focus mainly on inexpensive and moderately expensive wines. We both agree that few pleasures in this world equal that of finding an inexpensive wine that has qualities that remind us of a greater, more expensive wine.

Best wishes to you on this wonderful journey through the world of wine. May *The Everything Wine Book* serve as a useful guide.

— Danny and Andy

EVERYTHING

C H A P T E R 1

WINE AND
WESTERN CIVILIZATION

BOTTLED BY ADAMS MEDIA

NET CONTENTS: TWELVE PAGES

PRODUCT OF USA

The evolution and development of wine has closely paralleled that of Western civilization itself. Wine was probably discovered by accident somewhere in the Fertile Crescent, the agriculturally generous expanse of river valleys extending from the Nile to the Persian Gulf. Early civilizations in the region (4000–3000 b.c.) owed their existence to the rich soils, and it is here that the wine grape first thrived. As primitive agricultural settlements gave way to powerful city-states, the seafaring and territorially ambitious peoples of the ancient world—first the Phoenicians, then the Greeks, then the Romans—distributed grape vines and winemaking know-how throughout the Mediterranean and Europe.

After the Roman Empire finally collapsed in the fifth century A.D., Christian monasteries in the Frankish Kingdom (France, northern Italy, part of Germany) kept detailed accounts of their grape cultivation and winemaking. This meticulous record-keeping helped to match the optimal grape varieties with the appropriate regions. The powerful influence of Charlemagne, who ruled the Frankish Kingdom from 768 to 814, extended to wine. The great emperor oversaw the establishment of vineyards from southern France to northern Germany, and the *grand cru* Corton-Charlemagne vineyard of Burgundy was once his property.

Under the rule of Queen Elizabeth I, Great Britain emerged as a naval power with a substantial merchant-marine fleet. Her seaborne international trade brought wine to Great Britain from several wine-producing nations of Europe, and the English thirst for fortified wines—Sherry, Port, and Madeira—is largely responsible for the development of these wine types.

By the time of the American Revolution, France was recognized as the greatest of the wine-producing nations. Thomas Jefferson enthusiastically wrote of their wine quality in correspondence to friends and encouraged the planting of European wine grapes in the New World. These early attempts at wine cultivation in the American colonies were largely unsuccessful, and the transplanting back and forth of European and native American vines inadvertently brought a destructive vine louse to Europe. The result was the *phylloxera* blight of the late 1800s that destroyed most of the vineyards in Europe. This disaster, however, was not without a silver lining—the ravaged vineyards inspired new cultivation techniques and a re-distribution across Europe of winemaking expertise.

The beneficial development in the agricultural sciences after the turn of the century enabled winemakers everywhere to protect their crops from common grapevine afflictions such as molds and pests. Grape-growing and winemaking became increasingly scientific. The twentieth century has also seen the widespread enactment of wine laws that guarantee authenticity and quality. Today wine is produced in temperate climates around the world, and there is a tremendous variety of wines available to the consumer.

The progression of winemaking from the earliest agricultural societies to the present day is a fascinating saga that reveals the fundamental significance of wine in our culture.

Ancient Wine

The discovery of wine was almost certainly an accident. Although the grape was known to early man—grape seeds have been discovered in ancient cave dwellings—the juicy, sweet fruit of the vine was probably a nutritious staple in the prehistoric diet long before it was known to ferment. Inevitably, the skins of some grapes held in storage were accidentally split, and wild yeasts worked their magic. Legend has it that an ancient king kept his beloved grapes in an earthen jar labeled "poison," and a discontented member of his harem drank juice from the jar in a suicide attempt. Instead of dying, she found her spirits rejuvenated, and she shared the drink with her king, who took her into his favor and decreed that, henceforth, grapes would be allowed to ferment. Men have been buying their women drinks ever since.

Mesopotamia (Persia) and Egypt, the endpoints of the Fertile Crescent, were the twin cradles of ancient winemaking. Both kingdoms were producing wine around 3000 B.C. Ironically, neither area has produced any wine of note for hundreds of years, although Egypt is in the process of restoring her winemaking capacity.

The ancient Egyptians cultivated grapes and made wine in a surprisingly modern fashion. Vines were carefully tended in the fertile Nile delta, and grapes were stomped and fermented in large wooden vats. As scientifically advanced as the Egyptians were, they could not have understood the biological mechanism of fermentation.

The wine of ancient Egypt was mostly sweet white wine, probably made from the grape now known as the Muscat of Alexandria, and it was considered to be a gift from the god Osiris. As a matter of respect to the gods, the Egyptians used wine in their funeral rites. Depending on the status held by the deceased, his body and belongings were anointed with wine prior to entombment.

The wines of Egypt found their way abroad in the ancient world. Many centuries after the decline of the Egyptian dynasties, her wines still enjoyed a fine reputation and were roundly praised in Roman writings.

The Mesopotamian culture in Persia was advanced in mathematics, commerce, and agriculture. Around 3000 B.C. the early Persians were producing wine from vines probably originating in the Caucasus foothills to the north. Like the Egyptians, the Persians regarded wine as a divine gift and made toasts of praise to their gods. The Persians loved their wine, and rightly so—the grape varieties they used are believed to be the precursors of the finest *Vitis vinifera* species.

Situated between Egypt and Mesopotamia along the Fertile Crescent were the Phoenicians, who sailed the Mediterranean from what is now the coast of Lebanon. Thus the grapevine—and wine—found its way to Greece, Sicily, and north-central Italy. Here the Etruscans, immigrants from the Caucasus, began to make fine wines in the region that is now Tuscany.

That the Old Testament mentions wine so frequently is an indication of the importance of wine in early Hebrew culture. Noah is said to have established a vineyard after the flood. Much to the chagrin of his maker, he also got drunk. When Moses led his people out of Egypt, they regretted leaving behind the delicious wine produced there. Their fears were calmed, however, when Moses's spies returned from the Promised Land with a giant cluster of grapes they found growing there. Jewish Law requires Kosher wine—pure, unadulterated, and produced under rabbinical supervision—for Passover rites and other religious ceremonies.

When Greek civilization expanded to the many islands in the Aegean and the Mediterranean, the Greeks found grapes already there, brought centuries earlier by the Phoenicians. Wine played an important role in Greek civilization. Dionysus was the native god of fruitfulness and vegetation, especially with regard to vine-growing. Wine was considered to be a gift from Dionysus, and one of the semiannual feasts of Dionysia was held in late December to celebrate the new wine of the vintage.

For the most part, the wines of the ancient world would not be well received by modern wine drinkers. Greek wine was typically stored in clay vessels lined with pine pitch, a flavor component found in modern-day Retsina. Additionally, wines in ancient Egypt, Greece, and elsewhere were flavored with additives such as herbs and seawater. Romans returning from Marseilles bemoaned the "smoked" wine they found there. It was not uncommon for wine to be smoked in a fire-house or boiled down to a syrup.

How to Enhance Your Wine-Drinking Experience

1. Sit on comfortable furniture.

2. Exercise during the day to help heighten your senses.

3. Let your wine breathe if it needs to. Ten minutes often goes a long way.

4. Use crystal wine glasses to add a little to the wine and a lot to the ambiance. (We don't own crystal, but if we did we'd use it.)

5. Make sure the lighting isn't too dim or too bright. Poor lighting can stress your senses.

6. Have some food in your stomach so you don't get "buzzed" prematurely.

7. Have a glass of water readily available, and don't be thirsty when you drink wine.

8. Keep the wine you are drinking in your mouth long enough to really taste it. Don't be afraid to move it around a bit with your tongue.

9. Don't drink your wine, especially white, so slowly that it warms up too much.

10. Drink wine with good and appropriate food.

11. Drink wine with good and appropriate people.

The Roman Empire: The Beginnings of Quality Wine in Europe

The Roman Empire covered, at its greatest outward expansion, most of the Mediterranean lands and a good part of Europe. The Romans found grapes already under cultivation in many of their conquered lands, the wine culture having been widely distributed by their Greek and Phoenician predecessors. The Romans, too, loved wine and fostered its development throughout the Empire. Whereas the Romans initially shared the taste of their predecessors for adulterated wines, it is likely that pure, fine wines, both red and white, were being produced in Spain, France, and northern Italy. Rome was devoted to the cult of Bacchus (the god of wine), and the methodical Romans developed sophisticated vine-growing and wine-making techniques that were unequaled until the eighteenth century.

The Empire was awash with wine—so much so that in A.D. 92 Emperor Domitian ordered that the great vineyards of France be uprooted. Fortunately that order was not fully executed, and it was rescinded two centuries later. When the Roman Empire fell for good in A.D. 476, the great wine regions of Europe—in northern Italy, in Germany, and in France—were under vines.

What we have come to think of as the European grape species actually originated in Asia Minor; however, the wine culture diminished in its birthplace and elsewhere outside of Europe due to the rise of Islam. In 634 the prophet Mohammed conquered the Meccans in the first jihad, or Islamic holy war. At its zenith (around A.D. 900) the Islamic Empire stretched from Spain to northern India. The Islamic code of law and theology forbade the consumption of alcohol, and wine production effectively ceased in these lands. The responsibility for the further development of wine culture thus fell to the rulers of the successor states (Germany and France) and the increasingly powerful Catholic Church.

1989
CASTELLO DI AMA
DRY RED TABLE WINE OF TUSCANY
VIGNA IL CHIUSO

Da uve raccolte nel 1989 nella vigna Il Chiuso,
del vigneto San Lorenzo.

ESTATE BOTTLED BY CASTELLO DI AMA S.p.A.
GAIOLE IN C. - ITALY

NET CONT. 750 ML - PRODUCT OF ITALY - ALC. 12.5% BY VOL

Wine in Europe

The grapevine was introduced to southern Gaul (France) long before the Romans arrived. The Romans, however, taught their sophisticated cultivation methods to the native Gauls and introduced hardier varieties to the northern regions. Monastic orders thrived in the duchies of France and Germany, and they often owned considerable vineyards. Many centuries of keeping records—of rainfall, crop yields, and grape varieties—enabled the medieval monks to plant the ideal grape varieties in the major regions.

At the request of Pope Urban II, armies of Christian soldiers set out from Europe to liberate the Christian Holy Land from the hands of the Islamic Empire. Seven crusades and two hundred years later, the European Christian soldiers had succeeded only in bringing chess and new strains of *Vitis vinifera* back to Europe. During this period the two most important regions of France, Bordeaux and Burgundy, further developed their reputations for producing quality wines.

In A.D. 1152 Henry II of England married Eleanor of Aquitaine (coastal France), and her dowry included the vineyard areas of Bordeaux and neighboring Gascony. The light-red wine of these regions gained favor in England, where it became known as Claret. By 1350, the port city of Bordeaux was shipping out one million cases of wine per year. Though Bordeaux red wines are now among the most ageworthy, Claret in this era was drunk young: Long-term aging was not possible until the development of proper bottles and corks in the late 1700s.

As England's seafaring capacity grew, so too did her taste for wines from the far-away vineyards of the Mediterranean. Many wines, however, did not ship well and spoiled during their voyage. Some ingenious shippers in Spain and Portugal added brandy to the wine barrels prior to shipment, with the intention that the wines be rewatered upon arrival in England. The journey at sea jostled and heated these fortified barrels. But the wine, immune to bacterial activity at the higher alcohol content, actually improved greatly along the way. Rather than redilute them, the British preferred to drink these fortified wines at full strength. Port from Portugal, Sherry from Spain, and Madeira from the Portuguese island of the same name became very popular as soothing tipples in cold and foggy England.

The wine grape was propagated by the Romans in the northerly Champagne region long before Champagne had bubbles. The delightful fizziness we associate with the beverage was probably another accidental discovery. It gets very cold in the

Champagne region; red grapes struggle to mature fully and to develop color in such a climate. It is conceivable that a cold spell after the harvest might have arrested the fermentation process of a still wine from the region. Then after a few warm spring days the yeast left in the bottle may have awakened from its dormancy, and—boom!— the bottle exploded from the buildup of carbon dioxide. Actually, probably quite a few bottles exploded, over who knows how many years, before they figured it out.

Legend credits Dom Pérignon, the blind cellarmaster at the Benedictine Abbey of Hautvillers until his death in 1715, with harnessing the second fermentation. In the late 1600s he is reputed to have introduced to the production of sparkling wine replaceable cork stoppers, thicker glass, and the concept of blending. However, another Champagne producer, Nicole-Barbe Ponsardin (the widow of François Clicquot), is credited with developing the technique for removing dead yeast from the bottle. Along with fortified wine and Claret, Champagne found favor with the English.

The French Revolution in 1789 had a negative impact on wine production in Burgundy. The vineyards there were seized from the Church and the noblemen and given instead to the people—few of whom were given enough acreage to produce their own wine. Most growers had to sell their grapes to *négociants* (shipper-bottlers) who did little to maintain Burgundy's reputation for quality.

When native American vines were brought to France—perhaps to help determine whether American soil was somehow to blame for the problems associated with growing the European grape varieties—the destructive *phylloxera* louse came with them. This contagious vine malady destroyed vineyard after vineyard in Europe and eventually spread to other continents when vines were transplanted.

The solution to the *phylloxera* problem was to graft European vines onto American vine roots, which are naturally resistant to *phylloxera*. The upside during all this turmoil was the flushing out of French winemakers from France. These craftsmen took their talents to vineyards in other European countries. In particular, the Rioja region of Spain owes its reputation for high-quality, affordable red wines to the displaced winemakers of Bordeaux.

In an effort to establish consistent standards for all of the important aspects of wine production—including region of origin, grape varieties, minimum alcohol content, and maximum vineyard yields—France enacted a series of laws beginning in 1905 collectively known as the *appellation d'origine contrôlée* (AOC) laws. These laws guard the famous place-names of France and guarantee that wines bearing their names have met rigorous government standards. In 1963 Italy followed suit with her own set of laws—*denominazione di origine controllata* (DOC) and *denominazione di origine controllata e garantita* (DOCG), by name. With these laws, Europe set the standard for the entire wine world in legislating the integrity of wine.

From Scuppernong to Merlot: The History of American Wine

The European explorers who discovered the New World were delighted to find a landscape practically smothered with grape-vines. Upon closer inspection, however, they found vines unlike the Old World varieties. Just imagine the French Huguenots trying to make wine from the native scuppernong grape in Florida. This native variety looks more like some carnivorous plant from *Lost in Space* than it does a European grapevine. The grape, twice the size of a European wine grape, grows in clusters, not bunches, on a gigantic vine capable of producing literally a ton of fruit!

Needless to say, the resulting wine bore little resemblance to Old World wine. Up north, in Virginia and New England, colonists also made disappointing wines from the native varieties. In comparison to European wines, the native American wines were said to have a "foxy" flavor—that is, grapey. This flavor comes from the presence of methyl anthranilate, a naturally occurring organic compound.

In the early 1600s some settlers brought European vines to the eastern United States only to see them succumb to the harsh winters and unfamiliar pests. This failure, along with the disappointing native American wines, helped whiskey to become the national drink. Hard cider, which is relatively simple to produce, was also quite popular.

Meanwhile, unbeknownst to the settlers in the East, Spanish missionaries began to successfully cultivate European grapes for sacramental wine in the coastal land north of Mexico. Needless to say, the European grapes found a happy home in sunny California. In the eastern states, the native American grapes were eventually "domesticated," and new varieties—such as Catawba, Concord, and Isabella—were developed in a manner not unlike new roses at the Garden Club. The American wine industry was on its way, with the unlikely state of Ohio leading the charge.

In the early 1800s, the Ohio River Valley proved to be a favorable growing area for American hybrid grape varieties, particularly the Catawba. This versatile grape can be made into all manner of still wine—red, white, and pink—as well as sparkling wine. In fact, the first American "champagne" was produced in southern Ohio, and so high was its quality that it actually inspired Catawba-based imitations in California!

By 1859 Ohio was ahead of all other states in wine prodution and was responsible for nearly 40 percent of the national output. Shortly thereafter, a vineyard blight destroyed the industry in southern Ohio. The northern Ohio wine industry took hold along the shore of Lake Erie in the late 1800s, only to be crippled by prohibition.

The Gold Rush of 1849 brought many settlers to California, and the wine industry there expanded rapidly. Railroads came along a few years later and brought California wine to the eastern markets. By the turn of the century the American wine industry was healthy enough to satisfy the growing domestic market and to ship wine around the world as well. California shot ahead of all other states in wine production.

Just when the American wine industry began to gather momentum, so too did the Prohibition Movement. In 1920, the United States made virtually all alcoholic beverages illegal. The destruction of the American wine industry by the misguided zealots who supported the Eighteenth Amendment (yes, the Constitution was changed) was severe. Uprooted vineyards and abandoned equipment were common sights. However, many growers and producers found creative ways to remain in the business.

Medicinal wine and wine-based tonics were not outlawed. When chilled, the medicinal additives settled to the bottom, leaving a somewhat palatable wine. Cooking wine could still be produced, so long as it was salted (so as to be undrinkable).

Sacramental and religious wines were still sold, especially to newly minted "rabbis" whose "synagogues" were really private drinking clubs. Most significant of all was a loophole in the Prohibition law that allowed the home production of "fruit juice"—up to 200 gallons per year! Since it is easier to make wine than beer or whiskey, the demand for grapes soared until 1925, when a huge surplus pushed the bottom out of the grape market.

As the industry rebuilt itself after the repeal of Prohibition, it found a market much changed in its thirteen-year hiatus. The quality of wine was very poor, in part because California grape growers were

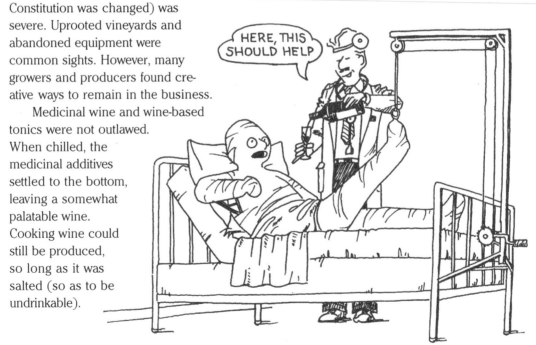

HERE, THIS SHOULD HELP

raising grapes that shipped well, rather than grapes that made fine wine. The public preferred "dessert wines"—fortified wines, actually—to dry table wines. Nonetheless, the American wine industry slowly recovered. Two changes took place in the late 1930s that helped this process.

First, French hybrids, crosses of native American and European vines, were brought back from Europe, where they had been developed to resist *phylloxera*. These new varieties were hardy enough to withstand a northeastern winter, yet yielded good-quality wine without a "grapey" taste. Second, varietal labeling became popular. In contrast to the French, who were drinking 40 gallons of wine per person per year in 1940, Americans were drinking a little less than 1 gallon of wine per capita. At the end of World War II the mass production of sweet Kosher wine began, as did the mass production of California jug wines.

The American wine boom really began with the affluence of the late 1950s. Wine was attractive to educated suburbanites, especially those wealthy enough to travel abroad. Wine, which to most of the wine-drinking world is a simple beverage, had become a status symbol in the United States. A few role models helped. When John F. Kennedy was sworn in he brought with him, among other things, a new sense of internationalism and his wife Jackie, who loved all things French. French restaurants—and French wines—became very trendy. In 1962, the film version of Ian Fleming's book, *Dr. No*, was released. The protagonist, British agent 007,

had expensive tastes in cars, women, and wine. From a kitchen in a Boston television studio, Julia Child taught a generation of Americans how to prepare French cuisine— and to match it with wine. By 1970, Americans were drinking well over a gallon of wine per person per year.

New products appeared in wine stores to meet the growing demand. Portuguese rosé, which perhaps blazed the trail for American white Zinfandel, hit the shelves around this time. Lancer's and Mateus, the two most common, were slightly fizzy, fruity, and sweet. The fact that they were imported from Europe gave these quaint wines sufficient cachet in the market. From West Germany came Liebfraumilch, a flowery, fruity, and slightly sweet blend of Riesling and other lesser grape varieties. Americans were switching back from the sweet, fortified Ports and Sherries to table wines, but they hadn't entirely lost their sweet tooth.

Meanwhile, California's reputation for world-class fine wines rapidly grew. In the early 1970s resourceful winemakers, many educated in their craft at the University of California at Davis, developed a whole new genre of California wine—high alcohol, big, fruity wine that took full advantage of the long California growing season. In a side-by-side blind tasting against fine French wines held in 1976, the American wines defeated the French wines and shocked the wine world with powerful, defeating finesse. American winemakers swelled with pride.

The market for varietal Cabernet Sauvignons was hot in that decade, whereas the market for varietal Zinfandel was not. Unfortunately, many growers had acre upon acre of Zinfandel vines whose grapes matured effortlessly in the California sunshine and provided blenders with a dependable workhorse of a grape. This surplus was the inspiration for "White Zinfandel." This fruity, pink, and slightly sweet rosé, a little classier than its Portuguese predecessor, found its way into every corner of the market. It was, for many customers, their first taste of wine. The popularity of white Zinfandel helped drive wine consumption in the United States up to 2 gallons per person per year.

The wine industry found it necessary to develop white Zinfandel because Americans in the 1970s showed a strong preference for white wine over red. While premium Cabernet Sauvignon was in demand and selling well, California growers found the Pinot Noir grape troublesome, and bothered little with Merlot which, they believed, had no future.

Why do the French—who smoke more than Americans, eat more red meat, and exercise less—have fewer heart attacks? Medical researchers who asked this question came back with a surprising answer to this "French paradox"—it is because the French drink red wine! Due to these findings, health-conscious Americans changed from white wine to red in the blink of an eye. And it was Merlot they turned to.

The Merlot grape has a well-deserved reputation for making soft, fruity wine—the perfect red wine for white-wine drinkers who never got used to the tannic edge of most Cabernet Sauvignons. Merlot has been used for centuries in Bordeaux to soften Cabernet-based wine, yet it was considered too insubstantial to make wine by itself outside of the Pomerol district of Bordeaux.

The rapidity and thoroughness with which Americans turned to Merlot is a measure of how highly they prize a "quick fix" to a medical quandary. "Drink red wine, live longer!" Simple. Except there wasn't nearly enough Merlot to go around. The price of Merlot grapes shot skyward, prompting growers to plant in less-than-ideal growing areas and to harvest grapes from younger vines. Winemakers, in turn, were financially induced to squeeze the expensive Merlot grapes harder (to get more juice) and to release the wine sooner.

All of this had an unfortunate result. Inexpensive Merlot can often be a harsh, angular wine instead of the soft, lush wine one associates with the Merlot grape. But the wine-buying public hasn't seemed to mind, and the Merlot boom is the legacy of the "French paradox."

There is good news for Merlot fans: All those recently planted Merlot vines are maturing, and this should result in better Merlot at stable prices. In the meantime, it is likely that the red-wine converts of the Merlot boom, looking for quality and value, will develop a taste for the other important U.S. red varietals: Cabernet Sauvignon, Zinfandel, and Pinot Noir.

EVERYTHING

C H A P T E R   2

An Introduction to Wine and Winemaking

BOTTLED BY ADAMS MEDIA

NET CONTENTS: TWENTY PAGES

PRODUCT OF USA

What Makes Wine Enjoyable?

We drink wine to stimulate our taste buds, alter our brains (via alcohol), and/or quench our thirst. If you are drinking wine to enhance your image, you need therapy, not wine. The human animal is designed to crave intellectual and physical stimulation. Stimulating the taste buds via food and beverages is a significant part of the so-called human experience.

Human taste is comprised of four basic components: sweetness, saltiness, acidity, and bitterness. Of major importance in both the production and enjoyment of wine is its natural acidity, the component against which the other taste components are balanced. In particular, the precise balance of acidity and sweetness—from natural sugars, "fruity" flavors, and/or alcohol—is the key factor that makes wine pleasant tasting. Too much acidity makes a wine taste unpleasantly sharp, whereas a lack of sufficient acidity results in an uninteresting wine that is neither clean tasting nor thirst quenching.

Flavors are detected by different taste buds in your mouth that individually perceive one of the four components of taste. The area most sensitive to sweetness is on the tip of the tongue, and the sensation is immediate. Taste buds that react to saltiness are on the sides of the tongue, with the acidity taste buds located toward the middle. The taste buds that detect bitterness are located at the back of the tongue, and are therefore the last to get involved with the food or beverage in your mouth. This is why people often note a bitter aftertaste when eating and drinking certain foods.

When tasting wine, a little stimulation of the bitterness-sensing taste buds is pleasant. Of course, what constitutes "too much" varies from one wine drinker to another, and also from day to day for any individual. People's mouths vary from day to day depending on what they ate today or yesterday, their physical health, the time of day, etc. If you burn your mouth on a hot slice of pizza, the acidity of any wine isn't going to feel good.

There are several different acids that occur naturally in wine—tartaric, malic, lactic, citric, and acetic acids. Therefore, when we speak of acidity in wines, we really mean the "acidity profile," the total and often complex acidic impression of the wine on the palate. The acidity profile and its corresponding balance of complementary components is of primary importance in white wines. Red and white wines with excessive acidity taste harsh, especially without food. Wines with too little acidity do not have an interesting taste and their flavor doesn't linger in the mouth very long. Although red wine is typically no less acidic than white wine, the acidity profile is often less apparent in reds because red wines usually display a more complex array of flavor components than do white wines. The difference is in the skins—white-wine grape skins are removed and discarded early in the winemaking process, whereas red-wine grape skins are generally kept in the fermenting vats long enough to give red wine its color, complex flavors, and tannin.

Tannin is an important component of red wine. Have you ever bitten into a grape seed? That dry, bitter taste is tannin. In moderate amounts tannin gives red wine an added flavor dimension as well as a natural preservative. Great red wines are often quite tannic in their youth; with aging the tannin softens and lends complexity to the mature red wine. In most red wines, tannin adds a pleasant, slightly bitter flavor that

is best balanced by rich fruit flavors. If you find it difficult to imagine bitterness as pleasant, think of expensive dark chocolate or rich espresso coffee; bitterness is certainly an important part of their flavors.

Red wine with too much tannin is bitter and unpleasant, and its fruit flavors may be hidden beneath the tannins. The correct amount of tannin doesn't mask other flavors, but instead gives the wine a little "grip" in the mouth and seems to hold all the flavors together. A low measure of tannin makes simple, fruity red wine more suitable for quaffing than sipping.

Generally speaking, a high level of tannin is an indication of a long shelf life, since tannin is a natural preservative.

The Wine Advocates Vintage Guide 1987-1995

REGIONS		1987	1988	1989	1990	1991	1992	1993	1994	1995
BORDEAUX	St. Julien/Pauillac St. Estephe	82R	87T	90E	98T	75R	79E	86T	89T	92E
	Margaux	76R	85E	86E	90E	74R	75E	85T	86T	86E
	Graves	84R	89E	89E	90R	74R	75E	87T	89E	88T
	Pomerol	85C	89T	92E	95E	58C	82R	88T	92T	92E
	St. Emilion	74C	88E	88E	98T	59C	75R	84C	86T	87E
	Barsac/Sauternes	70R	98T	90E	96T	70C	70C	70C	78E	85E
BURGUNDY	Côte de Nuits (Red)	85R	86E	87R	92R	86T	78R	87T	84E	87T
	Côte de Beaune (Red)	79C	86R	88R	90R	72E	82R	87T	84E	87T
	White	79R	82R	92R	87R	70C	92R	72C	89R	90E
RHONE	North-Côte Rôtie Hermitage	86E	92E	96E	92T	92E	78E	58C	88E	90T
	South-Châteauneuf du Pape	60C	88R	96T	95E	70C	78R	87R	89E	92E
	Beaujolais	85C	86C	92C	86C	90R	77C	86R	87R	89E
	Alsace	83R	86R	93R	93R	75E	85E	87R	93E	89R
	Loire Valley	82R	88R	92R	90R	75R	80R	86R	87R	88R
	Champagne	N.V.	88E	90R	96E	N.V.	N.V.	N.V.	N.V.	87E
ITALY	Piedmont	85E	90T	96E	96E	76E	74C	86E	85E	86E
	Chianti	73R	89T	72C	90E	85T	72C	86R	77C	90E
	Germany	82R	89R	90E	92E	85E	90R	87R	90R	87R
	Vintage Port	N.V.	N.V.	N.V.	N.V.	90E	95E	N.V.	92T	?
SPAIN	Rioja	82E	87E	90E	87E	76E	85E	87E	90E	87E
	Penedes	88E	87E	88E	87E	74E	82E	87E	90E	88E
AUST	New So. Wales & Victoria	87E	85E	88E	88E	89E	87R	87R	90E	87E
CALIFORNIA-N. COAST	Cabernet Sauvignon	90E	75E	84E	94E	94T	93E	91E	95T	90T
	Chardonnay	75C	89C	76C	90R	85R	92R	90R	88R	88R
	Zinfandel	90R	82R	83R	91R	91R	90R	90R	92R	90R
	Pinot Noir	86E	87R	85R	86E	86R	88R	88E	92R	88R
WASH/ORE	Pinot Noir	72C	88R	86R	90R	87R	88R	89R	92E	87E
	Cabernet Sauvignon	85E	88E	92E	87E	85C	89E	87E	90T	86E

KEY (General Vintage Chart)

- 90-100 = The Finest
- 80-89 = Above Average to Excellent
- 70-79 = Average
- 60-69 = Below Average
- Below 60 = Poor

EXPLANATION OF SYMBOLS

- C = Caution, too old or irregular in quality
- E = Early maturing and accessible
- T = Still Tannic and Youthful
- R = Ready to drink
- NV = Non-Vintage

Used with permission from Robert M. Parker, Jr., T/A The Wine Advocate, P.O. Box 311, Monkton, MD 21111 © copyright, 1996

How Wine Happens

Although winemaking has been raised to a fine art and an increasingly precise science over the last five thousand years, it remains, in essence, a relatively simple process. Wine grapes, *Vitis vinifera*, can grow with considerable ease in most warm-to-temperate climates. Ripe grapes contain a solution of natural sugar and water, with more sugar than in most other fruits. Additionally, the skin of the grape is an ideal medium for the accumulation of natural yeasts, one-celled plants that consume the natural sugar and convert it to ethyl alcohol and carbon dioxide. It is as if grapes *want* to become wine. Had we not evolved into humans, it is conceivable that apes could have learned to make wine—it is that simple. Of course, in the thousands of years since this process was first observed, technology has played an ever-increasing role in winemaking.

There are many technological options available to the modern winemaker. Equipment such as crushers, de-stemmers, and fermentation tanks come in so many shapes and varieties that each and every winery in the world might well have a unique configuration of them. However, whether the end product is red, white, or pink, and whether it is cheap or expensive, there are several principles common to all winemaking.

First of all, air is the enemy. Exposure to oxygen robs wine of its fresh-tasting qualities and also encourages the activity of acetobacters, which are naturally occurring microbes that consume ethyl alcohol and discharge acetic acid (vinegar). It is an ironic twist of nature that just as grapes wish to become wine, wine in turn aspires to become vinegar—again, with minimal effort. The winemaker, therefore, must take care to prevent air from ruining the wine. These precautions begin in the fields at harvest time.

It is crucial that the grapes are picked and transported to the winery without prematurely splitting the skins. While hand-picking is best, mechanical harvesting machines have been developed that can handle grape bunches with sufficient care. A judicious sprinkling of powdered sulfur dioxide (a sulfite), an effective anti-oxidant, is often applied to protect grapes prior to crushing.

Exposure to air is also minimized during fermentation, and nature lends a helping hand in this stage of winemaking. Carbon dioxide, which is discharged by the yeasts along with ethyl alcohol, provides a cushion of protection against the ambient air. This is especially important in the fermentation of red wine, which usually takes place in an open vat.

As a final precaution against the ill effects of exposure to air, many inexpensive wines are pasteurized—that is, heated to a high-enough temperature to kill the acetobacters. This is an effective way at least to delay the effects of oxidation, and it is the reason why jug wines enjoy such a long shelf life after opening. Inevitably, a new wave of acetobacters will find its way into the wine and begin the process of vinegar-making if the wine is kept too long. Because pasteurization is a harsh process that prevents the long-term evolution of wine in the bottle (*some* oxidation is actually beneficial!), this process is rarely used for high-quality wines. A famous exception is Château Corton-Grancey, a *grand cru* red from France's Burgundy region.

Clarity is another goal common to all winemaking, and the brilliant transparency of both red and white wines does not come naturally. Wine is, by nature, cloudy with dead yeast and tiny particulate matter. Several processes, including fining, centrifuging, filtration, racking, and cold stabilization, may be used to clarify wine.

Fining is one of the few processes in which foreign matter is introduced into the wine. Whipped egg whites have long been used as a fining agent for quality wines. Shortly after fermentation is complete, the wine is transferred to a large settling tank. When added to the tank of young, unfinished wine, the mass of whipped egg whites slowly sinks to the bottom, electrostatically attracting undesirable particles along the way. The clear wine is then drawn off, leaving the coagulated meringue at the bottom of

the barrel. In addition to egg whites, other fining agents are casein (milk protein) and bentonite clay (aluminum silicate).

Centrifuging and filtration are two quick and effective methods of clarifying wine. To centrifuge wine, a container of unfinished, cloudy wine is rapidly rotated so that heavy particles are separated from the wine by centrifugal force. Unfortunately, this process tends to strip wine of some desirable qualities as well, and centrifuging is being used less and less frequently for quality wines. Filtration is the simple and straightforward process of screening out unwanted particles from the wine by passing it through layers of filter paper or synthetic fiber mesh. Though less harsh than centrifuging, there are some fine wines with the term "unfiltered" on the label—the implication being that filtration also strips wine of some desirable qualities.

Compared to fining, centrifuging, and filtrating, the process of racking is a relatively passive means of clarifying wine. Racking works for the same reason as centrifuging: Unwanted particles are heavier than the wine itself and will eventually sink to the bottom if the wine is left undisturbed. The clear wine may then be "racked," that is, drawn off to another barrel. Again, air is the enemy, and unwanted exposure to air during the

POOF

racking process must be avoided. Red wines in particular, which are often held for many months in the barrel prior to bottling, may undergo multiple rackings.

Cold stabilization is a relatively harsh treatment used to clarify inexpensive wines. This process involves chilling a tank of wine almost to the freezing point. At this low temperature, minerals such as potassium acid tartrate (cream of tartar) become less soluble and precipitate out as crystals. Have you ever seen "wine crystals" on a cork? Though often mistaken for unwanted sediment, this accumulation of wine crystals is actually a good sign—it means that the wine has *not* been cold-stabilized, which would have eliminated the crystals prior to bottling.

HOW WHITE-WINE PRODUCTION AND RED-WINE PRODUCTION DIFFER

Although the prevention of oxidation and some process of clarification are common to all winemaking, there are fundamental differences between the production of red wine and that of white wine. In short, white wine is fermented grape juice—that is, the juice is extracted from the grapes prior to fermentation. Red wine, however, is the juice of fermented grapes, which are crushed into a thick mush—the "must"—from which the juice is extracted after fermentation. Interestingly, the finest rosés are often produced from red grapes handled like white grapes: The red grape skins, which provide color, are removed prior to fermentation, leaving only a slight blush of color in the wine.

The differences between the production of red wine and that of white wine begin in the vineyards. Most of the classic red-wine grape varieties—for example, Cabernet Sauvignon, Merlot, and Syrah—thrive in climates warmer than those that are ideal for the important white-wine varieties. Full ripeness is so crucial for red-wine grapes because the essential components of quality red wine—rich fruit flavors, tannin, body, and color—develop in the grape in the final stage of ripening. Paradoxically, these grapes must not ripen too quickly. If that happens, the resulting wine often lacks depth and harmony of flavors. The longer the growing season, the more complex the wine, and a prolonged growing season that doesn't bring the grapes to full ripeness until early autumn is ideal. Although most of sunny California's vineyards are planted in the warm valleys, the finest California reds usually come from grapes grown on the cooler slopes overlooking the valleys.

High-quality red and white grapes can often grow side by side, but in general the important white varieties perform best in climates too cool for great reds. Chardonnay, Sauvignon Blanc, and especially Riesling grapes tend to make uninteresting, low-acid wines in the same climates in which the great red grapes may thrive. But Chardonnay is made into the great white wine of the chilly Chablis region of France, an area whose red grapes rarely mature fully. Germany's Rieslings are among the finest wines in the world, yet German red wines are of little more than curiosity value. Riesling, along with an increasing amount of

Chardonnay, have been the only *Vitis vinifera* successfully grown in upstate New York where winter can be brutally cold.

Although the climates in which red- and white-wine grapes thrive may vary, the cultivation techniques are not that different. The real differences between red- and white-wine production begin after harvest.

White Wine

As soon as possible after picking, white-wine grapes are fed into a crushing machine that gently splits the skins. For most white wines, prolonged skin contact after crushing is not desirable, so the skins and other grape matter are quickly separated from the juice. However, in making some of the great white wines of the world the skins are allowed to remain in the juice for a day or so in order to lend additional body and character to the wine. A juicing machine uses pressurized sulfur dioxide gas to squeeze out the juice, which then goes to a settling tank, where undesirable solids such as dirt and seeds settle to the bottom. The juice might be centrifuged at this stage, but, as previously mentioned, the centrifuge can remove the good with the bad. The clarified white grape juice is now ready for fermentation . . . well, almost.

Some doctoring of the grape juice might be deemed necessary by the winemaker. Although regulations vary around the world, adjustments in acid and sugar levels are often called for. In cooler regions where even white-wine grape varieties struggle to achieve full ripeness, sugar may be added to the juice. This is called chaptalization.

Without enough sugar, the wine might not attain the desired alcohol level. Fully ripened grapes usually ferment to an alcohol content of 12 percent by volume. The acidity might also be adjusted at this point. Calcium carbonate may be added to reduce acidity, whereas tartaric or other acids may be added to raise it. In the final analysis, the sugar and acid must be in balance at the desired levels in order to make good wine. Now fermentation may begin.

Although wild wine yeast naturally accumulates on grape skins during the growing season, almost all winemakers prefer to control fermentation and therefore introduce carefully cultivated yeast to the juice. Fermentation proceeds—slowly, it is hoped, because a rapid fermentation might raise the temperature to a level that kills the yeast. Also, the yeast itself imparts character to the wine, so a slow fermentation, with longer contact with the yeast, is desirable. Most winemakers control the temperature of the fermentation by refrigeration and recirculation. The carbon dioxide that is produced during fermentation is permitted to escape from the enclosed vat without allowing ambient air back in—yet another precaution against oxidation.

Through this process, the white grape juice has become white wine—rough, unfinished wine that still needs some tinkering, including a filtration to remove any remaining sugar and particles. Just prior to fining, the winemaker may deem it necessary to add some sweet, unfermented grape juice in which the yeasts and acetobacters have been killed. This is done to add roundness to the flavor and to take the acidic edge off a harsh-tasting wine. However, the new wine has its own way of reducing its acidity: malolactic fermentation.

This process, like alcoholic fermentation, occurs naturally but is usually controlled by the winemaker. In the spring following the harvest, warm weather activates microbes in the wine that convert malic acid into lactic acid and carbon dioxide. Malic acid, which is naturally present in apples, is sharply acidic. Lactic acid, which develops naturally in dairy products, is only half as acidic as malic acid. Thus malolactic fermentation softens a wine's acidity profile. This process can be controlled by the winemaker to such a degree that one may find in the market clean, crisp white wines that have not undergone any malolactic fermentation; soft, fleshy white wines that have undergone full malolactic fermentation; and wines somewhere in the middle. Some wines have been known to undergo an unintended malolactic fermentation after bottling, resulting in a funny-tasting wine with an unwelcome trace of fizziness.

Up until a few decades ago, oak casks were the most economical storage vessels available. Oak imparts flavors to a wine, mainly vanilla and tannin. Because of the long history of wine storage in oak, these flavors have become accepted as basic components of wine. It is even likely that the style of certain wines, notably the Chardonnay-based white Burgundy wines, evolved in such a way that oak flavors are a necessary and expected facet of the wine's flavor; without oak, such wines might taste

incomplete. Now that less expensive storage vessels are available, such as those made of stainless steel, oak flavor is an additive of sorts. In fact, some producers of inexpensive wines circumvent the great expense of oak barrels by adding oak chips to wine held in stainless-steel tanks.

Virtually all wines benefit from a resting period after fermentation and clarification. A few months of aging, either in oak or steel, allows the flavor components in white wine to become more harmonious. Likewise, a resting period in the bottle is beneficial. An unfortunate consequence of the wine boom is that most wines are consumed long before they are at their best. Although red

Amazing Wine Facts

- Each year, over 40 percent of the wine produced in the world comes from either France or Italy.

- Over 30 percent of the wine consumed in the world is drunk in either Italy or France. Each year, residents and tourists in each of these two geographically small countries drink about 1/7 of the wine in the world.

- Wine consumption in both France and Italy is about twice that of the United States, yet twice as many people live in the United States than in France and Italy combined.

wines generally undergo a much more gradual evolution in the bottle than do white wines, a well-made white wine can improve for five or more years in the bottle. Chardonnays and Rieslings are known to age more gracefully than other white wines.

Red Wine

Red wine is not necessarily "better" than white wine, but well-made red wines have more flavor components and thus are typically more complex than white wines. Enjoyable white wine has a prominent acidity profile counterbalanced with a hint of sweetness, restrained fruit flavors, and maybe a touch of oak. That is why white wines are best served chilled—acidic beverages, such as lemonade, taste better at lower temperatures. If served warm, both lemonade and white

wine are less enjoyable because the prominent acidity becomes unpleasantly sharp at higher temperatures. Although red wine may be nearly as acidic as white, red wine usually has a wider range of fruit flavors as well as a noticeable amount of tannin, qualities best appreciated at warmer temperatures. The difference is skin deep.

Whereas all grapes contain the same greenish pulp, the skins of red-wine grapes give red wine its color, tannin, and assorted fruit flavors. So white grape skins, which add little to white wine, are removed early in the winemaking process, but red grape skins are kept in the fermenting vat for an extended period of time. It is therefore necessary to remove the stalks from red-wine grapes as they are crushed, lest the stalks impart excessive tannin on the wine. Thus a combi-

PRODUCE OF FRANCE

SAUVION & FILS

"LES BRÛLIS"

Sancerre

APPELLATION SANCERRE CONTROLÉE
LOIRE WHITE WINE

ALC. 12.5 % BY VOL.   750 ml

mis en bouteilles par

SAUVION ET FILS, LE CLÉRAY, VALLET (L.-ATL.) FRANCE

IMPORTED BY M.S. WALKER INC., SOMERVILLE, MA.

nation crusher/de-stalker is used to prepare red grapes for fermentation rather than the simple crusher used for white grapes.

The image of half-naked men stomping grapes in an open vat is familiar to many. Although technology has replaced the human foot in most corners of the wine world, the open vat is still widely used for red-wine production because grape skins tend to rise to the top of the fermenting must, forming a "cap" atop the juice. In order to extract the desirable qualities from the skins, this cap must be continuously mixed back into the juice. This may be accomplished by pumping juice from the bottom of the barrel over the cap (called "pumping over") or by manually punching the cap back into the juice with a special paddle (called "punched cap fermentation"). It is said that a punched-cap wine reflects the physical character of the wine-maker—a big, strong winemaker will force more extract from the skins, resulting in a big, strong wine. As in white-wine production, temperature control is important, though red wines benefit from a fermentation temperature a little higher than that which is ideal for whites.

After fermentation is complete, perhaps one to three weeks later, the new wine is drawn from the vat. This first run of juice, called "free-run" juice, comes forth voluntarily; forcibly squeezing the juice from the must would extract excessive tannin. Only after the free-run juice is removed is the remaining must squeezed, yielding "press wine," a portion of which might be blended with the free-run juice in order to carefully adjust the tannin level. The wine is then clarified in much the same manner as white wine and transferred to aging barrels, where it may slowly mature. Racking may be necessary every few months if the wine is held in the cellar for a length of time. Prolonged barrel aging before bottling is desirable for most types of red wine, since the broad array of flavor components generally needs more time to harmonize in red wines than in white wines.

Many wines, both red and white, are blends of several different grapes. Even in the case of wines made entirely from one variety, a winemaker may blend different "lots" (separate barrels) of wine in order to make the best possible wine. The "recipe" for such wines may vary from year to year, depending on the characteristics of the available lots in a given vintage.

When wine is deemed ready for release, it is transferred to bottles in a mechanized process notable for its sanitation. Once again, air is the enemy, and care is taken not to allow its contact with the wine during bottling. Germs and impurities are also mortal enemies, and the bottling process is often the most highly mechanized step in the entire operation, as sparkling-clean bottles are filled, corked, capped, and labeled with minimal human contact. For the finest wines it is often advantageous for the winery to then keep the bottles in storage for two or more years. This makes for better wine when it finally reaches the market, and in many cases the value of the wine will have increased greatly during its slumber.

Components of Wine

Water

Wine is mostly water—not added water but water gathered naturally in the grapes. Wine has long been consumed with food in regions where the local water is not reliably pure and safe. Wine may be described as "watery" when the other components, particularly acids, seem too understated.

Alcohol

Wine is ethyl alcohol (C_2H_5OH), 10–15 percent by volume. Fortified wine is usually 18–20 percent. Alcohol is an important flavor component—compare vodka to spring water if you don't think alcohol has flavor.

Tannin

This is a family of complex organic compounds extracted mainly from the grape skins (and thus a characteristic of red wines more than whites). Oak barrels also infuse wine with a touch of tannin. You can taste tannin when you bite into a grape seed. A wine with excessive tannin tastes like biting into a wool sweater. Tannin acts as a natural preservative, affording some wines the opportunity to improve with age. A moderate level of tannin also gives wine an added flavor dimension, albeit one that is often unpleasant to newer consumers of wine.

Fruit

The beauty of the noblest grape varieties, both red and white, is their ability to produce wine with a complex aroma of fruits other than grapes, particularly when young. Each noble variety of grape has its own set of typical fruit associations. During the winemaking process, the interaction of organic acids and alcohol forms compounds that imitate the aroma of other fruits.

Acid

There are several types of acid in wine. Together they form the wine's "acidity profile," which is balanced by sweet components. Tartaric, malic, and citric acids naturally form in grapes. After fermentation the malic acid may be converted to lactic acid (malolactic fermentation) through bacterial activity. The alcohol in wine may be converted to acetic acid (vinegar) by acetobacters, another bacteria found in wine.

Sugar

Not all of the natural fruit sugar in grapes is completely fermented. The residual sugar in dry wine is usually undetectable, but sweetness becomes noticeable in wines approaching 1 percent residual sugar.

Glycerine

This is the component that gives wines a desirable degree of viscosity (thickness). It is a complex alcohol, a by-product of the fermentation process.

Carbon Dioxide

This gas is produced during fermentation, and it is allowed to escape in the production of table wines. However, intentionally or not, some dissolved CO_2 may remain in the wine, giving a slight "fizz" to it. This can be a good thing in, say, an otherwise uninteresting rosé. Sometimes a minor second fermentation takes place after bottling, and the wine is ruined by the undesirable prickle. Sometimes a trace of fizz thus formed goes away with time. CO_2 is, of course, a very important component of sparkling wines.

Oak

Once a necessity, now an option, oak treatment—barrel fermenting; barrel aging; new oak or old, charred oak; French or American oak; oak chips—adds a flavor component to wine. Vanilla and tannin are two flavors given to wine by oak. Judicious use of oak complements the other components; too much oak can overpower the fruit. Just as a chef might try to dress up a mediocre fillet of fish with an interesting sauce, a winemaker might dress up an ordinary vat of Chardonnay with heavy-handed oak treatment.

These components—water, alcohol, tannins, fruit esters, acidity, sweetness, glycerine, carbon dioxide, and oak—are the ingredients that comprise wine as we know it. It is up to the winemaker who manages the process from vineyard to bottle to manipulate these components as he or she desires. For example, a gentle squeezing of the grapes extracts significantly less tannin than a powerful crushing. Acidity may be lowered by encouraging a malolactic fermentation, the process by which malic acid ("apple acid") becomes lactic acid ("milk acid"), and the wine consequently becomes less sharply acidic.

Nonalcoholic Wines

There are two basic ways to remove alcohol from wine. The high-quality and more expensive method calls for separating the water and alcohol from the rest of the wine by filtering it through very small pores and then rehydrating it. This is possible because water and alcohol molecules are smaller than the molecules of the other components. Such wines end up having about 0.5 percent alcohol. The other way to remove the alcohol from wine is to boil the alcohol and water off, and then reintroduce water to what is left.

A few different companies make nonalcoholic wine using the filtration process. Ariél wines are among the best of these, and they come in about half a dozen varieties, including sparkling.

"Contains Sulfites"

The sulfite known as sulfur dioxide (SO_2) is a compound consisting of sulfur and oxygen that occurs naturally during fermentation. However, because sulfur dioxide is helpful to the winemaking process, additional amounts of it are often added to wine. Its primary function is to inhibit wine from oxidizing during the winemaking process when it is exposed to air. It also helps prevent an unwanted second fermentation in bottles of sweeter wines by inhibiting leftover yeast from consuming residual sugars. Think of it as a food preservative.

With advances in technology, wine has been receiving less exposure to air, and so the need for sulfur dioxide has lessened. Winemakers today add less than before, but they are still adding a lot more than is produced naturally.

Some people with asthma have had life-threatening reactions to the sulfur dioxide in wine, so in 1988 the U.S. government mandated that all bottles of wine containing ten parts per million of sulfites carry the warning "Contains Sulfites." Other people have less dramatic reactions to sulfites, such as headaches and/or dizziness.

Even without the additional sulfites added by winemakers, most wines would exceed the ten parts-per-million threshold. Most people don't need to worry about sulfites, although the dire warning of their existence on a bottle of wine could make one think otherwise. The maximum allowable level of sulfites in wines sold in this country is 350 parts per million, but almost all wines contain less than half that amount.

If you want to enjoy wine and avoid sulfites, look for wines labeled "No Sulfites added." Some organizations that classify wines as organic actually allow wines that come from grapes grown without pesticides, but that have had sulfites added. Other such organizations do not. There is a good chance that your wine shop has a small selection of such wines, along with others labeled organic.

Sulfur dioxide is not the only additive contained in wine. Caramel, potassium sorbate, ascorbic acid, citric acid, and tartaric acid are some of the other things added to wine to help keep it stable.

Variety, Soil, Weather, and Winemaking Technique

There are four fundamental factors that endow wine with its characteristics: grape variety, soil, weather, and winemaking technique. Most winemakers would agree that luck is the fifth factor, since the art of winemaking is never completely subject to scientific controls.

GRAPE VARIETY

Think of white wines as cats and red wines as dogs. There are many different breeds of each, just as there are many different types of grapes within the species *Vitis vinifera*. Each breed of dog or cat has unique identifiying characteristics. Just as Golden Retrievers typically have long, orange-brown fur, Cabernet Sauvignon–based wines tend to display aromas of black currants, green pepper, and chocolate. We use the term "varietally correct" to describe wines whose qualities are consistent with their predominant grape variety. Some great wines, notably the whites of Alsace (France), are sometimes more identifiable for their region of origin than for their grape variety. However, there are some generally accepted varietal characteristics associated with the popular grape varieties. Here are two examples.

Cabernet Sauvignon
Aromas: black currants, green pepper, chocolate, mint, leather; jammy fruit when young, cedar and tobacco with age
Color: deep purple/red

Flavors: moderate acidity balanced by fruit flavors, firm tannin, long progression of flavors on the palate.

Sauvignon Blanc
Aromas: cut grass, fresh green herbs, asparagus and other vegetables
Color: pale gold, sometimes greenish
Flavors: crisp, prominent acidity, herbaceous rather than fruity flavors.

It would be a boring world of wine if all Cabernet Sauvignons and all Sauvignon Blancs were identical. That there are so many different styles of each is testimony to the importance of the other three factors. It is really a "nature vs. nurture" debate. Grape varieties have inherent characteristics that can be altered or re-interpreted by the soil, the weather, and the winemaker's technique.

THE SOIL IN WHICH GRAPES GROW

The rich, low-lying valley floors and river deltas where so many crops thrive are not the best locations for growing wine grapes. The grapevine grows well in rocky hillsides where no other crops will and seems to prefer gravel to earth. Abundant water, so vital to other crops, can be anathema to wine grapes. The vine will dig deep for its water, sometimes as much as 10 feet down. Irrigation is relatively uncommon in the vineyards of the world.

California wineries tend to emphasize grape variety and weather, whereas the French stress the importance of the geographical region of origin. Soil (*terroir*), they believe, gives wine its distinctive character. The established French wine-growing estates are not permitted to bring soil from elsewhere into their vineyards. Ironically, the soil in the Romanée-Conti estate, perhaps the most highly esteemed parcel of vines in France, was imported from France's Saône River banks two hundred years ago!

Each of the major wine regions of France has unique soil characteristics. For instance, the Graves subregion of Bordeaux gets its name from the notably gravelly soil deposited along the Garonne River by the most recent glacial advance. The red wines of the Graves are among the most powerfully flavored reds of Bordeaux, and the crisp, acidic whites are among the finest white wines in the world. The *goût de terroir*, the particular flavor imparted by the soil, is evident in both.

Limestone and chalk are common components of the soil in which Chardonnay performs well. Such soil is found in the Champagne region and the Burgundy subregions of Chablis and the Côte de Beaune. The Gamay grape is not highly regarded in the heart of Burgundy, where Pinot Noir holds court as king of the red grapes. However, south of Burgundy proper is the Beaujolais subregion, where the soil is especially rich in granite. In this medium, the otherwise lowly Gamay produces the beloved red wines of Beaujolais. The soil of Châteauneuf-du-Pape in the southern Rhône valley is notable for its large white rocks that retain and reflect heat toward the vines. As a result, the red grapes

grown there—Grenache, Syrah, and others—achieve a degree of ripeness not found elsewhere in France, and the wines from this area are correspondingly bold.

Weather

Soil is the most constant factor in winemaking; the mineral composition of a vineyard barely changes in a human lifespan. Although the weather is different in every growing season, general trends such as annual rainfall and temperature ranges may be somewhat constant. Thus the vineyard locations in France were probably chosen for their climate as well as their soil.

Geographically, soil and long-term weather trends are inextricably linked. Yet wine grapes grow for only about six months. The weather in a given growing season, though somewhat predictable (based on historical trends), is the reason that we have good years and bad years for wine. So soil is one-half of the "nurturing" process, and weather is the other half.

New vineyard sites are usually selected for their "microclimate," the weather trends in the vineyard plot itself. In the hilly regions where the grapes are grown, the weather can vary from one corner of the fields to the other. Vineyardists, especially those in California, have made an obsession of seeking the ideal climate for growing grapes.

THE VINEYARD YEAR

Spring

It is best that early springtime remain cool, with no early heat waves. Otherwise, leaf buds might prematurely develop, only to be killed by a cold night's frost. This period is one of the few opportune times for abundant rain, which becomes less desirable as the growing season progresses. Grape leaves unfurl in late April, followed by flower buds in late May. (Of course, we are referring to the Northern Hemisphere, where the vast majority of wine is produced. The vineyards of the Southern Hemisphere—in Australia, South Africa, New Zealand, and South America—harvest in March.) Hail, obviously, is a dreaded enemy of the vine during the critical month-long flowering. High winds and heavy downpours can also interfere with pollination during this period.

Summer

After the bees have completed their work of pollination, the grapes themselves require about three months to ripen completely. An occasional gentle rain is welcome in early summer, as it helps to fill the grapes with liquid to plump them up to the proper size. A drought year would result in small grapes with a high skin-to-pulp ratio, which in turn would make it a tannic, intensely flavored wine. As the grapes mature, dry and cool breezes are a blessing because they help to keep the grapes free of disease and to slow the ripening process. Grapes that ripen too rapidly tend to develop less flavor. As during the flowering stage, hail is a dreaded summertime enemy.

Autumn

September is a critical month. A warm and dry September can rescue a lousy vintage, and a cold and rainy September is sure to ruin a previously perfect growing season.

Phylloxera

Phylloxera is a disease that attacks and destroys the roots of *Vitis vinifera* grapevines. In the 1800s, this disease nearly wiped out most of the vineyards of Europe. Fortunately, the wine grapes indigenous to North America, *Vitis labrusca*, were resistant to *phylloxera*. Scientists in Europe were able to graft *vinifera* vines to the roots of *labrusca* vines. Not only did this work, but the characteristics of the individual *vinifera* grapes were not compromised by the foreign roots.

Phylloxera helped spread the art of winemaking throughout the world by forcing French winemakers to leave France for *phylloxera*-free pastures. Many winemakers from Bordeaux brought their expertise to the Rioja region of Spain when their own vineyards were destroyed.

Like germs that evolve into new forms that are resistant to conventional treatments, new strains of *phylloxera* have emerged to which the native American rootstock is not resistant. *Phylloxera* destroyed many of the California vines in 1996. This will cause the price of many California wines to continue to increase into the twenty-first century. Undoubtedly, the wine industry will team up with science and successfully respond to the latest strain of *phylloxera* with another genetically engineered solution.

All of the grapes in a vineyard do not ripen simultaneously—good thing! If they did, it would be impossible to pick and crush them simultaneously. A perfect September would be without rain while the pickers make pass after pass through the rows of vines, picking only the grapes at the exact point of ripeness. An impending rainstorm leaves a vineyardist with a difficult choice— either pick the grapes a few days shy of perfect ripeness or pick rain-swollen grapes after the storm and run the risk of rot.

After the harvest is complete, the weather can still be a factor. Cool weather is welcome during the fermenting period, especially for small wineries that don't have sophisticated, temperature-controlled fermenting tanks. The cool drafts around the tanks help to prolong the fermenting process and prevent over-heating. In Germany and Canada, a timely deep freeze makes *eiswein* (ice wine) possible. When crushed, the frozen grapes yield a nectar of incredible richness.

WINEMAKING TECHNIQUE

The skill of the winemaker is admirably utilized in solving problems associated with less than ideal weather, and the winemaker's ingenuity is often required early in the growing season. A frost following an early warm spell could well destroy the first vine buds, but a clever sprinkling of mist on the vines covers them with a protective shield of ice, which paradoxically insulates them from colder, more harmful temperatures. Frequent rainfall later in the season invites grape rot of various sorts, which can be combated with sensible use of chemicals. Each and every vintage will yield grapes of unique

character, and it is the task of the wine-maker to make the best use of each harvest. This is undoubtedly a delightful task after an ideal growing season; in reality, however, there are usually problems to be overcome.

A cold, damp summer—very rare in California and Australia, but common in France—is not conducive to full ripeness. Under-ripe grapes, both red and white, usually lack sufficient sugar to ferment to the desired alcoholic strength. The addition of sugar prior to fermentation is called chaptalization; it is permitted in some European countries but is unnecessary in California and other warm regions. Also, under-ripe red grapes usually lack the concentration of desirable components in the skin-pigment, tannin, and fruit flavor. A skilled winemaker might compensate for this deficiency by allowing the skins to macerate in the juice for a longer time than is usual.

After fermentation it may be desirable to adjust the acidity of the wine. The addition of calcium carbonate will soften the acidity associated with under-ripeness, whereas natural wine acids (tartaric, malic, etc.) may be added to sharpen a flaccid, over-ripe wine.

With one eye on quality and the other on cost, the winemaker has to make many choices: Stainless steel or oak? New oak or old oak? Oak costs money; will the wine be worth it? How much press wine should be blended back into a wine made from free-run juice? Ideally, in making these and other choices the winemaker brings out the best in the grapes, and from them crafts a wine that reflects the hereditary qualities of the grape variety and the unique composition of the soil, and addresses any problems caused by the weather.

Hybrids

A hybrid grape is a cross-breed of two grapes of different species. The classic European species, *Vitis vinifera*, is responsible for all of the great wines of the world. The early colonial settlers found many different grape species in the New World, most notably *Vitis labrusca*, *Vitis riparia*, and *Vitis rotundifolia*. In an effort to "domesticate" the native American grapes, the early American settlers cross-bred different native American species. Among these American Hybrids, the early successes include the Catawba, the Concord, and the Delaware.

Unbeknownst to the early American grape-growers, the American vines often harbored a vine louse, called *phylloxera*, in their roots. Whereas the native American species were resistant to its attack, the European species were not. When American grapes were foolishly transplanted in Europe, disaster struck. The vigorous vine louse attacked and destroyed most of Europe's vineyards in the late 1800s. The hybridization of *Vitis vinifera* and *Vitis labrusca* was an attempt to produce a quality grape that was resistant to *phylloxera*. These cross-breeds are known as French Hybrids.

As it turned out, the grafting of European vines onto American rootstocks proved to be a better solution to the *phylloxera* problem. However, French Hybrids remain with us and produce quality wines in the northeastern United States, where the climate is unsuitable for most European varieties. Baco Noir, a hybrid of *Vitis riparia* and the European Folle Blanche grapes, makes an enjoyable and surprisingly full-bodied red wine in New York and Canada. French Hybrids are now outlawed in France under appellation d'origine contrôlée laws.

Many attempts have been made to cross-breed grapes within the *Vitis vinifera* species. Ideally, a cross-breed will display the best qualities of each grape and none of its shortcomings. This hasn't really happened yet, although there have been some minor successes. Pinotage, a successful red variety grown exclusively in South Africa, is a cross of Pinot Noir and Cinsault, a minor red Rhône variety. The Flora grape is an interesting cross of Gewürztraminer and Semillon. Perhaps the most important cross-breed grown today is Germany's Müller-Thurgau, a cross of the noble Riesling and the prolific Sylvaner.

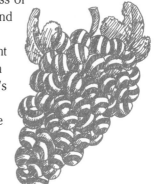

EVERYTHING

C H A P T E R 3

QUALITY ISSUES: HOW TO TELL GOOD WINE FROM BETTER TO BEST

BOTTLED BY ADAMS MEDIA

NET CONTENTS: TWELVE PAGES

PRODUCT OF USA

The winemaker, part artist and part scientist, manages the winemaking process from vineyard to bottle. There are variables every step of the way, and here the relationship between the quality of wine and the cost of producing it is clearly seen.

Let's look at the grapes. There are mediocre grapes, picked, perhaps, from very young vines growing in regions too warm or too cold for that particular variety. Maybe they were picked a few days too early to avoid a predicted thunderstorm. Or maybe they were picked after the storm and their rich fruit was diluted by an unwanted infusion of water.

Mediocre grapes in the hands of a skilled winemaker can make enjoyable, pleasant wines, priced for everyday drinking. These wines may even constitute a bargain. But they can *never* be great wine, any more than an expertly driven Ford Taurus can win the Indy 500.

Then there are good grapes, well grown in good regions under favorable conditions. These might be blended with lesser grapes to produce a decent wine at a particular price and quantity. Or they may be used alone to make a higher quality wine.

Great grapes, carefully tended to maturity in well-known vineyards, command the highest price and produce the most expensive wines. The labels on these bottles might proudly display the name of the vineyard.

Now grapes, whether purchased on the market or picked from the winery's own acres, must be crushed. The cheapest way is to press the grapes along with the leaves, stems, and whatever else has been picked by the machines (used because it's cheaper than hand-picking) and squeeze them until no more liquid remains. This extracts the most juice, of course, but it draws harsh tannins from the grapes as well. The most expensive method is to virtually let the grapes crush themselves with their own weight. The resulting "free-run juice" is prized and accordingly expensive. Again, wine from each process can be blended or not—choices must be made.

Other choices must also be made—such as new oak barrels versus old (new oak is better because it exerts more oak flavor), and barrel or steel-vat fermentation. Such decisions are made with one eye on quality and the other on cost. Each of these components contributes to the broad spectrum of wines costing from $3 to $500 per bottle.

The Quality Spectrum

CATEGORY 1: JUG WINES ($3–5 PER 750 ML)

These wines are named for their large bottles. Because they are usually made from blends of lesser grapes, their label will not indicate a grape variety. Jug-wine producers from California have borrowed famous names from Europe: Chablis, Rhine, Burgundy, Chianti, etc. This trend, however, is fading. Look for brand names or simply red, white, or rosé.

Most Americans know of the chablis (with a small "c"), the light, inexpensive, inoffensive, off-dry, white jug wine, before they, if ever, learn of Chablis, the wine village in France. True Chablis can be among the world's best Chardonnays. These wines are labeled Chablis, not Chardonnay, since the European custom is to name wines after regions and not grapes. This custom also applies to Burgundy, Chianti, and Rhine.

The Burgundy region of France produces Pinot Noirs of unsurpassed quality. This has nothing to do with California "burgundy," although they are both red wines. The Chianti district of Italy produces wine made from Sangiovese grapes, some of which are among the world's best red wines. California "chianti" is off-dry and simple red wine. Finally, Rhine is a German wine region famous for its Rieslings—flowery, off-dry, and complex. California "rhine" is merely white and off-dry.

These four names cause a great deal of confusion for the novice wine drinker. When the knowledgeable wine consumer hears or reads about one of these four regions, he or she thinks in terms of great quality and great tradition. The American novice on the other hand, thinks of mass-produced, generic wines. This is just one of the many examples of the wine language barrier that makes entering the wine world difficult.

Despite this misuse of famous European wine place names, California jug wines aren't all that bad. These wines are made to be inexpensive but good tasting—two good qualities in any beverage. In fact, these wines can be an excellent value when the occasion calls for a simple wine.

I FIND IT HAS AN OPULENT BOUQUET BUT WITH A TOUCH OF IMPUDENCE

CATEGORY 2: "FIGHTING" VARIETALS ($5–8)

These inexpensive wines are labeled and sold under varietal names—Chardonnay, Merlot, Cabernet Sauvignon, Chenin Blanc, and Pinot Noir, to name some of the most commonly offered types. Unfortunately, they are often recognizable in name only, as the signature qualities of the grape varieties rarely appear in this price range. This doesn't mean these wines can't taste good, but the good-tasting $7 Merlot may not taste very much like a Merlot.

They do, of course, comply with labeling laws. However, these wines are not usually produced from better lots of the indicated variety; they instead represent the bottom of the heap. It is also safe to assume that a hefty portion of your wine dollar frequently goes to waste on the varietal name. Suffice it to say that people who demand cheap Chardonnay and Merlot get what they deserve. However, a bargain-rich country like Chile does produce some pretty good Merlot for $7 or $8.

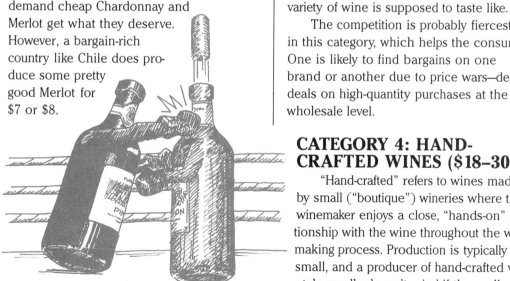

CATEGORY 3: MID-RANGE VARIETALS ($8–18)

Mid-range varietals fill a need in the wine market that went unmet until the mid-1980s—affordable, "good" wines labeled according to grape variety. Like fighting varietals, midrange varietals don't vary much from year to year. The majority of such labeled wines sold in North America come from California. What, then, is different? For a couple of dollars more, you can buy a Chardonnay that is varietally recognizable. These wines are better, and they allow you to understand what a particular variety of wine is supposed to taste like.

The competition is probably fiercest in this category, which helps the consumer. One is likely to find bargains on one brand or another due to price wars—deep deals on high-quantity purchases at the wholesale level.

CATEGORY 4: HAND-CRAFTED WINES ($18–30)

"Hand-crafted" refers to wines made by small ("boutique") wineries where the winemaker enjoys a close, "hands-on" relationship with the wine throughout the winemaking process. Production is typically small, and a producer of hand-crafted varietals usually doesn't mind if they sell out

of wine in a given year. In contrast, midrange, volume-oriented producers usually have stockholders to satisfy, and selling out of wine would present a business problem. Such wineries have been known to purchase bulk, unfinished wines, even from other countries, and blend, bottle, and sell it under their own label.

Hand-crafted wines also differ from large, midrange producers in terms of consistency from year to year. Whereas the large producer is inclined to strive for a uniform product from each vintage, hand-crafted wines may vary from one vintage to the next because the wine reflects the idiosyncrasies of each vintage.

CATEGORY 5: RESERVE WINES ($30 AND UP)

The reserve designation, without legal meaning in the United States, is often used to indicate a wine of greater quality than the winery's regular offering. It usually means that better grapes, or better lots of blending wine, were used in its manufacture. Because the term may be used without legal restriction, the term

"reserve" might well appear on a very ordinary and inexpensive bottle of wine in the United States.

CATEGORY 6: NONVARIETAL WINES (USUALLY UNDER $10)

"Nonvarietal" has two meanings. One meaning is that the wine in your bottle doesn't contain an overwhelming amount of any single grape variety. The other meaning is that the label doesn't specify the grape variety, if any, from which a wine is made. The latter case is common practice in European wines.

Worldwide, the vast majority of inexpensive wine is sold without a grape variety listed on the label. Jug wines and table wines are labeled red, white, or rosé, with no varietal indicated. Most Italian and French wines, from ordinary table wines to the finest wines, indicate the geographical source rather than the grape variety. Varietal labeling is most common outside of Europe, where consumers have become accustomed to purchasing specific varieties instead of wines from a specific region.

A high-end exception to this generalization is "Meritage" wines. According to United States law, wines comprised of less than 75 percent of any one variety must be called "table wine" (nonvarietal). The California wine industry coined the term "Meritage" to indicate a level of quality of nonvarietal wine far superior to ordinary "table wine."

Vintages

Because wine is an agricultural product that can keep for several years, most quality wines give the year of harvest on the label. Yet, the vintage date is a frequently misunderstood piece of information. The year of harvest tells you two things: how old the wine is, and, because climate conditions vary from year to year, whether or not the wine was produced in a "good year." But a "good" year can be many things: an abundant harvest, a high-quality harvest, or both. Growing conditions might have been excellent in one area but below average in a neighboring area; that's why we call them *micro*climates. Also, growing conditions might have been terrific for one grape variety but not another.

The vintage date, especially for inexpensive wines, can serve as a "freshness date." Most white and rose wines are best drunk before their second or third birthday. Even inexpensive red wines are made to be consumed right away rather than aged for several years. It is a truism yet to be refuted that red wine is either enjoyable in its youth or enjoyable in full maturity, but not both. Great chardonnays, especially those from Burgundy (France) can improve for several years in the bottle, as can sweet dessert white wines. Aside from these exceptions, younger is probably better for inexpensive wines.

For the great wines of the world, some years are much better than others. There are many different regions in the world that produce great red wine. However, until recently, a "good year" meant a good year for red wine in Bordeaux, France, where 1961 was regarded as "the vintage of the century." A unique year it was. The grape crop in Bordeaux was nearly destroyed by bad weather early in the season, but a gorgeous summer ripened the remaining grapes to perfection. Thus the 1961 Bordeaux reds were both superb and scarce. Thirty-five years later, some of them are still improving in the bottle.

The year 1964 was a split-personality year in Bordeaux. In Pomesol and Saint Emilion, where the earlier ripening Merlot grape predominates, the wines were outstanding. However, across the river in Medoc and Graves, heavy rains fell before the Cabernet Sauvignon was harvested, and the Cabernet-Sauvignon based wines from these districts were rather thin. It is likewise true in California that the quality of a vintage may vary somewhat from one microclimate to another and from one grape variety to another.

California has remarkably consistent growing weather and "bad years" just don't seem to happen. Some years, however, have been better than others, and there has recently been a succession of very good years beginning in 1990.

So, unless you are shopping for expensive wine of the "vintage-sensitive" type—Piedmontese and Tuscan red wines from Italy, Red Bordeaux, or Red and White Burgundy—do not place too much stock in the vintage date. Do use the vintage date to make sure that the wine you are buying is still young enough to enjoy as it was intended to be.

$25 Bottles of Wine Worth Buying and Worth Saving

1. *Champagne on sale.* Champagnes are often discounted as much as 20 percent. If you like Champagne, you may want to splurge on a $30 bottle marked down.
2. *White Burgundy.* There are some wonderful and ageworthy French Chardonnays. If you like to have good Chardonnay with good food, these are worth it.
3. *Riesling from Alsace, France.* Bottles in this price range will make you realize what the Riesling fuss is all about. Trimbach and Hugel are two of the top producers.
4. *Dessert Wines from Germany or France.* Dessert wines aren't for everyone, but if they are for you, then try a half bottle of German dessert wine or a Sauternes from France for $25.
5. *Super-Tuscans.* These blends of Sangiovese and Cabernet Sauvignon from Italy can be aged a long time. If you like a big mouthful of red wine, and you also like some subtlety and complexity, then you'll like these reds.
6. *Nebbiolo-based Piedmont wines.* Also worth the money in this price range, these wines are fairly big reds and are terrific with Northern Italian cuisine.
7. *Châteauneuf-du-Pape red wines.* These can be made from any or all of thirteen wine-grape varieties. French quality really shows in the finest examples.
8. *Pinot Noir from the Carneros region of California.* These wines are excellent with food and easy to drink.
9. *Vintage Port.* These are a treat, especially during the colder months. Dow and Croft are two excellent producers. It is available in half and full bottles. Spend less and/or get more with a Warre's Warrior Port.

The Price Components of Expensive Wines

An expensive wine doesn't start out like ordinary wine. By this we mean that it isn't discovered, nor does it develop by chance. It is expensive to make, and it is made to be expensive.

The best grapes grow in the best vineyards. The best vineyards don't have the most fertile soil, but they do have the best soil for growing wine grapes. These soils pass on elements of mineral flavor to the grapes and thus to the wine. These vineyards also have good climates for growing wine grapes. The concept of microclimate is very big in the wine world. The amount of sun and cooling breezes can vary from acre to acre in areas with hilly terrain.

These differences contribute to differences in grape flavors. The better the vineyard, the more expensive the land. Vineyards worthy of individual recognition are few in number, so the cost associated with a limited resource that is in demand certainly comes into play. Unlike the contrived scarcity of diamonds, the scarcity of top vineyard acreage is quite real.

In addition to the vineyard factor is the vine factor. Older vines produce fewer but better grapes. So it is more expensive to have older vines in the ground because they yield fewer bottles. Some wine labels that claim old vines are stretching the truth. There is no accepted standard as to just what constitutes "old vines."

All grape juice isn't created equal. The best wines are made from the best juice. This juice costs more than lesser juice, especially when it is bought on the open market. Free-run juices come from grapes that are lightly crushed or allowed to crush themselves under their own weight. Often grapes whose best juice has been drained off are then more thoroughly crushed. That juice is used for lesser wines.

The top juice is often put into the best oak barrels that money can buy—made from French Limousin Oak. A new oak barrel can add a dollar or more to the cost of producing each bottle of wine from that barrel. After the best juice is allowed to ferment and/or age in the best barrels, the winemaker comes along and chooses the best of the best to be his top wine. The rest of the best will probably become the second-string wine, which is still going to be very good and quite expensive, but not the best.

Many top wines are crafted to be aged many years to bring out the best a grape has to offer. This cellar aging in a barrel or a bottle certainly doesn't help cash flow. This, therefore, is another factor in pricing.

Top wines from top winemakers have a loyal following who support the pricing of these wines. If the quality falls off, then these winemakers lose the necessary buyers. They can't afford to cut quality, even if it means producing far fewer bottles of these expensive wines in an off year. Some of these top wines may not be produced at all in some years, yet much of the cost is still incurred.

Why Expensive Wines Are Worth It to Some People

If you've ever been to a good wine store, you probably have looked at the expensive wines and wondered a few things. The biggest puzzle to you might be why anyone would spend hundreds of dollars for a bottle of wine.

Getting a wine neophyte to understand this practice is like trying to get an atheist to believe in God. It takes a leap of faith. If you have never tasted a good $20 bottle, the leap to a $100 bottle is gigantic. Think of it as listening to a symphony orchestra performance in person at symphony hall versus listening to the same music on your home stereo. Going from a $10 bottle to a $20 bottle is like buying better speakers for your stereo. When you get to a certain level of wine quality, buying a great wine becomes like buying tickets to a live performance.

However, just because the music sounds better doesn't mean you will enjoy it any more. The same is true for wine. Just because you are drinking a better wine, it doesn't mean you are going to enjoy the wine-drinking experience more. If

you love music, you know that just being able to listen to your favorite song on any music system can be one of life's most enjoyable experiences.

There are a lot of expectations when one goes to the symphony, and there are a lot of expectations when one pulls the cork on a $100 bottle of wine. It is hard to enjoy anything in life if you aren't relaxed, receptive, and prepared to enjoy it to the fullest.

Now that we all feel good about not being able to justify spending $100 on a bottle of wine, let's talk about such precious bottles.

In April 1984 we sat in a $180-per-month college apartment and drank a $150 bottle of wine. It was La Tache 1978, a Pinot Noir from France's Burgundy region.

Was this wine worth the money? Wine like this is a luxury item. Six $25 bottles may make more sense to you. Maybe six $10 bottles and a great new spring jacket would be the best use for your $150. But we both enjoyed that bottle more than any other bottle of wine we have ever had. Two factors were what made this wine-drinking experience so phenomenal. (Actually three, if you count the fact that neither of us had to pay for the wine.)

The first factor was the startling evolution of the wine during the sixty minutes from the time we opened the bottle until the last delicious mouthful. Upon opening the bottle, the wine tasted quite harsh, as if it had gone bad in the bottle. But after five minutes the flavors snapped into focus. It seemed that the flavors, ever wonderful, changed dramatically every ten minutes or

Wine and the Internet

The Internet is a great resource for people who have an interest in wine. Why? Because in addition to the advertisements from various producers of wine, there is an amazing amount of free, specific, and accurate information.

Web pages come and go, but it looks like www.winevin.com, a computer industry Web-site award winner, will be around for awhile. This is a good place to start in your on-line wine odyssey.

The Internet may become the first place the wine industry ever seriously attempts to target younger adults. The Internet is cheap, hip, and unstuffy—adjectives people don't usually use to describe the wine world.

We don't recommend you order wine on-line and have it shipped, because of the cost of shipping and the uncertainties of temperature and handling of your wine. You may also encounter some unpleasant legal consequences if the wine is shipped across a state line.

What you can do is to find a review of a good wine on-line, and then go out and get it. If you want a good wine from Zimbabwe, however, you may want to risk the shipping and handling consequences rather than spend the time trying to track down such a wine in the real world.

so. The experience in its entirety was like tasting five or six very good wines.

The second factor was the flavor (or flavors!) of the wine itself. A gentle framework of soft tannins with an overlay of a fleshy, mouthfilling, glycerine body supported a palette of nuances—raspberry, cherry, smoke, coffee, and soil, among others. And the flavors lingered in the mouth.

Good wines have structure (firmness without harshness), balanced components (so the wine isn't "too" anything), complexity in the mouth (so it thoroughly stimulates the taste buds on both a sensual and an intellectual level), and body (not too thick, not too thin)—and they taste good. A great wine does all of these things, but it is the level of balanced complexity in its flavors and components that puts it into a different league, a league most people will never know exists (and may not ever care to know).

Sticking with the music analogy, let's take a shot at this complexity thing. Think of the components of a good wine as if they were the instruments in a six-piece ensemble. Maybe you can pick out the violin, the cello, and the other instruments while you listen to and enjoy the music, both as a total entity and as six individual entities.

When you have a symphony orchestra, you up the ante. Rather than one violin, there are many violins. This gives the music a fuller sound, and it adds a thickness to it. It's like going from a two-dimensional world to a three-dimensional world. The violin section plays as one, yet the sound is quite different from that of a single violin. It has an underlying richness. It's the difference between a square and a cube. That is why large orchestras exist. A great wine is like a great orchestra, with its components having a thickness of dimension, a thickness that can be better savored than described.

EVERYTHING

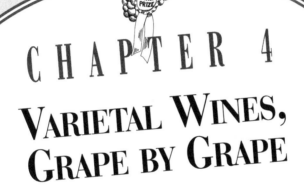

C H A P T E R 4

VARIETAL WINES, GRAPE BY GRAPE

BOTTLED BY ADAMS MEDIA

NET CONTENTS: FORTY-SIX PAGES

PRODUCT OF USA

Wine is made from grapes unless otherwise labeled as pear wine, blueberry wine, etc. Grape varieties vary greatly in color and character as well as in winemaking potential. Although there are many species of grapes, most of the world's wines come from the *Vitis vinifera* family, the classic European grape family whose vines were first brought to America prior to the American Revolution. Due to the vine disease *phylloxera*, the *vinifera* vines didn't produce much wine in the New World for over a century. Early American wine came from the *Vitis labrusca* and the Ohio River Valley's *Vitis riparia* species of grapes. The Scuppernong grape, thought to be the first native grape American settlers tried to turn into wine, is a member of the *Vitis rotundifolia* species of grape.

Vitis labrusca's most famous family member is the Concord grape. Today, it is not given much serious consideration by the

wine world. However, decent wine can be coaxed out of it. Generally, these grapes are used to make grape juice and grape jelly rather than wine. Other *labrusca* grapes used more in the past than in American winemaking today are Catawba, Delaware, and Niagara.

The biggest contribution *labrusca* grapes have made to the wine world is to be an organ donor for disease-prone *vinifera* vines. Many of the *vinifera* vines around the world today are grafted onto *labrusca* roots. (See the *phylloxera* section for the details of this medical miracle.)

The *vinifera* family of grapes, which come in red, black, and green varieties, is used to make the vast majority of the world's wine. It is believed that these grapes originated in Asia Minor. The wine world has a term for a small subset of the *vinifera* family that produces the world's top wines: noble grapes. Cabernet Sauvignon, Pinot Noir, Merlot, Syrah, Sangiovese, and Nebbiolo are the noble red grapes.

Riesling, Chardonnay, and Sauvignon Blanc are the noble white grapes.

Varietal wines—those labeled and sold according to the grape variety from which they are made—must meet government-determined minimum varietal percentages. This is the minimum percentage of a wine that must be made from the grape variety under which it is being sold. Although your bottle says Chardonnay, there is a very good chance that juices from other grapes are also in the bottle. These minor-percentage grapes are not usually credited on the bottle.

Varietal Correctness

Wine grapes have certain signature characteristics. Body, flavors, and textures are the most obvious. If you buy an inferior wine made from inferior grapes, you will not be able to recognize the grape because its signature characteristics are missing. When you drink the following wines, have your tongue and nose on the lookout for their signature flavor characteristics:

Cabernet Sauvignon: Cassis, mint, bell peppers
Merlot: Blueberries, plums, tar
Pinot Noir: Cherries, fresh ground coffee, soil, rasberries
Zinfandel: Berries, black pepper
Gamay: Strawberries
Chardonnay: Apples, pears, pineapples, bananas
Gewürtztraminer: Lychee nuts, spices
Semillon: Figs

Cabernet Sauvignon

Main growing regions: Bordeaux (France), Australia,
California, Washington State, Chile, and Tuscany (Italy)
Aromas and flavors: Black currants, green peppers, chocolate, and spice
Acidity: Moderate
Tannin: Moderate to prominent
Body: Moderate to full
Major mixing partners: Sangiovese (Tuscany),
Merlot (Bordeaux), Shiraz (Australia)

Cabernet Sauvignon is indeed a noble variety. Although its precise origins are unknown, Cabernet Sauvignon first became noteworthy as a grape variety in Bordeaux in the late 1700s. Today this variety is at or near the top of every connoisseur's great red varietal list. Appearing either alone or in combination with other varietals, Cabernet Sauvignon generally makes rich, tannic wines capable of commanding high prices. The most expensive and well made of these tend to need a few years of aging in order to openly display their fine qualities—multiple layers of fruit flavors and a smooth but firm tannic structure. Typical tasting comments on young Cabernets usually praise the black currant, bell pepper, chocolate, and spice flavors. With its forthright fruit flavors, Cabernet Sauvignon benefits from contact with new oak, which lends balance and further complexity.

There are several exquisite versions of Cabernet Sauvignon from California, particularly from the Napa Valley, that are not blended with other grapes. One of the most famous and expensive of these is Heitz Cellar "Martha's Vineyard" Cabernet Sauvignon. President Ronald Reagan proudly served the 1974 vintage of this wine to the president of France at a state dinner. Many top California wine producers have recently begun to combine Cabernet Sauvignon with other grapes offering complementary flavors.

As a blending grape, Cabernet Sauvignon successfully shares a bottle with Syrah (Shiraz) in wines from Australia, and with Sangiovese in "super-Tuscan" wines from Italy. In Bordeaux, Cabernet Sauvignon is usually blended with a combination of Merlot, Cabernet Franc (a relative), Malbec, and Petite Verdot. It is this Bordeaux blend that has found favor in California. In fact, a typical Bordeaux blending ratio—say, 60 percent Cabernet Sauvignon, 30 percent Cabernet Franc, and 10 percent Merlot—could not be labeled as Cabernet Sauvignon in California. United States law requires a minimum of 75 percent of a particular grape variety in order to qualify for varietal labeling. In response to this quandary, the California wine industry coined the term "Meritage" in order to distinguish these fine blended wines from ordinary table wines.

In any wine shop one might find varietal Cabernet Sauvignon from Chile, Australia, Californina, Washington State, Italy, Spain, or France. Expensive as great Cabernet Sauvignon can be, the bargains are out there. Look for varietal wines from the south of France (labeled *vin du pays d'oc* or Languedoc) and also from Chile. The Cabernet/Shiraz blends from Australia are often excellent values. The finest and most sought-after versions of Cabernet Sauvignon come from several different countries.

There are a handful of ultra-expensive, reserve Cabernet Sauvignons and Meritage wines from Napa Valley, California: the previously mentioned Heitz Cellar "Martha's

Good Cabernet Sauvignon in Ascending Order of Price

1. Santa Rita Cabernet Sauvignon (Chile) $7
2. Monterey Vineyard Cabernet Sauvignon (Monterey, California) $9
3. Terra Rosa Cabernet Sauvignon (California) $11
4. Liberty School Cabernet Sauvignon (California) $13
5. Franciscan Cabernet Sauvignon (Napa, California) $18
6. Pride Mountain Cabernet Sauvignon (Napa, California) $24
7. Jordan Cabernet Sauvignon (Alexander Valley, California) $32
8. B. R. Cohn "Olive Hill" Cabernet Sauvignon (Sonoma, California) . . $34
9. Spottswoode Cabernet Sauvignon (Napa, California) $45
10. Beringer Private Reserve Cabernet Sauvignon (Napa, California) . . . $60

Vineyard," Beaulieu Vineyard "Georges Latour Private Reserve," Caymus "Special Select," Far Niente, Opus One, Niebaum-Coppola "Rubican," and Stag's Leap "Cask 23." From Penfold's in Australia comes the noteworthy Cabernet Sauvignon Bin 707. Winemakers Miguel Torres and Jean Leon are producing high-quality Cabernet Sauvignon in the Penedés region of north-eastern Spain, and the iconoclastic wine-maker Gaston Hochar planted Cabernet Sauvignon in Lebanon, where it is blended with Syrah and Cinsault in his famous Château Musar wine. We have good reason to expect premium Cabernet Sauvignon from Chile in the near future.

It is in the Bordeaux subregions of Médoc and Graxas where the most elegant, ageworthy, and expensive Cabernet Sauvignon-based wines are produced. Two of the top–rated Bordeaux châteaux,

Château Mouton-Rothschild and Château Latour, rely on Cabernet Sauvignon for 70 percent of their blends. These and other highly rated Bordeaux châteaux produce wines that can age well for many decades and command hundreds of dollars for a bottle from a great year.

The assertive flavors of Cabernet Sauvignon—young or old—match nicely with lamb, beef, and other red meat dishes. Young Cabernet Sauvignon is especially well paired with meats from the grill because the youthful fruit flavors are a perfect counter-point to the pleasantly bitter scorch imparted by the open fire.

So what does Cabernet Sauvignon do for an encore? Some of the finest rosé wines in the world are made from this wonder grape. Look for Simi Rosé of Cabernet Sauvignon from the Sonoma Valley.

Pinot Noir

Main growing regions: Burgundy (France), California, and Oregon
Aromas and Flavors: Cherries, raspberries, and smoke
Acidity: Moderate to high
Tannin: Low to moderate
Body: Light to medium
Major mixing partners: None

If it were not so difficult to grow, Pinot Noir would enjoy a reputation for greatness equal to that of Cabernet Sauvignon. It is the noble red grape of France's Burgundy region where, under ideal conditions, it yields ruby-colored wines whose velvety richness has seduced wine lovers for centuries. Whereas the great Cabernet Sauvignons of Bordeaux may be predictably excellent, great Pinot Noirs of Burgundy overwhelm one's senses every time with their striking beauty.

Cabernet Sauvignon traveled with ease from Bordeaux to California's warmer valleys, where it thrives in sunshine. However, except for a few pockets (Santa Barbara and Carneros, to name two), Pinot Noir seems to be more at home up north in Oregon, where the long, cool growing season allows the Pinot Noir fruit flavors to develop slowly. Pinot Noir ripened quickly on the hot California valley floors tends to be flat and uninteresting.

Less pigmented than most red grapes, Pinot Noir has a brick-orange cast rather than a deep purple color. At its best, Pinot Noir is low in tannin and high in glycerine (hence, the "velvet"), and has a lively acidic backbone that gives length and focus to the typical Pinot Noir flavors of raspberries, cherries, and smoke. Such structure makes Pinot Noir a highly versatile food wine.

Full-bodied red Burgundy from the Côte de Nuits subregion is made entirely from

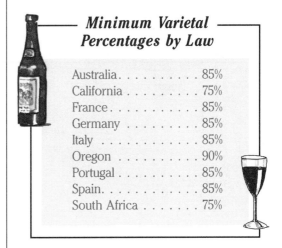

Minimum Varietal Percentages by Law

Region	Percentage
Australia	85%
California	75%
France	85%
Germany	85%
Italy	85%
Oregon	90%
Portugal	85%
Spain	85%
South Africa	75%

Pinot Noir and is a classic accompaniment to beef roasts. The lighter red Burgundies from the Côte de Beaune are perfect with game birds such as pheasant and partridge. The Pinot Noirs from Oregon can be very Burgundian in structure and range from a light Côte de Beaune style to a richer Côte de Nuits style; they match with food accordingly. The light, clean acidity and modest tannin of typical Pinot Noir makes it suitable with all but the lightest of seafood dishes. Open one of the jammy Californian interpretations of Pinot Noir—from Santa Barbara, Carneros, or the Russian River Valley in Sonoma—in place of Merlot. You'll find that these generously fruity and mildly acidic wines might be more enjoyable.

Perhaps the best use of Pinot Noir grapes in California is as the main component in brut rosé–style, Blanc de Noirs sparkling wines. Several of the great French Champagne houses, in order to meet growing world-wide demand, opened shop in California. Here they found that Pinot Noir, a vital component of Champagne in France, grows to full ripeness in the California sunshine. More ripeness means more color in the skin and more fruit flavors as well. When gently pressed and quickly removed from the vat, Pinot Noir skins lend a delightful "blush" of copper color to Champagne-method sparkling wine. In France, such ripeness is quite rare, and brut rosés from the Champagne region are accordingly uncommon and expensive. The California versions are usually a better value.

Decent Pinot Noir is never cheap. A good way to get to know this grape is by trying varietal-labeled Pinot Noir from the big, reputable Burgundy (Bourgogne as it's known in France) houses. These will usually be labeled "Bourgogne Pinot Noir." If you feel like paying for it, move up-market from there to the better red Burgundies, although this region is very difficult (and expensive) to get to know. The Chalonnais subregion of Burgundy offers two inexpensive and enjoyable Pinot Noir–based wines: Givry and Mercurey.

ADELSHEIM VINEYARD

OREGON PINOT NOIR 1995

ALCOHOL 13.5% BY VOLUME

Most Oregonian interpretations of Pinot Noir are closer in style to their Burgundian brethren than they are to their Californian neighbors. Ask a reliable wine merchant for his or her suggestions for a varietally correct (yet affordable) Pinot Noir. Oregon Pinot bargains are definitely available, especially in comparison to the fabulously expensive *grands crus* and *premiers crus* of Burgundy.

Good Pinot Noir in Ascending Order of Price

1. Fireskeed Pinot Noir (Oregon) $10
2. Villa Mt. Eden Pinot Noir (California) $12
3. Louis Latour Bourgogne Pinot Noir (Burgundy, France) $12
4. Elk Cove Pinot Noir (Oregon) $14
5. Estancia Pinot Noir (Monterey, California) $15
6. Sterling "Winery Lake" Pinot Noir (Napa, California) $18
7. Byron Pinot Noir (Santa Barbara, California) $18
8. Steele Pinot Noir (Carneros, California) $23
9. Joseph Drouhin Mercurey (Burgundy, France) $23
10. Gary Farrell (Sonoma) $24
11. Truchard Vineyards Pinot Noir (Napa, California) $26
12. Hanzell Pinot Noir (Sonoma, California) $28
13. Eyrie Vineyards Pinot Noir Reserve (Oregon) $30
14. Domaine Drouhin Pinot Noir (Oregon) $36
15. Louis Latour Gevrey-Chambertin (Burgundy, France) $50

Merlot

Main growing regions: Bordeaux (France), California,
Washington State, Australia, Chile
Aromas and flavors: Plums, blueberries, and cherries
Acidity: Low
Tannin: Low to moderate
Body: Medium
Major mixing partner: Cabernet Sauvignon (Bordeaux)

It is difficult to discuss Merlot without mentioning Cabernet Sauvignon. Just as Cabernet Sauvignon gained recognition in the Médoc subregion of Bordeaux in the late 1700s, so too did Merlot become prominent in the cooler Bordeaux subregions of Pomerol and Saint-Emilion. These two subregions are cooler and wetter than the Médoc; Merlot grows much better in cooler climates than does Cabernet Sauvignon, although not *too* cool; Merlot has yet to gain a foothold in chilly Oregon where Pinot Noir is king.

Merlot is a distant relative of Cabernet Sauvignon. The biggest difference is that the skin of the Merlot grape is thinner than that of Cabernet Sauvignon; therefore, Merlot is the earlier ripening and less tannic of the two. Merlot has a reputation for making soft, round, and drinkable wines with low acidity and generous fruit flavors of plum, blueberry, and cherry along with a pleasantly chalky texture. Yet, according to many experts just

a few short years ago, Merlot had no future as a varietal wine in California.

Except for in Pomerol, Merlot has rarely been a soloist: Until recently, its primary role had been in blends with Cabernet Sauvignon. In the past few years, however, the Merlot grape has made the transition from being an assistant to Cabernet Sauvignon in blended wines to being a star in its own right. Consequently, it has become a somewhat overrated and misunderstood varietal. How did this happen?

When the word went forth from the medical journals that red wine was good for your heart, the resulting boom in red-wine sales was equivalent to sales of Beatles records upon rumors of Paul McCartney's death. The wine-drinking public, already hooked on white Zinfandel and Chardonnay, switched en masse to red wine. Non-wine drinkers, perhaps mindful of an unpleasant experience with dry, tannic, red wine, wanted a soft, supple, drinkable red wine.

These consumers turned to Merlot, due to its reputation for low acid and its softness.

California was unprepared for this market shift, with only a few acres of this variety planted since the mid-1970s. It seems that every winery so capable planted additional Merlot acreage as soon as possible, and the resulting wines were often disappointing. Too often, one buys a Merlot shaped more by market forces than by the winemaker's art. Grapes from very young vines growing in marginal areas are usually pressed too hard (the better to extract every drop of pricey nectar, with the inevitable concentration of unwanted tannin). It is now almost impossible to buy delicious, varietally correct Merlot for under $8.

In the meantime, the best bargains in varietal Merlot are the Languedoc and *vin de pays* wines of France. South America (Chile and Argentina) produces good, affordable Merlot as well. If you like soft and fruity red wines, experiment with Pinot Noir or perhaps *cru* Beaujolais made from Gamay. *Cru* Beaujolais comes from ten villages in Beaujolais. Unlike ordinary Beaujolais, these wines can improve with a couple of years of aging. Pinot Noir and Gamay are both relatively easy to match with food.

What are the characteristics of a good Merlot? Look for rich, plum-like fruit, almost jammy in its concentration, and low levels of acid and tannin. Merlot does not get particularly complex; yet because of its soft tannin and gentle acidity profile, its pleasing fruit flavors are more accessible than those in sturdier reds.

The soft tannin also makes Merlot an enjoyable match with a broad variety of foods. Even seafood, especially from the grill, can be a lovely pairing with Merlot's unobtrusive flavors. Its somewhat bland personality allows Merlot to fit nicely with all types of well-seasoned ethnic dishes.

Because Merlot has become such a popular varietal wine, we have assembled a detailed Merlot buying guide for several price ranges.

GOOD MERLOT

Now that red wine is supposed to be good for you, more Americans are looking to drink the stuff. Because it is easy to drink in comparison to other red-wine varieties, Merlot has become many red-wine neophytes' wine of choice. This has caused a tremendous "Merlot boom." Like many fads, this one will cost you if you want to be a part of it. Comparable (in quality, not taste) red wines made from different grapes often cost less.

In response to the Merlot boom, the wine market now offers us an enormous selection of choices from around the world, many of which did not exist a decade ago. Merlot is becoming an industry within an industry. Since Merlot is very popular with new wine drinkers, and this book is written with such people in mind, we felt an expanded Merlot wine–buying section was warranted. As such, here is a list of recommended Merlots at various prices.

THE MERLOT SPECTRUM

Group 1 Under $10
Cheap, enjoyable, and the label says Merlot

These wines would be difficult to recognize as Merlot if tasted blind, but they nonetheless taste pretty good. Note that there are few California wines in this group—the economics of grape growing and winemaking make it difficult to produce good, cheap Merlot in California. Just about every winemaking country is represented in Group 1, making for some interesting (and affordable!) comparison taste testing.

Group 2 $10–15
The threshold of varietal correctness

Once you pass through the $10 barrier, you can find Merlot that is easily identifiable as such. Although there are a few Californians (they are in higher brackets!), you will notice a fair amount of Washington State wines. Merlot is an early ripening grape and thus does well in the cooler growing regions of Washington.

Group 3 $16–19
Fruity, full-bodied, and complex

This price range is where truly delicious Merlot begins. Sadly, these same wines were in the $10–15 range not too long ago.

At these prices, winemakers can afford to use higher quality grapes (not just Merlot in name only) and the more expensive winemaking techniques such as proper cooperage (barrels) and gentle pressing.

As a result these wines are fruity, full-bodied, and complex. Most importantly, they have the velvety texture that is the signature of good Merlot.

The Merlot Spectrum

Group 1 Recommendations

1. Marcus James (Brazil) $5
2. Lirico (Veneto, Italy) $6
3. Domaine Caton (France) . . . . $7/1.0 liters
4. Santa Rita (Chile) $7
5. Hardy's "Nottage Hill" (South Australia) $7
6. Georges Duboeuf Domaine de Bordeneuve (France) $7
7. Rene Barbier Mediterranean Select Merlot (Penedés, Spain) . . . $8
8. Emerald Bay (California) $8
9. Dulong (France) $8
10. Concha y Toro (Chile) . . . . $9/1.5 liters
11. Dunnewood (California) $9
12. Swartland (South Africa) $9
13. Mezzacorona (Italy) $9
14. Fortant de France Kosher Merlot (France) $9

Group 2 Recommendations

1. Christian Moueix Merlot (Bordeaux, France) $10
2. Forest Glen (California) $11
3. Blackstone (California) $12
4. Covey Run (Washington) $13
5. Columbia Crest (Washington) $14
6. Château Ste. Michelle (Washington) $15
7. Hyatt (Washington) $15

Group 3 Recommendations

1. Estancia Vineyards (Alexander Valley, California) $16
2. Clos du Bois (Sonoma, California) $18
3. Falesco (Latium, Italy) $18
4. Swanson (Napa, California) $19
5. Havens (Napa, California) $19
6. Franciscan (Napa, California) $19

Group 4 $21–29
Hand-crafted masterpieces

In this price range we escape the dollar-driven feeding frenzy and enter more exclusive territory—sort of like leaving the department store for a pricey boutique.

Notice the two French wines in this price range; Pomerol and Saint-Emilion are two subregions of the Bordeaux region. Unlike Médoc and Graves, Pomerol and Saint-Emilion wines are predominantly Merlot. Like most fine French wines, they seem light bodied in comparison to their California counterparts. No one disputes their subtlety and finesse.

Group 5 $30–50
Power Merlot—you have to know somebody to buy these

Among the professional elite in many vocations—the legal profession comes to mind—the ability to procure certain rare wines is

regarded as manly. Accordingly, the feeding frenzy for these tightly allocated wines is every bit as rabid as that for lower-priced Merlots. Fortunately, this foolishness is generally confined to the wines of California, and the four Pomerol wines on this list are more widely available.

If you wish to continue your journey upmarket, you must leave California. With the exception of the one "super Tuscan" from Italy, Pomerol (France) is the promised land.

1990	Fattoria di Ama Merlot "Apparita" (Tuscany)—$100
1990	Château Trotanoy (Pomerol)—$170
1990	Vieux-Château-Certan (Pomerol)—$170
1990	Château Certan-de-May (Pomerol)—$170

1990 was a particularly good year.

Still not satisfied? Perhaps Château Petrus is the wine for you. As of this writing, the 1994 is being released at about $375/bottle. Considering that the 1990 Petrus now sells for over $1,000/bottle in some places, this wine is a safer investment than most mutual funds. A prisoner of its own popularity, Château Petrus is generally regarded as too expensive to drink at any point in its life.

Rarer yet is Château Le Pin from Pomerol. Only 500 cases (6,000 bottles) of the 1994 was produced, as opposed to 3,200 cases of Petrus. Even Donald Trump would have a hard time getting his hands on some. If he could, he would shell out $400 per bottle.

The Merlot Spectrum

Group 4 Recommendations

1. Château St. Jean (Sonoma, California). $20
2. Kiona Vineyards (Washington). $21
3. Pride Mountain (Napa, California). $22
4. Justin (Paso Robles, California) $23
5. Lolonis Reserve (Mendocino, California) $24
6. Chateau Haut-Segottes (Saint-Emilion, France). $25
7. Kenwood "Jack London" (Sonoma, California) $27
8. Stonestreet (Sonoma, California). $28
9. Clos du Val Estate Bottled (Stags Leap; Napa, California). $29
10. Château La Pointe (Pomerol, France) $29

Group 5 Recommendations

1. Sullivan (Napa, California). $30
2. Château Clos L'Eglise (Pomerol, France) $30
3. Château Gazin (Pomerol, France). $35
4. Duckhorn (Napa, California) $35
5. Château Beauregard (Pomerol, France) $36
6. Newton "Unfiltered" (Napa, California). $38
7. Duckhorn "Three Palms" (Napa, California) $43
8. Avignonese (Tuscany, Italy) $48
9. Matanzas Creek (Sonoma, California) $50
10. Château L'Eglise Clinet (Pomerol, France). $50

Syrah/Shiraz

Main growing regions: Rhône (France), Australia, and California
Aromas and flavors: Prunes, spices, and berries
Acidity: Low to moderate
Tannin: Moderate to prominent
Body: Medium
Major mixing partners: Grenache (Rhône) and Cabernet Sauvignon (Australia)

The Syrah grape, known as Shiraz in Australia and South Africa, is a noble grape variety held in high esteem by many red-wine lovers. The great and age-worthy wines of the northern Rhône—Hermitage, Côte Rôtie, St. Joseph, and Cornas—are produced from unblended Syrah. The finest wine produced in Australia is Penfold's Hermitage, another example of unblended Shiraz at its finest. Australian varietal Shiraz is as common as Shiraz/Cabernet Sauvignon blends; the latter are remarkable bargains.

Although its exact origin is not known, the Syrah grape is believed by some to have originated in ancient Persia. It gets its name from the city of Shiraz in the foothills of the Zagros Mountains in what is now Iran. Syrah seems to have brought along a whiff of exotic Eastern spices in its travels to France, Australia, and California. The subtle spiciness in its aroma, often a combination of cinnamon, rose petals, and orange rind, complements flavors of raspberry and black pepper.

These qualities require bottle aging in order to emerge; youthful Syrah wines usually exhibit more power than finesse. Well-aged Syrah is rare in the wine market, but experience shows that mature Syrah is well worth the wait.

California got a late start with this variety. It seems that another grape from the Rhône valley, perhaps the Duriff grape, was transplanted by accident rather than Syrah. Today that grape is known in California as Petite Sirah, and the true Syrah is a relatively recent arrival in California. Some California Syrahs are quite good, but Australia, with a hundred-year head start, is the source for bargains in Shiraz.

In general, the French version is higher in acid and better with food than the Australian version, which shows more fruit. This is because of the difference in climate. The warmer weather of Australia leads to a more thorough ripening of the grape, which in turn leads to more fruitiness and a lower acidity in the wine. Whereas the French Syrahs tend to display raspberry-like fruit aromas, the Australian versions are often more suggestive of raisins.

Although California is unlikely to produce an inexpensive varietal Syrah worthy of mention, there have been some noteworthy successes with this latecomer. In particular, the warm climate in the Santa Barbara area seems to bring out a new degree of delicious fruitiness in Syrah.

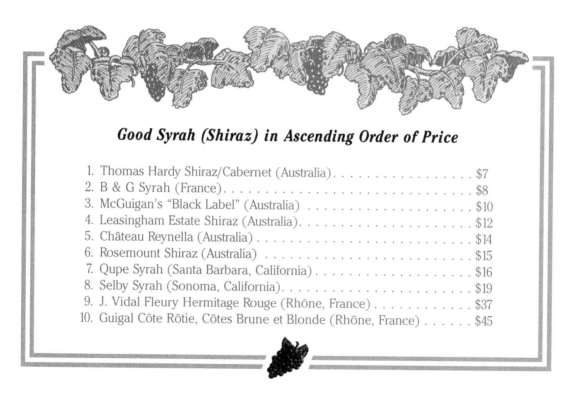

Good Syrah (Shiraz) in Ascending Order of Price

1. Thomas Hardy Shiraz/Cabernet (Australia). $7
2. B & G Syrah (France). $8
3. McGuigan's "Black Label" (Australia) $10
4. Leasingham Estate Shiraz (Australia). $12
5. Château Reynella (Australia) $14
6. Rosemount Shiraz (Australia) $15
7. Qupe Syrah (Santa Barbara, California) $16
8. Selby Syrah (Sonoma, California). $19
9. J. Vidal Fleury Hermitage Rouge (Rhône, France) $37
10. Guigal Côte Rôtie, Côtes Brune et Blonde (Rhône, France) $45

Zinfandel

Main growing region: California
Aromas and flavors: Blackberry jam and black pepper
Acidity: Low to moderate
Tannin: Moderate, can be substantial in some versions
Body: Medium to full
Major mixing partners: Often blended, but rarely credited (California)

This popular grape, of unclear origin (probably an obscure European variety) showed up in California in the mid-1800s and has been growing like a weed since then. No other *vinifera* grape so thrives on California heat and sunshine. Unfortunately, the evolution of Zinfandel got sidetracked by the creation of the wildly popular rosé, white Zinfandel, the inspiration for which evolved during a period of slack demand for red wine in the early 1970s.

As a result of this, wine lists must now use the retronym "red Zinfandel" to indicate the varietal in its original form. Zinfandel is as versatile as it is prolific, capable of a broad range of styles. In addition to white Zinfandel, which is actually a rosé, Zinfandel can range from a light, Beaujolais-like quaff to late-harvest brutes that practically ooze pepper and jammy fruit. Although $5 won't get you a bottle of Zinfandel, $10 bottles do exist and they are often quite good.

If you suffer sticker shock from a reserve Cabernet Sauvignon or Meritage, opt for an estate-bottled "old vines" Zinfandel ($15–20). Its complexity, power, and balance should impress you for the money. These wines are especially well matched with roasted lamb and other Mediterranean dishes, even hearty vegetable dishes. Zinfandel stands up well to garlic and powerful seasonings. These buxom, fruity wines are great alone or with a wine-friendly snack of cheese and crackers.

White Zinfandel was wildly popular for a few years after it first reached the market in the early 1970s, and it is still the wine of choice for people who otherwise would not drink wine. The noticeable residual sugar (around 1.5 percent), lower alcohol content (10 percent or so), and fresh strawberry fruit flavor give white Zinfandel its broad appeal.

Contrary to what many wine snobs would have you believe, there are several white Zinfandels of quality on the market. The key to good white Zinfandel lies in the color. While many of the palest pink versions are rather bland, the darker versions tend to have more fruit flavors.

Although white Zinfandel is generally a so-so match with most foods, it is rarely a bad choice at the dinner table. It is actually a good choice to have with spicy Pacific Rim cuisine because its sweetness can help put out the fire in people's mouths caused by spicy dishes. The uncomplicated flavors of white Zinfandel, and of most rosés for that matter, are a good match with the intricate seasonings of Far-Eastern cuisine.

There is, we believe, one particular "match made in heaven" with white Zinfandel—Thanksgiving dinner! An American holiday deserves an American wine, and the fruitiness and residual sugar of white Zinfandel will help to wash down even the most dried-out turkey breast. Because Thanksgiving dinner—turkey and root vegetables, usually—is so inexpensive to prepare, white Zinfandel represents an intelligent price matching. Finally, if you celebrate this annual feast with elderly relatives who are not wine buffs, they will probably find White Zinfandel more enjoyable than any other wine.

Good (Red) Zinfandel in Ascending Order of Price

1. Talus (California) $10
2. Gallo-Sonoma Frei Ranch (Sonoma, California) $12
3. Buehler (Napa, California) $14
4. Mazzocco (Sonoma, California) $15
5. Rodney Strong "old vines" (Sonoma, California) $16
6. David Bruce (Santa Cruz Mountains, California) $18
7. Deloach Estate (Napa, California) $19
8. Ravenswood (Sonoma, California) $20
9. Sky (Napa, California) $23
10. Storybook Mountain Estate Reserve (Napa, California) $29

Good White Zinfandel in Ascending Order of Price

1. Beringer (California) $5
2. Talus (California) $6
3. Buehler (Napa, California) $8
4. Deloach (Napa, California) $9

Nebbiolo

Main growing regions: Piedmont (Italy), some California
Aromas and flavors: Raspberries, plums, and earth
Acidity: High
Tannin: Prominent in youth, "dusty" with age
Body: Medium
Major mixing partners: None (Some minor, local grapes are blended with Nebbiolo in certain Piedmont wines.)

Named for the dense fogs so prevalent in the vineyards of Piedmont, Italy, the Nebbiolo grape is responsible for several of Italy's—and the world's—finest red wines. The great red wines of Piedmont—Barolo, Barbaresco, Ghemme, Gattinara—are regarded by afficionados as members of the exclusive club of the greatest wines in the world. Nebbiolo grapes have not as yet done well when grown away from their native soil. Somewhere outside of Italy there is perhaps a piece of land just waiting to be converted into a great Nebbiolo vineyard. Some growers in California have begun experimenting with Nebbiolo.

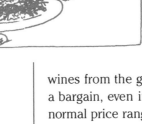

In the past the best of these wines, like many Cabernet Sauvignons, were too tannic to drink in their youth and required a decade or so of mellowing. Perhaps more than any other variety, Nebbiolo rewards patience. However, more Nebbiolo-based wines are being vinified to be enjoyable in their youth. If you want an affordable way to get to know Nebbiolo, try an entry-level Barolo or a Nebbiolo d'Alba selected by a wine merchant or reviewer you trust. Unfortunately, entry level for these wines is $12–15. If you see one of these wines from the great year of 1990, it may be a bargain, even if it is a little out of your normal price range.

Despite their powerful flavors, Barolo and other Nebbiolo-based Italian wines need to be served with food because they are quite acidic. Indeed, most Italian wines, red and white, belong at the dinner table, not the coffee table. The California versions have more fruit flavor, which cuts the prominent acidity somewhat. The Italian Nebbiolos are a natural match with rich, earthy dishes such as game and red meat with mushrooms. Even chicken can hold its own with most of these wines.

Because Nebbiolo has not been transplanted with widespread success from its native Piedmont, it is difficult to differentiate between the characteristics of the grape and those of the region. Look for Piedmont Nebbiolos to be very dry, flavorful but not heavy on the palate, and surprisingly subtle and complex. Look for the California version, which should become more prevalent in the years ahead, to have stronger plum and raspberry fruit flavors than those from Italy.

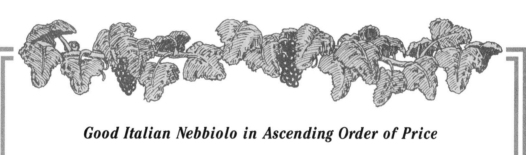

Good Italian Nebbiolo in Ascending Order of Price

1. Dessilani Spanna (Piedmont, Italy) $10
2. Filipetti Nebbiolo d'Alba. $11
3. Vietti Nebbiolo d'Alba $16
4. Fontanafredda Barolo $20
5. Monsecco Le Colline Barbaresco $25

Sangiovese

Main growing regions: Tuscany (Italy), some California
Aromas and flavors: Cherries, raisins, earth, and violets
Acidity: Moderate to high
Tannin: Moderate
Body: Light to medium
Major mixing partners: Cabernet Sauvignon (Italy) and Cannaiolo Nero (Italy)

Sangiovese is an Italian grape that, like the Nebbiolo, hasn't made a significant impact on the wine world when grown outside of Italy. It is the most important grape variety in central Italy, especially in Tuscany. It is in this region where the surprisingly sophisticated Etruscans made delicious wine well before the rise of the Roman Empire. The Sangiovese grape tends to generate closely related mutations. The Brunello and Sangiovetto grapes are close enough relatives of Sangiovese that they are usually considered to be Sangiovese itself.

It might be said that, in terms of style, Sangiovese is to Nebbiolo as Pinot Noir is to Cabernet Sauvignon. Like the great Pinot Noirs of Burgundy, great Sangiovese-based wines from Tuscany—Chianti Classico, Brunello di Montalcino—are somewhat light in body and color yet can improve for many years in the bottle. Also like these great Burgundies, many of these same great Sangiovese wines can be perfectly enjoyable before their fifth birthday.

Like all great varietals, Sangiovese can be a prince or a pauper, and the pauper, a varietal-labeled Sangiovese from one of Italy's many regions, is frequently a bargain. Early attempts at this varietal in California tend to cost like the prince but taste like the pauper. So far, California winemakers have had a difficult time getting Sangiovese acclimated to the warmth and sunshine of their vineyards. However, a few producers have produced some good Sangioveses.

Sangiovese with a varietal label can be surprisingly inexpensive. Look for the typical cherry fruit, high acid, and low tannin and glycerine. Because of this combination of characteristics, Sangiovese has few equals as a red wine to accompany seafood. When matching food and wine, remember also to match price along with other characteristics. In this sense, inexpensive, varietally labeled Sangiovese is a good pizza and spaghetti wine. These wines are usually better than those inexpensive, silly-looking, straw-covered bottles of cheap Chianti you see at Italian restaurants.

The Sangiovese (Brunello) grape stands alone in the potentially great Brunello di Montalcino Riserva; this is an expensive wine that can improve with age for several decades. In Chianti wines, the Sangiovese grape has historically been blended with the local Cannaiolo grape as well as two white grapes: Trebbiano and Malvasia. Presently, the top producers are omitting the white grapes, in favor of more Sangiovese.

The "super-Tuscan" red wines that first came to the market in the 1980s are a blend of Sangiovese and Cabernet Sauvignon. These superior wines lie outside of Italy's wine classification system, but they are more intensely flavored than Chianti and are worth a try if you are looking to splurge.

The great Chianti Classico and Brunello di Montalcino wines go well with veal, beef, lamb, and hearty chicken dishes. Sangiovese-based wines also stand up well with tomato sauce. Super Tuscans, with their sturdy framework of Cabernet Sauvignon, are generally best reserved for red meat and game.

Good Sangiovese in Ascending Order of Price

1. Lirico Sangiovese (Veneto, Italy) $6
2. Moris Farms Morellino di Scansano (Tuscany, Italy) $8
3. Conti Contini Sangiovese (Tuscany, Italy) $11
4. Il Cuore Rosso Classico (Sangiovese/Zinfandel blend; California) . . . $11
5. Rabbit Ridge Sangiovese (Sonoma, California) $13
6. Castello di Gabbiano Chianti Classico (Tuscany, Italy) $13
7. Fattoria di Ama Chianti Classico (Tuscany, Italy) $20
8. Swanson Sangiovese (Napa, California) $20
9. Avignonese Vino Nobile di Montepulciano (Tuscany, Italy) $25
10. Antinori Tignanello (Sangiovese/Cabernet Sauvignon blend; Tuscany, Italy) $45
11. Biondi-Santi Brunello di Montalcino 1990 . . . . $60

Grenache

Main growing regions: Spain, Rhône (France), and California
Aroma and flavor: Raspberry
Acidity: Moderate
Body: Medium to full
Major mixing partners: Syrah (France) and Tempranillo (Spain)

The southern Rhône valley of France is famous for its sturdy, drinkable and affordable red wines. Many different, grape varieties are grown here, but Grenache is the predominant variety and is the primary grape among the many used to make Côtes-du-Rhône rouge. This popular wine has ample body, meaty structure, and a straightforward fruit flavor of raspberry jam. Côtes-du-Rhône is a genuine bargain among French red wines, usually retailing for less than $10 per bottle. The dry rosés of the neighboring Provence region are also made primarily from the Grenache grape and are considered by many experts to be the finest pink wines in the world.

Under the local name Garnacha, Grenache is extensively planted in Spain and Portugal. It lends fruit to the relatively austere Tempranillo grape in the red wines of Rioja (Spain). In California it is vinified in bulk for use in rosés and red jug wines, although some wineries are experimenting with upscale rosés. California Grenache varietal wines, although somewhat scarce, can be quite good.

To experience Grenache in its purest state, look for Château Rayas from Châteauneuf-du-Pape. Although AOC law allows the use of as many as thirteen different grape varieties for Châteauneuf-du-Pape red, most such wines are predominantly Grenache, and Château Rayas eschews all other permitted varieties to make a 100-percent Grenache wine. To experience this it will cost you about $80 per bottle.

Well-made Grenache-based wines tend to have enough body and character to be enjoyable with or without food. Hearty beef and lamb dishes, especially stews made with Côtes-du-Rhône as an ingredient, seem to bring out the delightful spiciness in Grenache. The most powerful versions of Châteauneuf-du-Pape stand up well to steak au poivre and other powerfully seasoned dishes, whereas tamer bottlings match well with goose, duck, and the like—not summer food, and not summer wine. In hot weather, try pairing a French Tavel or a California rosé with a salad or simple picnic fare.

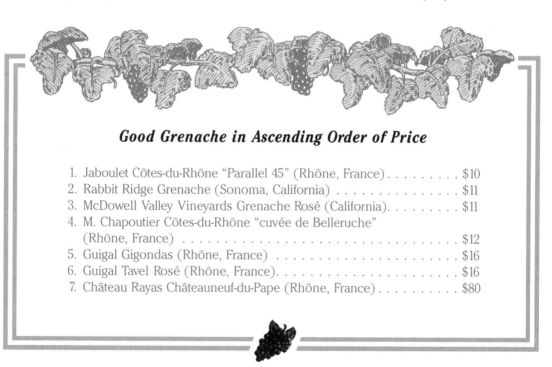

Good Grenache in Ascending Order of Price

1. Jaboulet Côtes-du-Rhône "Parallel 45" (Rhône, France) $10
2. Rabbit Ridge Grenache (Sonoma, California) $11
3. McDowell Valley Vineyards Grenache Rosé (California). $11
4. M. Chapoutier Côtes-du-Rhône "cuvée de Belleruche" (Rhône, France) $12
5. Guigal Gigondas (Rhône, France) $16
6. Guigal Tavel Rosé (Rhône, France). $16
7. Château Rayas Châteauneuf-du-Pape (Rhône, France) $80

Gamay

Main growing region: Beaujolais (France)
Aromas and flavors: Strawberries and raspberries
Acidity: Low to moderate
Tannin: Low
Body: Light
Major mixing partners: None

The granite soil of the Beaujolais, the southernmost subregion of Burgundy, brings out the best qualities of the Gamay grape. The red wine of Beaujolais is fresh, light, and fruity, and it is enjoyed all over the world. The lively fruit flavors—strawberry and raspberry—show well in the absence of substantial tannin. These qualities lend themselves well to carbonic maceration (fermentation in the complete absence of oxygen). This process protects the delicate fruit components and readies the wine for early release.

Beaujolais Nouveau, the first release of red Beaujolais, reaches the market the third Thursday in November, immediately following the harvest. It is eagerly awaited by the wine world as the first indication of the quality of the entire vintage, so a delicious Beaujolais Nouveau is cause for rejoicing among the French. With its pleasant balance of fruit over tannin, a Gamay-based wine can take a slight chilling and may be offered with just about any food, from poached salmon to barbecued pork ribs. These wines, with their overt fruitiness, are also enjoyable alone.

The Gamay grape reaches its summit of quality in the *"cru* Beaujolais" wines. These are red wines produced from Gamay grapes grown within the ten townships regarded as superior to the rest of the subregion: Moulin-à-Vent, Brouilly, Côte de Brouilly, Fleurie, Chiroubles, Morgon, Chénas, Juliénas, St-Amour, and Régnié. Taken together, these townships comprise the heart of the Beaujolais subregion. It has been observed that these wines, unlike other wines from Beaujolais, can benefit from two or three years of aging.

California does produce, albeit sparingly, two wines whose names imply Gamay—Napa Gamay and Gamay Beaujolais. Napa Gamay is actually the lowly Gros Auxerrois grape from southwest France, and Gamay Beaujolais is an inferior mutation of Pinot Noir. For price and quality, stick to the French version, especially during the Nouveau season when California "Gamay Nouveau" labels are intentionally deceiving and the wines are decidedly inferior to the real thing.

Georges Duboeuf is the king of Beaujolais wines. The quality and pricing of these wines are more than fair. Louis Jadot is another reliable bottler of Beaujolais. This firm bottles all manner of wine from this sub-region—Beaujolais Nouveau, Beaujolais-Villages, and all of the *crus*.

Tempranillo

Main growing region: Rioja (Spain)
Aromas and flavors: Not very fruity; leather, spice, cherries, and raisins
Acidity: Low to moderate
Tannin: Low to moderate
Body: Medium
Major mixing partner: Grenache/Garnacha (Rioja)

One rarely sees Tempranillo bottled as a varietal, but it is included here because of the importance of Rioja, an affordable treasure from Spain. Tempranillo-based Rioja-region wines range from very inexpensive and enjoyable to fabulously expensive, world-class red wine. The inexpensive versions often display the body of Pinot Noir without the flashy fruit. The subtle cherry fruit of Tempranillo is often well masked by smoke flavors and oakiness. Grenache (Garnacha) is the minority blending partner in Rioja, and it adds some fruitiness to the wine. The greatest versions of Rioja cost as much as any great wine and show a depth and length of flavors that justify their price.

As a light- to medium-bodied red with modest acidity, red Rioja matches well with grilled fish, well-seasoned vegetable dishes, and pasta, and also goes well with chicken and red meats. As such, Rioja might accurately be called a fool-proof red wine.

The Tempranillo-based Rioja wines are a great value, and they are easy to appreciate. Rioja is a good place for the neophyte to start in his or her exploration of red wine.

Good Tempranillo in Ascending Order of Price

1. Navarra Tempranillo $7
2. Bodegas Montecillo Cumbrero Tinto $9
3. Campo Viejo Crianza a Tinto $10
4. Bodegas Montecillo Reserva $14
5. Marques de Riscal Tinto Gran Reserva $35
6. Vega Sicilia Unico 1970 . . . . $180

Chardonnay

Main growing regions: Burgundy (France), California, Oregon, Washington State,
Australia, South Africa, Chile
Aromas and flavors: Varies greatly by region; peas, vanilla,
tropical fruits, toast, and nuts
Acidity: Moderate to high
Body: Light to moderate
Major mixing partner: Semillon (Australia)

The wine-drinking public is so accustomed to saying, "I'll have a Chardonnay!" that it is worth a reminder that Chardonnay is the name of a white-wine grape variety. In fact, Chardonnay is the most popular and most versatile white grape in the world, though it is not the most widely planted one. That distinction belongs to Spain's Airén grape.

Chardonnay grapes are used to make the austere, bone-dry wines of France's Chablis subregion; they are truly great seafood wines. Chardonnay is a crucial component of Champagne and the sole grape in the premium Champagne labeled Blanc de Blancs. Chardonnay makes the great white Burgundies from France—the most expensive dry white wines in the world.

It also makes the best white wines in California; they are fruity and sometimes syrupy, high in alcohol, and often framed in oak. Chardonnay can even accommodate a dose of noble rot and yield a gloriously rich and sweet dessert wine. Finally, Chardonnay blends well with other grapes,

especially with Semillon, as commonly blended in Australia.

What makes Chardonnay so versatile? Perhaps Chardonnay has little indigenous character of its own and instead displays the best characteristics of the soil and climate in which it is grown, like a lawyer who can argue any side of an issue. However, in all of its incarnations Chardonnay does display a propensity for both glycerine and acid, whose interplay results in the most velvety, sensually delightful texture of all white wines. So, under all its trappings, Chardonnay is mostly about texture. That is what one looks for in even simple Chardonnays. Unlike the red-wine kingpin Cabernet Sauvignon, Chardonnays can be of high quality in the $8–10 price range.

So what does Chardonnay taste like? It depends on whom you ask. It is difficult to define a standard of varietal correctness in a grape variety with so many personalities. However, some generalizations about Chardonnay can be made.

The astringent flavor imparted by oak barrels marries well with Chardonnay in different regions. So well, in fact, that it can be difficult to separate in one's mind the flavor of the grape and the flavor of the oak. If you want to taste a pure, unoaked Chardonnay, look for a California Chardonnay that is labeled "Stainless Steel Fermented." This implies no oak.

Far to the south of Chablis in France is the Burgundy subregion of Côte de Beaune, where Chardonnay grapes become the world's greatest Chardonnay wines. Corton-Charlemagne, Meursault, and the various Montrachet vineyards produce beautifully structured Chardonnays, that are brilliant and clean, with acidity, mouth-filling body, and aromas of toast, nuts, butter, and a variety of subtle fruits. When ripened in the California sunshine, the fruit aroma becomes more apparent.

Napa Valley, the first California appellation to excel with Chardonnay, tends to produce high-glycerine, well-oaked versions with ample fruit—apple and pear aromas intermingled with oak is a frequent observation. Drive over the Mayacamas mountain range into Sonoma Valley and you will find a more tropical element in Chardonnay, usually pineapple. The Santa Barbara growing area, far south of Napa/Sonoma, tends to bottle an even riper Chardonnay. The fruit impression there is even more tropical, and the acidity profile is quite soft. For yet more fruit flavor, you must go to Australia.

The grape-growing climate in Australia is unique to wine-producing countries. The Hunter Valley in southeastern Australia experiences intense sunshine. This would normally over-ripen wine grapes, but the ripening effect of the sun in this region is greatly tempered by cool breezes. This combination of plentiful sunlight and refreshing air brings grapes to a full ripeness slowly, so as to develop the most intense flavors imaginable in Chardonnay. Suggestions of pineapple, coconut, and bananas spring forth from this deep-golden wine. These wines used to lack the necessary acidity, but innovative winemaking techniques seem to have solved this problem.

Because Chardonnay has such a range of styles, one needs to consider the type of Chardonnay when trying to find the right wine for a particular meal. Chablis is the driest, most acidic interpretation, and belongs with seafood, especially shellfish and delicate white fish like Dover sole. The rounder white Burgundies from the Côte de

Chateau Ste Michelle

COLUMBIA VALLEY

CHARDONNAY

PRODUCED AND BOTTLED BY CHATEAU STE. MICHELLE®
WOODINVILLE, WA • USA • ALC. 12.8% BY VOL. • CONTAINS SULFITES

Beaune are also seafood wines but can accompany meats such as chicken and veal. Seafood doesn't match so well with fruitier Chardonnays such as those from California and Australia.

If you insist on a fruity Chardonnay with your fish, California cusine comes into play. The flavorful ingredients used in California cuisine—generous additions of fresh herbs and various chili peppers, and wood grilling—can transform a delicate piece of fish into a jam session of loud flavors. A big wine is called for; California Chardonnay is ideal. In fact, big Chardonnays like these can stand up to many dishes not normally paired with white wine—even grilled meats!

Finally, if you want to drink Chardonnay without food, the Australian versions, with their generous fruit and mild acidity, are an excellent choice.

Good Chardonnay in Ascending Order of Price

1. Monterey Vineyard Chardonnay (Monterey, California) $7
2. Georges Duboeuf Saint-Véran (Macon, Burgundy, France) $9
3. Meridian Chardonnay (Santa Barbara, California) $10
4. Kendall-Jackson Vintners Reserve Chardonnay (California) $13
5. Cambria "Katherine's Vineyard" Chardonnay (Santa Barbara, California) $18
6. Robert Mondavi Chardonnay (Napa, California) $20
7. Rosemount "Show Reserve" Chardonnay (Australia) $24
8. Matanzas Creek Chardonnay (Sonoma, California) $27
9. Hanzell Chardonnay (Sonoma, California) $34
10. Domaine Leflaive Puligny-Montrachet (Burgundy, France) $43

Sauvignon Blanc

Main growing regions: Bordeaux (France), Loire (France), California,
Washington State, and South Africa
Aromas and flavors: Cut grass, herbs, and lemon
Acidity: High
Body: Medium
Major mixing partner: Semillon (Bordeaux)

In comparison to Chardonnay, it may take a little more wine knowledge to appreciate a great Sauvignon Blanc. That is because the hallmark of quality Sauvignon Blanc—bright, crisp acidity—is not as sensually pleasing as the seductive texture of good Chardonnay. Yet this high acidity makes for a great pairing with seafood—Sancerre from the Loire; Graves Blanc from Bordeaux; and varietal Sauvignon Blanc from California, South Africa, and even New Zealand are perfect with fish. "Grassy" and "herbaceous" are common descriptions of Sauvignon Blanc's fruit components.

An alternative vinification style of Sauvignon Blanc yields a richer wine. "Fumé Blanc" is the name for a style created in California in the 1960s by Robert Mondavi. Styled after the legendary Pouilly Fumé of the Loire region in France, Fumé Blanc has a richer, fuller style. Whereas the Sauvignon Blancs are excellent with seafood, the more substantial Fumé Blanc may be paired with a wider variety of dishes, including chicken, veal, and pasta.

There are a few world-class wines made from Sauvignon Blanc that earn this variety its place beside the other white noble grapes, Riesling and Chardonnay. Château Haut-Brion blanc of Graves is universally regarded as the finest of its type and an equal to the great white Burgundies. Close on its heels is Domaine de Chevalier, also from Graves. Sauvignon Blanc is blended with a lesser amount of Semillon in most Graves whites. This formula is reversed in

the dessert wines from neighboring Sauternes.

In spite of its legitimate claim to nobility, Sauvignon Blanc might well have an inferiority complex. The public hasn't taken to this variety like it has to Chardonnay. Some winemakers have even employed a heavy-handed oaking to make Sauvignon Blanc seem more like Chardonnay. Fortunately, low demand has kept the prices down somewhat. Try serving a good Sauvignon Blanc with an uncomplicated seafood dish without telling your guests what they are drinking. You will look very wine smart.

Good Sauvignon Blanc in Ascending Order of Price

1. Kronendaal Sauvignon Blanc (South Africa) $6
2. Canyon Road Sauvignon Blanc (California). $8
3. Matua Valley Sauvignon Blanc (New Zealand) $10
4. Sterling Sauvignon Blanc (Napa, California) $10
5. Frog's Leap Sauvignon Blanc (Napa, California) $16
6. Michel Redde Sancerre (Loire, France) $18
7. Duckhorn Sauvignon Blanc (Napa, California). $20
8. Robert Mondavi Fumé Blanc Reserve (Napa, California) $24
9. Pouilly Fumé La Doucette (Loire, France) $30
10. Pavillon Blanc du Château Margaux (Bordeaux, France) $45

Riesling

Main growing regions: Germany, Alsace (France), and California
Aromas and flavors: Apricots, citrus, peaches, and flowers
Acidity: Moderate to high
Body: Light; medium to heavy for dessert wines
Major mixing partners: None (Riesling is often blended with lesser
varieties in nonvarietal German QbA wines.)

Just as Pinot Noir rivals Cabernet Sauvignon for preeminence among noble red varieties, the Riesling grape has a following who regard it as superior to Chardonnay. Like Pinot Noir, Riesling has not traveled as well as its rival. Both Pinot Noir and Riesling turn shy in the warmth of California and require a cooler climate in order to perform well. Whereas the demand for quality Pinot Noir has motivated American winemakers to seek out promising vineyards for it, Riesling has never been in high demand in the United States. Perhaps if Riesling had been widely planted in France it would have found its niche in French gastronomy and secured its immortality. However, only in the Alsace region of France is Riesling permitted to grow in French soil.

Riesling's alleged sweetness has also kept it out of the fast lane in today's wine market. Riesling grapes can make sweet wine. Their prominent acidity provides the perfect balance for late-harvest sweetness, and they can produce the sweetest dessert wines in the world. However, some excellent Rieslings, notably those from Alsace, can be nearly bone dry. The aroma of well-made Riesling is flowery as well as fruity. Riesling *smells* sweeter than Chardonnay.

Riesling has long been the basis for the finest wines of Germany. The steep slopes along the Rhine and Mosel rivers retain warmth and incubate the Riesling to full ripeness in the otherwise chilly climate. To attain the necessary sweetness and become a good dessert wine in such a northerly climate is a victory over nature.

Although the Semillon-based dessert wines from Sauternes, France are equally noteworthy as world-class dessert wines, these wines need some acidic Sauvignon Blanc blended in to balance the flaccid sweetness of *Botrytis*-affected Semillon. Sweet Riesling need not be blended.

Some of the best values in the wine world today are the German Rieslings designated QbA and labeled "Riesling." The superior QmP white wines from Germany are by definition made from Riesling unless labeled otherwise. (See Chapter 6, "Wine Around the World," for a complete explanation of the intricate wine laws of Germany.) If you insist on a very dry Riesling, the Alsace versions are definitely worth exploring.

There have been some notable successes with Riesling in North America, many outside of California. Oregon, Washington State, Idaho, New York State, and Canada all produce quality Rieslings.

Be wary of imitations! Several lowly grape varieties, including Gray Riesling and Welschriesling, are deceptively named and have nothing to do with the real thing. Look for wines labeled "Riesling," "White Riesling," or "Johannisberg Riesling." Don't be afraid of an older bottle. Rieslings have demonstrated a capacity to improve with age, much more so than Chardonnays. This is especially true of the Alsace and German Rieslings.

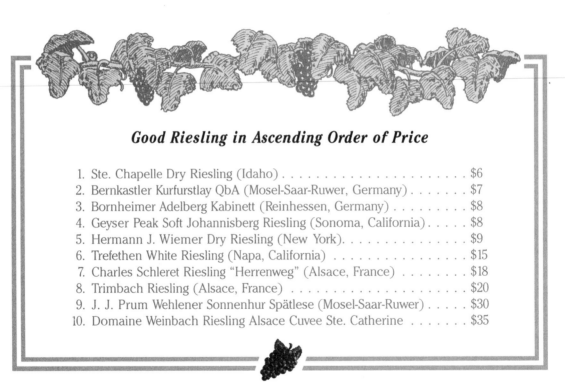

Good Riesling in Ascending Order of Price

1. Ste. Chapelle Dry Riesling (Idaho) $6
2. Bernkastler Kurfurstlay QbA (Mosel-Saar-Ruwer, Germany) $7
3. Bornheimer Adelberg Kabinett (Reinhessen, Germany) $8
4. Geyser Peak Soft Johannisberg Riesling (Sonoma, California) $8
5. Hermann J. Wiemer Dry Riesling (New York) $9
6. Trefethen White Riesling (Napa, California) $15
7. Charles Schleret Riesling "Herrenweg" (Alsace, France) $18
8. Trimbach Riesling (Alsace, France) $20
9. J. J. Prum Wehlener Sonnenhur Spätlese (Mosel-Saar-Ruwer) $30
10. Domaine Weinbach Riesling Alsace Cuvee Ste. Catherine $35

Chenin Blanc

Main growing regions: Loire (France), South Africa,
New Zealand, and California
Aromas and flavors: Somewhat muted; bread, pine, and orange
Acidity: Very high
Body: Light to medium
Major mixing partner: Chardonnay

Chenin Blanc is widely grown around the world and has several distinct personalities. In the Loire Valley of northwestern France, where it has been cultivated for over a thousand years, Chenin Blanc is responsible for the acidic white wines of Anjou and Touraine. The best known of these is Vouvray, which itself can take several forms.

Vouvray, whose name comes from the village in Touraine where it is produced, is probably the most weather-sensitive table wine in the world. Whereas winemakers elsewhere usually attempt to produce a somewhat consistent style from vintage to vintage, Vouvray is made in very different styles depending on the weather. A pleasant, sunny summer brings the Chenin Blanc grapes in Vouvray to full ripeness. In such years demi-sec (half-dry) wine is usually produced. These wines have a pleasant level of residual sugar, but they are dry enough to enjoy with dinner. Chenin Blanc's inherent bracing acidity provides ample balance to the sweetness in demi-sec wines. These

wines match well with a wide variety of light dishes.

A cold and rainy summer is unwelcome in any vineyard. Rather than gnash their teeth, though, the winemakers of Vouvray respond by making Vouvray sec. This dry version of Chenin Blanc is *very* acidic. Such wine is nearly impossible to drink without food and is difficult to match with anything other than shellfish.

Vouvray sec does have a following, however, among connoisseurs who prize naked acidity. On the other end of the sweetness spectrum is Quarts de

Chaume, a melony, honeyed dessert wine made from *Botrytis*-affected Chenin Blanc from Anjou in the Loire Valley. These sweet wines are said to live indefinitely in the bottle, as do the sweeter versions of the Vouvray demi-sec.

High acidity is the backbone of well-made sparkling wine, and the naturally acidic Chenin Blanc grape is used to make high-quality sparkling wine in the Loire region. Semi-sparkling wine labeled "Vouvray Mousseux" is common, and the great Champagne firm of Taittinger produces its Bouvet Brut from Chenin Blanc in the Loire. These sparkling wines, though not as complex as true Champagne, are often as well made and offer excellent value.

Chenin Blanc has traveled abroad with success. It was brought to South Africa in the 1600s by Dutch settlers and is widely grown there under the name of Steen. In California, Chenin Blanc is extensively cultivated for use in brandy-making and as part of the mix in jug wines.

There have also been many pleasant and enjoyable California Chenin Blancs sold as varietal wines, but their popularity is fading. The best of these display the same honey and melon aromas as Quarts de Chaume with moderate acidity—perfect summer wines. As well as its use in California jug wines, Chenin Blanc is sometimes blended with Chardonnay in New Zealand and in Loire.

In general, Chenin Blanc–based wines match well with summer foods. Because of their high acidity, restrained fruit, and balance, well-made versions can be a welcome respite from your usual white wine. These wines have a natural affinity with sweet shellfish like sea scallops, but are also enjoyable with anything light, such as pasta, fish, and chicken.

Good Chenin Blanc in Ascending Order of Price

1. Landskroon Steen (South Africa) . . . . $ 8
2. Matua Valley Chenin Blanc/Chardonnay (New Zealand) . . . . $ 9
3. Dry Creek Chenin Blanc (Sonoma, California) $9
4. B&G Vouvray (Loire, France) $10
5. Mark Bredif Vouvray (Loire, France) $14
6. Domaine Baumard Quarts de Chaume (Loire, France) $30

Pinot Blanc

Main growing regions: Burgundy (France), Alsace (France), Italy, and California
Aromas and flavors: Somewhat subdued almonds and apples
Acidity: Moderate to high
Body: Medium to full
Major mixing partner: Chardonnay (Burgundy)

Also known as Pinot Bianco in Italy, Pinot Blanc is known for its simple, full-bodied, clean structure and forward acidity. It is used (in combination with other grapes) for some premium sparkling wines in California. Not widely produced in California, Pinot Blanc can be a good value among Alsace wines. Because it usually makes a relatively uncomplicated wine, Pinot Blanc is enjoyable with a wide variety of dishes and does not require particularly careful matching.

Pinot Blanc is more notable for its history and heritage than for the wines made from it. Originally cultivated in ancient Burgundy, Pinot Blanc has long been cultivated side by side with Chardonnay. Indeed, some mutations of Pinot Blanc are capable of producing a Chardonnay-like wine. But for the most part, Pinot Blanc makes a rather nondescript wine with weak aroma—good with food and boring without. Although we encourage occasional daring and uninformed purchases in the wine store, for Pinot Blanc we suggest you start with our recommended bottles.

Good Pinot Blanc in Ascending Order of Price

1. Mirassou White Burgundy (Monterey, California) $9
2. Hugel "cuvée les Amours" Pinot Blanc (Alsace, France) $12
3. Eno Friulia Pinot Bianco (Friuli, Italy) $12
4. Chalone Pinot Blanc (Monterey, California) $24

Semillon

Main growing regions: Bordeaux (France), Australia, and California
Aromas and flavors: Figs, honey, and lemon
Acidity: Low to medium
Body: Full
Major mixing partners: Chardonnay (Australia) and Sauvignon Blanc (Bordeaux)

The Semillon grape rarely stands alone as a varietal. It is often blended in the Graves subregion of Bordeaux, France, with Sauvignon Blanc. Its silky richness complements the acidity of the Sauvignon Blanc. In Australia Semillon is used in Semillon/Chardonnay blends. These wines are pleasant and inexpensive.

Semillon is the main variety in Sauternes, the dessert wine–producing subregion of Bordeaux. These wines also have Sauvignon Blanc mixed in to give them a little acidity.

Good and affordable dessert Semillon, in its pure form, is produced in Australia.

Its signature characteristics are low acidity and thick body, and its aromas and flavors of figs, honey, and lemon are restrained. This set of qualities does not add up to an exceptional table wine, but good, inexpensive varietal Semillon is available. However, Semillon's propensity for richness and its susceptibility to "noble rot" make it a useful grape variety, albeit one with limited applications.

Good Semillon in Ascending Order of Price

1. Penfolds Semillon/Chardonnay Koonunga Hill (Australia) $8
2. Indian Hill Semillon (Sierra Foothills, California) $10
3. Château Haut-Gravier (Graves, France) $11
4. Peter Lehmann Sauternes-Semillon (Australia) . . . . $13/half bottle
5. Château Raymond-Lafon (Sauternes, France) . . . . $25/half bottle

Viognier

Main growing regions: Rhône (France) and California
Aromas and flavors: Apricots, wood, peaches, and flowers
Acidity: Low to medium
Body: Medium to full
Major mixing partners: None

The unheralded Viognier grape has been producing some fine alternatives to Chardonnay in France's upper Rhône. Viognier's popularity is fairly recent as a varietal from California. Its apricot/peach flavors are a refreshing alternative to the repetitive pear/vanilla flavors of California Chardonnay. In fact, Viognier's biggest asset may be its vastly different flavor structure compared to Chardonnay, making it a good choice for those seeking an alternative to Chardonnay.

The northern Rhône valley of Condrieu is the home turf for Viognier. The smallest recognized appellation in France is Château Grillet, a single estate within Condrieu. The Viognier grape approaches world-class status at this tiny property: A bottle of Château Grillet fetches $100 or more, and is said to age well *forever* in the bottle. Less expensive but certainly noteworthy versions of Viognier come from the surrounding Condrieu vineyards.

At its best, Viognier has aromas and flavors of peach, apricot, and flowers, though it is not as overtly flowery as Riesling. With the aromas and flavors of these particular fruit,

The Vitis Vinifera Family (most notable members)

Red-, Purple-, or Black-Skinned Grapes (Red Wine):
Cabernet Sauvignon, Gamay, Grenache, Merlot, Nebbiolo, Petite Sirah, Pinot Noir, Sangiovese, Syrah, Tempranillo, Zinfandel

Green-Skinned Grapes (White Wine):
Chardonnay, Chenin Blanc, Gewürztraminer, Pinot Blanc, Pinot Grigio, Riesling, Sauvignon Blanc, Semillon, Viognier

Viognier is a natural match with pork, which has an affinity for both. However, if you substitute Viognier for Chardonnay in any food-wine pairing, you won't be disappointed.

California Viognier is not cheap. For bargains, look for varietal Viognier from big French producers. Inexpensive *vin de pays* varietal Viognier has caught on in the French countryside, at least for export. These are often good values in terms of quality when compared with similarly priced Chardonnay.

Good Viognier Blanc in Ascending Order of Price

1. Georges Duboeuf Viognier (France) $9
2. B&G Viognier (France) $10
3. Rabbit Ridge Viognier (Sonoma, California) $16
4. Arrowood Viognier (Sonoma, California) $33
5. Guigal Condrieu (Rhône, France) $37
6. Château Grillet (Condrieu, Rhône, France) $100

Pinot Grigio/Pinot Gris

Main growing regions: Italy, Alsace (France), Oregon, and California
Aromas and flavors: Somewhat muted; minerals, pine, and orange rind
Acidity: Medium (generally higher in Europe)
Body: Medium (generally heavier in the United States)
Major mixing partners: None

A close relative of Pinot Blanc, Pinot Grigio has recently become a very popular varietal wine from Italy. In Friuli and Aldo Adige, two northern regions of Italy, Pinot Grigio can produce a well-structured and acidic match for seafood, with somewhat muddled aromas. In warmer climates, however, the acidity level can be undesirably low. Pinot Grigio is a relatively recent visitor to California, where it has yet to succeed in making wines comparable to those in northern Italy.

Alsatian soil brings out the best in several white varieties, and Pinot Grigio, known there as Tokay Pinot Gris, is one of them. This pink-skinned variety is not very strong-willed and is a perfect vehicle for the Alsace *terroir*—rich, minerally soil flavors mingle with the substantial acidity.

The Oregonians call their version Pinot Gris. The cool Williamette Valley appears to be a Pinot Gris–friendly growing region. These wines have stonger than usual Pinot Gris flavor, rich body, and the signature pine and orange aromas of Pinot Grigio. These wines tend to be more expensive than the Italian versions.

Because it doesn't have prominent fruit flavors, Pinot Grigio is relatively easy to match with food. The drier, more acidic versions are excellent with shellfish and other seafoods, whereas the fuller-bodied versions can accompany chicken and pasta dishes well.

Good Pinot Grigio/Pinot Gris in Ascending Order of Price

1. Lirica Pinot Grigio (Veneto, Italy) $6
2. Castello d'Albola Pinot Grigio (Tuscany, Italy) $9
3. Eno Friulia Pinot Grigio (Friuli, Italy). $13
4. Gustave Lorenz Pinot Gris Reserve (Alsace, France). $15
5. Eyrie Vineyard Pinot Gris (Oregon) $19
6. Puiatti Pinot Grigio (Friuli, Italy). $22

Gewürztraminer

Main growing regions: Germany, Alsace (France), and California
Aromas and flavors: Strong lychee-nut fruit and grapefruit rind
Acidity: Low to medium
Body: Full
Major mixing partners: None

A mouthful, literally, Gewürztraminer (gah-VERTS-truh-MEEN-er) can be as difficult to enjoy as it is to pronounce. Rich, pungent, spicy flavors with fruit notes of lychee and grapefruit rind make for a difficult food-wine pairing. As such, Gewürztraminer is often suggested with spicy Asian food—an awkward blind date at best. Regional tradition in Alsace matches Gewürztraminer with sausage and ham. Because of its low acidity and bold flavors, Gewürztraminer can be enjoyable all by itself, without food. Alternatively, a

Good Gewürztraminer in Ascending Order of Price

1. Geyser Peak Gewürztraminer (Sonoma, California) $8
2. Durkheimer Feuerberg Gewürztraminer QbA (Rheinfalz, Germany) . $11
3. Chateau St. Jean Gewürztraminer (Sonoma, California) $12
4. Charles Schleret Gewürztraminer "Herrenweg" (Alsace, France) . . . $18
5. Domaine Zind-Humbrecht Gewürztraminer Turckheim
   (Alsace, France) $26

simple, creamy cheese provides a good background for the complex, full personality of this grape.

Gewürztraminer is a pink-skinned clone of the much older Traminer vine that probably originated in northern Italy. The "Gewürz-" is German for "spicy" or "pungent" and reflects the powerful aromas of Gewürztraminer wines. It is the least subtle of all the well-known *vinifera* grapes.

Although it grows best in Alsace (France), it plays second fiddle there to the Riesling grape. Its share of vineyard space in Germany has been on the decline, again being out-muscled by the Riesling grape. California and Pacific Northwest versions of this quirky variety tend to lack the complexity of their European counterparts, but can be both enjoyable and affordable.

Minor Grapes

The *Vitis vinifera* family of grapes, which is responsible for wine as we know it, is indeed a very large family. There are thousands of such grape varieties, yet most are unknown to wine drinkers and wine-store shelves. Vines grow all over the world, but relatively few varieties are used for the commercial production of wine. The well-known wine grapes are famous because they produce good or balanced wine, and to grow them requires little-to-reasonable effort. But maybe someone will conduct winemaking experiments with an obscure or yet-undiscovered variety of grape and give the world a new Chardonnay or Pinot Noir.

However, there are some grapes that are used as blending grapes for the family big wigs. This is done to make a wine taste less tannic or acidic, to make it more complex, to save money, or any combination of these reasons. The minor wine grapes used in commercial wine production are often red grapes that are blended with other red grapes. Cabernet Franc, although rarely found alone, is considered by many to be Cabernet Sauvignon's best friend.

Malbec is a more typical example of a minor grape. It is used in wine production throughout the world. Malbec makes simple, sturdy wine. The skins and seeds are thoroughly removed from the juice of this and most of the other minor commercial grapes.

This is because the flavors of the acids and tannins are not as desirable in the minor grapes as those of the major grapes like Cabernet Sauvigon. Remember, the skins of red-wine grapes give a wine some of its signature characteristics. If people liked the signature characteristics of Malbec, Cinsault, Cannaiolo, Kerner, and the many other grapes most people have never heard of, then we'd be drinking wines featuring those grapes.

Don't dismiss these grapes as meaningless. Some of the famous wines of Italy, France, and Spain have some minor grapes blended in for the sole purpose of making the wine better. Different countries have different laws concerning the legal percentages of these grapes in the wine. A grape variety that accounts for 5–25 percent of a wine, depending on the country, doesn't need to be credited. Of course, most European wines don't even credit the star grape on the wine label. It is hoped that all this secrecy will be eliminated someday. After all, each can of soda sold in the United States has its ingredients listed.

There are relatively minor grapes from which wines are made, but they are rarely sold outside the region in which they are produced. In Germany, the easy-to-grow and early-ripening Müller-Thurgau grape is made into a simple white wine enjoyed mostly in Germany. In Argentina, Criolla is used to make a simple white wine for Argentineans to enjoy. The red Periquita grape is popular in Portugal.

Italy is by far the biggest producer of decent Barbera, which makes a very drinkable, food-friendly red wine. It's a good pizza wine, and it is currently enjoying some success outside of the homeland. Italy also has many lesser known grape varieties that are used to produce wine for the locals.

The Muscadet grape of Loire, France, is a grape that is used to make wines that go very well with shellfish. It is hardly ever grown elsewhere.

Spain's white Arien grape, the most widely planted wine grape in the world, is unfamiliar as a variety to most wine buffs.

These minor grape varieties have a few things in common. For the most part, they have not found a worldwide following because they lack distinctive, high-quality characteristics. They do grow easily in their home regions, where they have long been enjoyed as inexpensive everyday wines. As such, they tend well with the local cuisine, and that is probably the best way to enjoy them. If they are well made, they can be excellent values. Several of these varieties have been successfully transplanted to the New World and are becoming popular as varietal wines.

Some Minor Varieties Worth Looking For:

Red

Barbera (Piedmont, Italy)
Malbec (Argentina; originally from
    Bordeaux, France)
Lemberger (Washington State;
    originally from Germany)
Carmenere (Chile; originally from
    Bordeaux, France)
Periquita (Portugal)

White

Grüner Veltliner (Austria)
Aligoté (Burgundy, France)
Sylvaner (Germany)
Furmint (Hungary)
Chasselas (Switzerland)

EVERYTHING

C H A P T E R 5

SPECIAL OCCASION WINES

BOTTLED BY ADAMS MEDIA

NET CONTENTS: TWENTY PAGES

PRODUCT OF USA

Sparkling Wine (Champagne)

"Come, for I am drinking stars!"

So said cellarmaster Dom Pérignon, according to legend, when he tasted the first Champagne. The bubbles in Champagne and sparkling wines set them apart from all other wines, lending a sense of frivolity and joy-ousness not otherwise associated with wine-drinking. Champagne has long been virtually a requirement for celebrations such as New Year's Eve, sports victories, and weddings. People who normally do not drink wine nonetheless enjoy Champagne at such occa-

sions. Presently, however, the wine boom has not extended to Champagne and sparkling wines; as the wine-drinking public becomes more interested and knowledgeable in the still wines of the world, consumption of bubbly has slackened in favor of demand for Chardonnay and Merlot. It remains for those consumers following this trend to discover that Champagne and sparkling wines are not just for celebrations—they can be as well made, affordable, and appropriate with good food as any other wine.

Sparkling wine starts out as white (or pink) wine. It is then put in a bottle or barrel with yeast and sugar for a second fermentation, which produces a little more alcohol (1 percent of volume) and a lot of carbon dioxide (bubbles). The alcohol kills the yeast, which is eventually removed with great care so as not to lose the carbonation.

The result is white wine or rosé enhanced by natural carbonation and the complex flavors developed during the second fermentation. If the second fermentation occurred in the same bottle in which it is sold, then it was made via the Champagne method, or *méthode champenoise* as it is known in France where it was supposedly invented by the blind monk named Dom Pérignon. This is the best, but most labor-intensive, way of making sparkling wine.

The best sparkling wines in the world, according to the French and many other people, come from Champagne, a wine-producing region in northern France. Only sparkling wines produced in this region via the Champagne method are denoted as Champagne. Therefore, the only true Champagne comes from Champagne, France.

Champagne has become to sparkling wines what Kleenex is to facial tissues in terms of name use and recognition. Much to the fury of the French, some cheap sparkling wines made in the United States, Canada, and Australia can legally call themselves champagne (with a small "c") in those countries. The French have long jealously guarded this place-name. The treaty of Versailles specifically forbade the Germans from appropriating the name, and the EEC nations honor the French label law.

Sparkling wine should be served well-chilled, so that the carbonation will last longer and feel smoother. However, those who are drinking very expensive Champagne will want to serve it at a slightly warmer temperature so that they may, at least theoretically, taste why they paid so much for a bottle of sparkling wine.

For around $10–15, pretty good California or Spanish sparkling wine can be had. (Spanish sparkling wine is known as cava.) We consider California sparkling wine to be a very good wine value; it is fruitier and less dry than French versions. If you don't like your sparkling wine to be very dry, you may not even like the *real* stuff from Champagne.

The driest of Champagnes and sparkling wines often contain a high proportion of Chardonnay and are appropriate with any light seafood dish. Pale bubbly (that is not Rosé bubbly) is rarely *incorrect* with any dish. Historically this has been an easy way

Champagne & Sparkling Wines Buying Guide

Good Inexpensive Stuff
Feist-Belmont Blanc de Blancs (France) $8
Paul Cheneau Blanc de Blancs (Spain). $9
Domaine St. Michelle (Washington State) $10
Culbertson (California) $10
Bouvet Brut (Loire, France) $11
Rotari Brut Riserva (Italy) $13

Better Less Inexpensive Stuff
Gloria Ferrar Brut (Sonoma, California). $15
Domaine Chandon Brut Cuvee (Napa, California) $16
Scharffenberger Brut (Mendocino, California) $17

Best of California
Jordan "J" Sparkling Wine (Alexander Valley, California). $18
Scharffenberger Blanc de Blancs (Mendocino, California) $23
Iron Horse Brut (Sonoma, California). $27
Domaine Chandon "Etoile" (Napa, California) $29
Roederer Estate "Brut L'Hermitage" (Anderson Valley, California) $40
Schramsberg J. Schram Brut (Napa, California). $54

Recommended French Champagnes
(all from Champagne, France, of course)
Moët et Chandon "White Star" (extra dry) $25
Pol Roger Brut. $33
Laurent-Perrier Brut. $37
Moët et Chandon Brut Imperial, 1990 . . . . $48
G. H. Mumm "Rene Lalou," 1985. . . . . $65

Champagne & Sparkling Wines Buying Guide

Champagne for Rock Stars
Perrier-Jouët Flower Bottle, 1989 . . . . $90
Dom Pérignon, 1988. . . . . $95
Louis Roederer "Cristal," 1989 . . . . $145

Champagne for True Connoisseurs
Pol Roger "Cuvée Sir Winston Churchill". $100
Krug Grand Cuvée $110
Laurent Perrier Grande Siecle $115
Bollinger R. D. Extra Brut $125
Salon Le Mesnil $130
Taittinger Comtes de Champagne Blanc de Blancs $145
Krug (vintage) $165

Good Pink Stuff, California
Mirabelle Brut Rosé (North Coast) $14
Gloria Ferrar Blanc de Noirs (Sonoma) $15
Mumm Cuvée Napa Blanc de Noirs (Napa) $16
Schramsberg Brut Rosé Cuvée de Pinot (Napa) $28
Iron Horse Rosé Brut (Sonoma) $30

Really Good Pink Stuff, Champagne
Jean Vesselle Brut Rosé. $30
Moët et Chandon Vintage Brut Imperial Rosé $60
Billecart-Salmon Rosé $65
Taittinger Comtes de Champagne Brut Rosé. $145
Louis Roederer "Cristal" Rosé $220

Sweet Sparkling Wine
Saracco Moscato d'Asti (Piedmont, Italy) $15
Schramsberg Cremant Demi-Sec (Napa, California) $30
Vueve Clicquot Demi-Sec (Champagne, France) $50

out of the food-wine matching game for many a host.

SWEET SPARKLING WINE

People who don't enjoy dry table wines often do enjoy two types of wine—sweet, and sparkling. Sweet sparkling wine offers a way to double their wine-drinking pleasure. The sweetness usually comes from a high amount of added sugar—almost all sparkling wines have at least some sugar added after the dead yeast is removed. Sweet sparkling wine, usually labeled demi-sec, is usually drunk without food, although it matches well with simple creamy cheeses and many desserts.

PINK CHAMPAGNE/ BRUT ROSÉ

The better sparkling wines, including Champagne, are usually made from both green-skinned grapes (Chardonnay) and black-skinned grapes (Pinot Noit and Pinot Meunier). If pigment from the black-skinned grapes is permitted to lend color to the wine, the result is pink-colored sparkling wine, also called brut rosé. There is a broad price spectrum of pink-hued bubbly, ranging from the $4 pink "champagne" (with a plastic cork) from bulk producers in California to exquisite and rare French versions that cost over $200. The growing climate in California brings Pinot Noir to full ripeness and is especially well-suited to the production of affordable and well-made brut rosé. The fuller-bodied of these are sturdy enough to enjoy with traditional red wine dishes such as beef and game birds.

Dessert Wine

Dessert wine is very sweet white wine that usually has a rich golden color. It can be made several ways. In most cases the residual sugar in these sweet wines is the result of the "noble rot," the *Botrytis cinerea* fungus on grapes left on the vine to become overly ripe. This "affliction" draws water from the grapes and adds complex flavors. The resulting crop of grapes has a high concentration of sugar, not all of which converts to alcohol during fermentation. Other types of dessert wines are made from over-ripe grapes that are simply very high in sugar content.

Because the grape juice used to make dessert wines has so much sugar, the fermentation process can potentially produce a high level of alcohol. The high sugar content also helps preserve the wine, so it can improve in the bottle for many years. Unlike most dry white wines, these wines can last for several days after being opened. They are best served at around 50°F (10°C).

If you are interested in trying a dessert wine, you probably should start with a half bottle. Two people together are very unlikely to drink a half bottle

Botrytis Cinerea (Noble Rot)

In certain regions, grapes are allowed to stay on the vine after they are ripe to contract a fungus called *botrytis cinerea*. Unlike *Phylloxera*, this condition is desirable and controllable. What this fungus does is cause the grapes to dehydrate (lose water), thus concentrating the juice and sugar. This affliction often referred to as the Noble Rot, yields an extremely thick and sugar-laden juice for the winemaker to work with. The grapes are apt to pick up some complex flavors that complement the sweetness. These sweet white-wine juices are turned into thick sweet wines called dessert wines.

In France these dessert wines come from the small but famous area of Sauternes. Like most wines in France, these wines are named after the region in which they are made. Germany's most coveted wines are dessert wines from *botrytis*-infected grapes from vineyards of the Rhine and Mosel. These are not the only two countries that use *botrytis*, but they are the sources of the very best dessert wines in the world. California, Austria, Hungary, and Australia also produce dessert wines made from grapes afflicted with the Noble Rot.

in a sitting. In fact, if you are just experimenting, you can probably stretch a half bottle to four people.

These wines are better served alone as dessert, rather than as an accompaniment to dessert. They are often too sweet to match with dessert food. Ironically, they are often served as an appetizer!

In the United States, Sherry and Port may be labeled "dessert wine" even if they are somewhat dry. They are not dessert wines in the same sense. This is one of the many annoying cases of misleading information on wine bottles. Make sure you are getting a real dessert wine. If you have a sweet tooth, you may really find them to be wonderful.

Good Dessert Wines in Ascending Order of Price (375-ml bottles)

1. Andrew Quady Essencia (California). $11
2. Peter Lehmann Botrytis Semillon Sauternes (Australia) $13
3. Ceretto Moscato d'Asti "Santa Stefano" (Piedmont, Italy). $13
4. Schramsberg Cremant Demi-Sec (Napa, California) $15
5. Lolonis "Eugenia" Late Harvest Chardonnay (Mendocino) $22
6. Château Raymond Lafon Sauternes (Bordeaux, France) $25
7. Veuve Clicquot Demi-Sec Champagne (Champagne, France) $25
8. Domaine Coyeaux Muscat Beaumes-de-Venise (Rhône, France). . . . $25
9. Disznoko Tokaji Aszu 6 Puttonyos (Hungary) $33
    (500-ml bottle)
10. Château des Charmes Riesling Ice Wine Bosc Estate $50
    (Ontario, Canada)
11. Château d'Yquem Sauternes (Bordeaux, France) $100
12. Schneider, Niersteiner Hipping Trockenbeerenauslese $175
    (Rheinhessen, Germany)

Fortified Wine

There are four primary types of fortified wines: Port, Sherry, Madeira, and Marsala. The popular drinking wines are Port and Sherry. The Madeira and Marsala are better known for being cooking wines, but there are good bottles of each for drinking. "Fortified" refers to the addition of alcohol in the production process. The wine's alcohol content is boosted from 10–14 percent up to 18–20 percent by adding grape brandy that is usually made from the same grape as the original wine.

When brandy is added after fermentation, the fortified wine is dry (has no residual sugar). If added before fermentation is complete, the fortified wine is sweet because the extra alcohol stops the yeast from converting the sugars. Fortified wine runs the gamut from bone-dry Fino Sherry to rich, sweet Port and Madeira. All four of these fortified wines have lengthy stories, as do most things in the wine world.

PORT

Port, or Porto, comes from Portugal. The name, however, comes not from the country but from the city of Oporto at the mouth of the Douro River. As the only red fortified wine it has natural appeal among red wine lovers who prize Port's capacity to improve with age in the bottle for many decades.

Port is sold in several different styles— Vintage, Tawny, and Ruby are the principal versions. Vintage Port, the most expensive of these, is also the easiest to produce—as long as nature cooperates; Tawny Port, so named for its brownish cast, is the result of long barrel-aging; and Ruby Port, named for its bright unoxidized color, is an inexpensive style that is perfect for neophytes and fine cooking.

Port is made from several different red varieties that grow to extreme ripeness in Portugal's hot Duro valley. The fruity Souzão grape, the dark-colored "Tintas"—Tinta Cao and Tinta Francisca—and the cabernet franc-like Touriga are blended along with other varieties in various proportions. A white Port is produced, although it is not nearly as prized as the red versions. All (red) Port, then, starts out as "musts" from these varieties, which are allowed to ferment half-way to dryness before the addition of brandy. Since half of the natural sugar remains unfermented, the resulting fortified wine is sweet. It then begins its life in "Port pipes" (138-gallon storage casks).

Vintage Port

After two years in storage a vintage may be "declared" by agreement of a majority of the Port producers. This means that the Port from that particular vintage is deemed to be of sufficient quality to justify offering it as top-of-the-line Vintage Port. Vintage Port is then bottled and is best aged for at least a decade. Because Vintage Port ages in the bottle, often for several decades, it deposits a substantial amount of sediment in the bottle.

Vintage Port has always been quite popular among the British, and a "match made in heaven" is Vintage Port and a wedge of Stilton, the deluxe cheese of England. The pungent saltiness of the cheese complements beautifully the sweet richness of Vintage Port.

Tawny Port

Unlike Vintage Port, which is transferred to bottles in its youth, Tawny Port may remain in the cask for 10, 20, or even 30 years. "Tawny" refers to the pale brown hue of these fortified wines after so long in the cask, where oxidation occurs more readily than in the bottle. With the high alcohol guarding against the formation of vinegar, the oxidation in this case improves the flavor over time. The fruit flavors of youth evolve into mellower, more subtle flavors, and the Port becomes seemingly less sweet.

Tawny Port requires far more blending skills then does vintage Port. Unless labeled "Port of the Vintage" (another form of Tawny Port), most Tawny's are blends of ports from several different years chosen for their complementary characteristics.

Ruby Port

Ruby Port, named for its bright crimson color, is a blend of young, lesser lots of Port. Again the blender's art is of importance—lesser lots (casks) of Port may be skillfully blended to produce an inexpensive and delicious Ruby Port.

The forthright flavors of Ruby Port make it a perfect choice for recipes that call for Port—the flavors of Ruby Port will endure the cooking process far better than will the other types. Also, Ruby Port is a perfect introduction to Port as you begin to explore fortified wines.

SHERRY

Like the other types of fortified wine, Sherry owes its popularity to the British. In fact, the name "Sherry" is an Anglicization of "Jerez," the port city on the coast of Spain from which Sherry is shipped.

Sherry is made by fortifying dry white wine made from the Palomino grape grown in southern Spain. Among wine lovers, Sherry is not as well respected as Port, perhaps because Sherry is generally less "wine-like" and complex than Port. As a result, quality Sherry is often overlooked and underpriced. And yet, quality Sherry can be an ideal substitute for a variety of hard liquor drinks:

- Serve a well-chilled fino Sherry in place of a martini;
- Offer a dark, dry Oloroso Sherry (at room temperature) after dinner instead of Cognac;
- Replace sweet liqueur with a sweet cream Sherry.

Whereas Port, particularly vintage Port, is perceived as closely akin to fine wine by consumers, quality Sherry is regarded as a manufactured product by many people, more like liquor than wine. Indeed, the aging, fortification, and blending processes for Sherry are far more involved than those for Vintage Port.

How Sherry Is Made

All Sherry begins its life in the warm, dry vineyards of southern Spain. Here the Palomino grape, a variety of little use aside from Sherry production, is made into dry, still wine. This wine, called *mosto*, is initially fortified with brandy to an alcohol level of 15 percent and permitted to age in the presence of air. While contact with air would destroy most wines at this stage, the partially fortified *mosto* thrives on it. In most (but not all) of these huge barrels, a cushion of spongy yeast, called *flor*, develops on the surface of the wine.

In barrels with ample flor development, the wine beneath the layer of yeast is protected from oxidation and remains pale in color. The *flor* yeast also imparts flavor on the wine and further concentrates the alcoholic content. Sherry from these barrels is generally called "fino" and may become one of the three paler types of Sherry—Fino itself, Mauzauilla, or Amontillado.

The barrels that develop little or no *flor* yeast yield "oloroso" Sherry, which is finished as one of the darker styles—dry Oloroso itself, sweet Amoroso, or very sweet cream Sherry. An especially rare type of Sherry is Palo Cortado, an Oloroso that develops *flor* yeast late in its life and can combine the finest qualities of both Finos and Olorosos.

Because the alcohol in Fino Sherries is concentrated by the *flor* yeast, these types of Sherry are given additional fortification only as required by importers worldwide. In Spain, Fino Sherry is often not additionally fortified and can be found at 16 percent

alcohol. As such, this type of Sherry will not survive indefinitely in an opened bottle.

The darker Oloroso Sherries usually receive a second fortification that raises the alcoholic strength to 18–20 percent. Because of this, Olorosos can live for a long time in the bottle after it is opened.

The blending process used in Sherry production, called the "solera" process, is unique. Barrels of young Sherry are connected to older barrels in such a manner that Sherries from different years are blended; this is why these are no vintage sherries. You may, however, find an expensive Sherry with a year on the label. This is usually the vintage year of the oldest Sherry in the solera blend and may be over 100 hundred years old.

Types of Sherry

The Fino Family
Manzanilla—This is a pale, dry, fino Sherry that comes from the coastal town of Sanlúcar de Barrameda. Because it matures in casks stored near the sea, it acquires a tangy salty flavor from the coastal air. Serve it with *tapas*.

Fino—Fino is both the general name of the unfinished *flor* Sherries and the name of one of the finished products within that group. This Sherry is pale, dry, and best served chilled as an apéritif in the hot summer.

Amontillado—Made famous by an Edgar Alan Poe short story ("The Cask of Amontillado"), this style of Sherry is most notable for its nut-like flavor and aroma. These characteristics, along with a light brown color, can develop when a fino-type Sherry ages. Like the other fino types, Amontillado is a before-dinner drink, though better served at room temperature. While the paler fino types are most enjoyable in the hot summer, Amontillado is something of an autumn apéritif with its darker, richer flavors.

The Oloroso Family
Oloroso—There is a popular perception that darker Sherries are, by definition, sweeter—not so. Oloroso Sherry itself is, in its natural state, quite dry. (Like Fino Sherry, Oloroso Sherry is both the name of a category of sherries—those unaffected by flor— and the name of one of the finished products in this category. Good Oloroso is dry, richly flavored, and full-bodied, and is medium-brown in color.

Amoroso—Dry Oloroso Sherry is sometimes sweetened by the addition of sweet, concentrated wine made for this purpose from Moscatel or Pedro Ximenez grapes. The result is Amoroso Sherry, a sweet after-dinner drink. Similarly, Amoroso may be darkened by the addition of specially prepared "coloring wine." Brown sherry is an especially dark version of Amoroso sherry.

Cream—The sweetest of Sherries, if not the darkest, is Cream Sherry, first developed in Bristol, England. The widespread success of Harvey's Bristol Cream notwithstanding, Cream Sherry (even Harvey's!) can be an enjoyable after-dinner drink.

MADEIRA AND MARSALA
Whereas Port and Sherry are generally enjoyed as beverages, Madeira and Marsala are more commonly used for cooking. If you find that you enjoy Sherry and Port, you might want to experiment with these.

Madeira
Madeira is a small Portuguese-governed island in the Atlantic Ocean off the northwest coast of Africa that produces fortified wines named after the island. The most common of these wines are used for cooking, but the better ones are consumed as cocktails. The early American colonists used to drink Madeira, so the island has a long history of producing and exporting its goods. Madeira is heated during the production process. It was discovered that heat improved the taste of the wine in the 1600s when Madeira was shipped across the Atlantic in hot cargo ships.

Light brown in color, Maderia can be sweet or dry. The four primary types of Madeira are Sercial, Verdelho, Bual, and Malmsey. If you don't see one of these four names on the bottle, you are getting a lesser Madeira. If you are going to venture into the world of Madeira wines, compare a pale Sercial to a dark Malmsey and figure out what style you like. The best Madeira is often aged for many decades and is a rare treat.

"Malmsey" is a British corruption of "Malvasia," and all Madeira labeled "Malmsey" is, in fact, made from Malvasia grapes. Plan on spending around $15 for your first Sercial Madeira.

Marsala

Named for the town on the western tip of Sicily, Marsala is a brown-colored fortified wine made from the green-skinned Catarralto grape, a local variety. After harvesting, the grapes are dried prior to fermentation, which raises the sugar level. After fortification, Marsala is often sweetened and darkened with grape juice syrup. Barrel-aging mellows its flavors.

Of all the fortified wines, Marsala is the least distinctive as a beverage and is best kept in the kitchen. Marsala comes in two styles, dry and sweet. Both are used for cooking.

FORTIFIED WINES WORTH TRYING

1. *Very Dry Fino Sherry.* Recommended producer is Tio Pepé (Spain). Serve chilled, with appetizers.
2. *Amontillado Sherry.* Recommended producer is Savory & James (Spain). Drink it alone or with snacks. It tastes like nuts and smells like an autumn forest.
3. *Vintage Port.* Recommended producers are Smith-Woodhouse, Dow's Croft, and Quinta do Noval. These can be very expensive, often $50 or more.
4. *Tawny Port.* Recommended producer is Taylor-Fladgate. Also recommended is Château Reynella Tawny port from Australia. It tastes like both Port and Sherry and is great with Swiss cheese.
5. *Bual Madeira.* Recommended producer is Cossart's (Madeira). Sweet, but not too sweet. Good for cooking and as a before-dinner drink.
6. *Malmsey Madeira.* Recommended producer is Cossart's (Madeira). Sweet, rich, and nutty (just like a favorite uncle). Good as an after-dinner drink.
7. *Dry or Sweet Marsala.* Recommended producer is Florio (Sicily). Used for cooking.
8. *Croft Late.* Bottle vintage Tawny Port. Reminiscent of a great Vintage Port, only much cheaper.

Note: There are many price points for fortified wines from the same producer.

WINE COOLERS AND BOONES FARM

A wine cooler is not wine. It is a commercial product made with white wine, carbonated water, and other natural and artificial flavors and sweeteners. It's like soda pop with an alcohol content similar to beer, 5 percent or so. Wine coolers are consumed at the same temperature as a cola.

Boones Farms is the name of a company and a product. It contains wine, along with other natural and artificial flavors. It isn't carbonated and can be consumed warm or cold.

If you have the chance to have a sip of either type, give it a try. There is no substitute for experience. Just don't make the same mistake twice.

Kosher Wine

Kosher wine doesn't have to be bad, but bad Kosher wine is a North American Jewish tradition. Jewish wine in North America was originally made from the acidic Concord grape and sweetened with sugar to cut the acidity.

Today, Kosher wines are made in California, France, Italy, and Israel, using "normal" wine grapes like the Cabernet Sauvignon and Chenin Blanc. The history of ceremonial wine in all cultures is one rich in red wine, with little or no attention paid to whites. That is still true today, but Kosher whites do exist. The best introduction to good Kosher wines are the Baron Herzog wines from California. They are good and widely available (by Kosher-wine standards). Weinstock Cellars also makes good California Kosher wines, including a white Zinfandel. The Kedem

winery in Upstate New York still produces Concord grape–based Kosher wines. If you want a traditional red Concord wine that doesn't have sugar added to it, look for the Kedem Concord Natural. If you are looking for a very sweet wine, maybe for children, then Kedem Malaga is a logical choice.

Kosher dietary law dictates that only Jews who observe the Sabbath can physically touch the wine. In the case of wine, once the bottle has been opened, the wine is being touched. In order to allow a wine to remain Kosher after being touched by a non-Jew or a non-Sabbath-observing Jew, the wine needs to be pasteurized (boiled). This process is called Mevushal, which dates back to a time when wines produced for Jewish ceremonies were prevented from being used in pagan rituals.

Additionally, the equipment used to make Kosher products may be used only for making Kosher products. Anything added to the wine during production, like yeast or sulfur dioxide, must also be Kosher. Wines that are Kosher for Passover need not be Mevushal wines. Mevushal is a higher level of Kosher, for Jewish people who observe the Sabbath and keep Kosher year-round rather than just on the Sabbath.

Kosher Wine Buying Guide

Château Grillon (Bordeaux, France) $13
Yarden Chardonnay (Israel) $16
Baron Herzog White Zinfandel (California) $8
Kedem Concord Grape Wine $4.50
Manischewitz (New York) Concord Grape Wine $5
Georges Duboeuf Kosher Beaujolais (Burgundy, France) $9

Mevushal
Emerald Hill Cabernet Sauvignon (Israel) $10
Emerald Hill Sauvignon Blanc (Israel) $10

10 Lesser Known Treasures

1. MOSCATO D'ASTI (ITALIAN WHITE)

There's nothing like it. It tastes like Italian wedding cake. It has a slight fizz, is low in alcohol (5.5 percent), and is pleasantly sweet. Enjoy it with fruit, fried rice, or Italian wedding cake. *Price:* $8–15

2. GERMAN RIESLING

Most Rieslings are less sweet than you think and are a great match with spicy Asian foods. Look for the German word *trocken* on the label, which means dry. Beware of *halbtrocken*, which means half dry, unless you are interested in a sweeter wine. *Price:* $9–12

3. AUSTRALIAN SHIRAZ/CABERNET SAUVIGNON BLENDS

This isn't as much a secret as the other treasures on the list. It is very hard to find a bad wine of this type. These two high-powered grapes bring out the best in each other. These wines are great alone, without food. The Shiraz/Cabernet combo is unique to Australia, but expect to see imitators soon. *Price:* $9–12

4. OREGON PINOT NOIR

These light, delicate reds resemble good French Pinot Noirs that sell for much more. *Price:* $9–12

5. ARGENTINA MALBEC

These wines are rumored to be the next big thing. They are somewhat similar to the wildly popular Merlot wines in flavor and softness, but much less so in cost and demand. *Price:* $8–10

6. CALIFORNIA JUG WINES

These are the 1.5-liter bottles that are mass produced, inexpensive, and sell like crazy. California makes the best jug wines for the dollar in the world. Don't be a snob; try a couple. You'll be pleasantly surprised. They're normally pasteurized, so they'll last a long time. *Price:* $8–12

7. CALIFORNIA SPARKLING WINES ("BRUT ROSÉ" AND "BLANC DE NOIRS")

The French counterparts of these wines, which are made from mostly Pinot Noir, sell for much more. *Price:* $10–20

8. FRENCH ALSACE WHITES

Riesling vines are at their best in the Alsatian soil, yet these wines are overlooked by wine drinkers scrambling for Chardonnay. Here is a chance to enjoy very high quality wines at bargain prices. *Price:* $8–18

9. PORT

This is a good way to bring the hard liquor and wine drinkers together. It's good wine with a kick. Serving Port is a cost effective, fun way to be a bit less pedestrian in this era of generic malls and pizza chains. Smith-Woodhouse and Dow's are two solid producers. A great half bottle or a good full-size bottle go for the same money. *Price:* $10–20

10. PORTUGUESE REDS

The demand for Portuguese non-Port wine is almost nonexistent in North America. Couple this with a favorable exchange rate and you have the makings of a bargain. You may not know the grape varieties, and it may be a bit of a hit-or-miss proposition, but try a few middle-priced reds. You may hit the jackpot. *Price:* $7–12

WHITES at a glance...

	CHEAP	BETTER	GREAT	OFF DRY	DRY	WITH FOOD	WITHOUT FOOD
Chardonnay	🍷	🍷	🍷🍷		🍷	🍷	🍷
Riesling	🍷	🍷	🍷🍷	🍷	🍷	🍷	🍷
Sauvignon Blanc	🍷	🍷	🍷		🍷	🍷	
Chenin Blanc	🍷	🍷		🍷	🍷	🍷	
Pinot Blanc		🍷			🍷	🍷	
Pinot Grigio (Gris)	🍷	🍷			🍷	🍷	
Gewürztraminer			🍷	🍷			
Semillon		🍷	🍷	🍷		🍷	
Trebbiano (Ugni Blanc)	🍷				🍷	🍷	

Cheap: Under $10   *Better:* $10–$19   *Great:* $50 and up   🍷🍷 Extrodinary performance within category

WHITES AT A GLANCE

The authors have assigned a 🍷 to almost all of the wine grapes in the *Better* category. In this price range we feel that personal preference is the strongest variable in the equation. A "double" 🍷🍷 means "especially so."

White wine generally isn't as complex as red wine. This is why we have so few in the *Without Food* category. On the flip side, it tends to be acidic (in a good way), which gives it a thirst-quenching quality. That is why whites go so well with food.

Gewürztraminer is often recommended as a good complement to Chinese food, but the authors prefer a simple Riesling. Most Gewürztraminers are a little too quirky to be matched up with food. Drink them without food or with simple food that doesn't require careful matching, like bread or cheese.

REDS AT A GLANCE

The authors have assigned a 🍷 to almost all of the wine grapes in the *Better* category. In this price range we feel that personal preference is the strongest variable in the equation. Cabernet Sauvignon, more than any other grape, benefits from aging. Additionally, it makes (arguably) the best red wines in the world. So although we have given it a 🍷 in the $10–19 category, you shouldn't expect greatness in those bottles. Usually the Cabs are very forward, with perhaps too much tannin for some people. You may want to look at the Aussie

REDS
at a glance...

	CHEAP	BETTER	GREAT	LESS DRY	DRY	WITH FOOD	WITHOUT FOOD
Cabernet Sauvignon		🍷	🍷🍷	🍷	🍷	🍷	🍷
Merlot		🍷		🍷	🍷	🍷	🍷
Gamay	🍷🍷	🍷		🍷		🍷	🍷
Pinot Noir		🍷	🍷🍷	🍷		🍷	🍷
Syrah (Shiraz)	🍷🍷	🍷	🍷	🍷	🍷		🍷
Petit Sirah		🍷			🍷	🍷	
Grenache	🍷				🍷	🍷	
Nebbiolo		🍷	🍷🍷		🍷	🍷	
Sangiovese	🍷	🍷	🍷		🍷	🍷	
Zinfandel		🍷		🍷			🍷
Tempranillo	🍷	🍷			🍷	🍷	

Cheap: Under $10   *Better:* $10–$19   *Great:* $50 and up   🍷🍷 Extrodinary performance within category

Cab/Shiraz blends in this price range. However, if you like a strongly flavored wine, then you shouldn't hesitate to try some straight Cabernet.

There are good wine values in all price ranges for almost all varietals. This chart is meant to be a general guide of what to look for. It reflects general quality and quantity of wines available at the various price levels.

The right $8 Syrah can be a very eye-opening experience for a wine novice or a person on a budget. It will have a boldness and complexity that imitates the qualities found in many higher priced wines. *Beware:* If you don't like tannin, some Syrah/Shirazes are apt to be too tannic for your tastes.

If you just want a cheap red that tastes good, Gamay-based Beaujolais from France is the way to go.

Tempranillo is grown almost exclusively in Spain and is the principal grape of the red wines from the Rioja region of that country. Riojas are light bodied and very compatible with food.

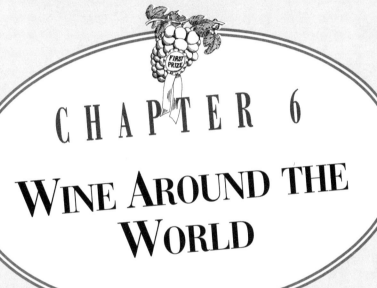

EVERYTHING

CHAPTER 6

WINE AROUND THE WORLD

BOTTLED BY ADAMS MEDIA

NET CONTENTS: FORTY PAGES

PRODUCT OF USA

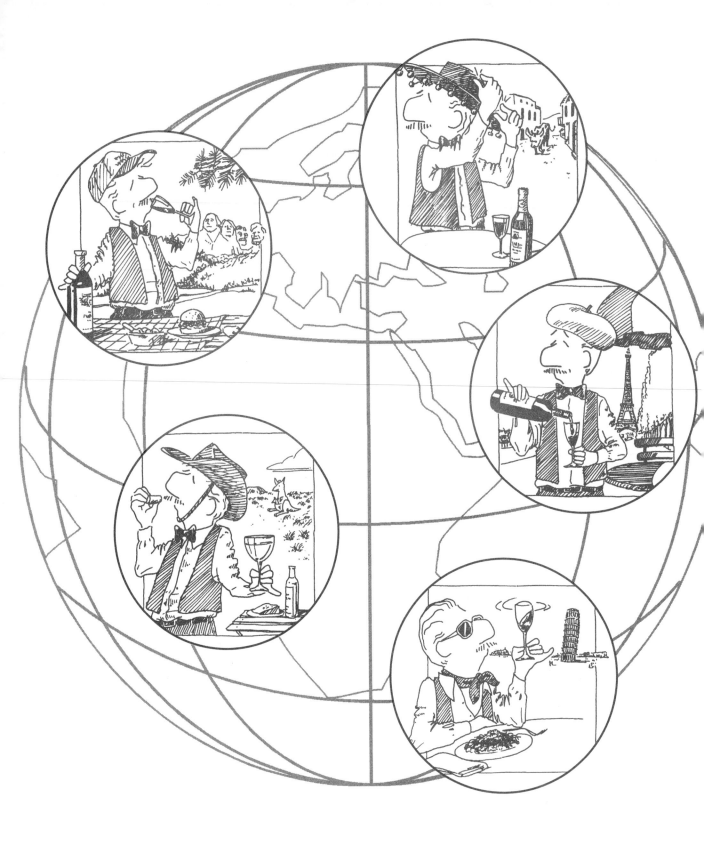

France

France is to wine what Microsoft is to personal-computer software.

As Julius Caesar concluded two thousand years ago, France is a pretty good place to grow wine grapes. Through trial and error, after centuries of careful cultivation and meticulous record-keeping, particularly by the Church, the French learned how to make very good wine. Indeed, it is not farfetched to say that they have defined good wine. The wineries in California, South America, and Australia strive to produce wine that will compare favorably with French wines. These New-World regions, especially California, have succeeded in producing beautiful wines that often exceed their French counterparts in sheer power, but never in finesse.

It is generally accepted among wine experts that France produces many "best-of types":

The best Champagnes are the finest sparkling wines in the world.

Alsace Gewürztraminer is the best version of this quirky wine.

The Pauillac and Margaux districts of Bordeaux produce the finest Cabernet Sauvignon–based wines in the world.

Merlot best displays its qualities in the Bordeaux subregions of Saint-Emilion and Pomerol.

The *grand cru* vineyards of the Côte de Beaune produce the finest Chardonnays.

The most refined Sauvignon Blanc–based wines are produced in Sancerre and the Graves subregion of Bordeaux.

Chenin Blanc is in its glory along the Loire River.

Sauternes, from the town of the same name, is widely acclaimed as the world's finest dessert wine.

The prototype Pinot Noir comes from the vineyards of Côte de Nuits in Burgundy.

For a simple, acidic shellfish wine, Muscadet is without equal.

Finally, the dry rosé wines of Provence are considered to be the best of their type.

The only gap in the spectrum of French wines is a selection of fruity, low-acid wines that go best without food. This might well be by design, as the French rarely drink wine without food, nor do they often enjoy food without wine. Also, the cool climates of France are not conducive to achieving the degree of ripeness required for rich, fruity wines. The Gamay-based wines from southern Burgundy are a notable exception.

Although it is widely accepted that France produces the best wines in the world, it does not have a monopoly on good, inexpensive wines. The French section in the wine shop might offer a $50 bargain, but $8 bargains are more difficult to find. Recently, French producers have begun to respond to the American desire for inexpensive variety-labeled wines. In addition to the usual suspects—Chardonnay, Merlot, Cabernet Sauvignon—one may find Viognier, Syrah, and others at prices below $10.

While most of these wines are simple food wines, they can represent good value. These wines are usually labeled, in accordance with French law, as country wine *(vin du pays)*. It is difficult to find better Merlot anywhere in the world for under $8 than those from the Languedoc region.

Other wines worth finding in the $8–10 range are Côtes-du-Rhône reds; Burgundy (Bourgogne) Pinot Noir (usually a better buy than American Pinot Noir); white Bordeaux made from Sauvignon Blanc; and Saint-Véran, a simple white Burgundy made from Chardonnay.

Except for those varietal wines aimed directly at the American market, French wines are usually labeled by geographical region (i.e., Bordeaux) rather than grape variety. This reflects the French view that soil is of supreme importance in producing quality wines. Except for the inexpensive *vin de pays* (country wine) varietals, only the wines from the Alsace region are labeled by variety.

In order to understand the degrees of specificity of French wine labeling, think of an archery target. The outer circle is all of France; the next-largest circle is a region of France such as Bordeaux; the next circle is in the district of, say, Médoc; within

that is the commune name, say, Pauillac; finally, the bull's eye—the individual producer, a château or domaine. The better (and more expensive) the wine, the more specific is the indicated source of the wine.

Just as French society is hierarchical, sometimes ridiculously so, so is her classification of her beloved wines. A general understanding of the classification of French wine is vital to your wine knowledge, since France long ago invented the wines that the rest of the world imitates. Even the bottle shapes of the different wine styles and wine regions of France are imitated by California winemakers to indicate the intended style of wine.

Label Law:

Appellation d'origine contrôlée (AOC or AC): the most widely applied standard used on French wine labels. It indicates that the wine meets the legal standards (per French wine law) for the area indicated. The more specific the area of origin, the higher the standards.

Vins délimités de qualité supérieure (VDQS): a second set of standards for wines in areas not covered by AOC law. Although a notch down in quality, VDQS is still a reliable government guarantee of quality.

Vin de pays/vin de pays d'oc: "country" wines from outlying areas. Most varietal wines (name of grape is on the bottle) come under this heading.

Think of France as six major regions, each with its own system of organization and classification: Bordeaux, Burgundy (Bourgogne), Rhône, Loire, Alsace, and Champagne.

BORDEAUX

Bordeaux, an industrial city in southwestern France, is the center of the world's most famous wine region. Several types of wine are produced here:

Dry white wines: Blends of Sauvignon Blanc and Semillon.

Sweet dessert wines: Blends of Sauvignon Blanc, Semillon, and Muscadelle afflicted with *Botrytis cinerea* (noble rot), a grape mold that concentrates the natural sugars.

Medium-bodied red wines: Blends of Cabernet Sauvignon, Merlot, Cabernet Franc, Malbec, and Petit Verdot. Some subregions produce wine made primarily from Cabernet Sauvignon, whereas the Merlot grape is dominant in other areas. Here are the most important subregions of Bordeaux and the wines they produce:

Sauternes—sweet dessert wines
Pomerol—Merlot-dominant reds
Saint-Emilion—Merlot-dominant reds
Entre-Deux-Mers—light, simple whites
Graves—fine dry whites, Cabernet
　　Sauvignon–based reds
Médoc—Cabernet Sauvignon-
　　based reds

The Médoc, a subregion of Bordeaux, is a relatively large area and contains four "communes" (wine-producing areas, kind of like small towns) that are entitled to their own appellation:

Saint-Estèphe
Saint-Julien
Margaux
Pauillac

You will find on the market a great number of châteaux-bottled Bordeaux wines. A château is literally a piece of land. In anticipation of an agricultural exposition in 1855, the local government in Bordeaux asked representatives of the wine trade to rate the red wines of Médoc according to price history. Those wines that over time had fetched the highest prices were given

FRANCE LABEL—BORDEAUX

CHATEAU PICHON LONGUEVILLE COMTESSE DE LALANDE: The name of the chateau where the wine was produced.

PAUILLAC: The appellation of origin, Pauillac is a commune (or village) within the Medoc subregion of Bordeaux.

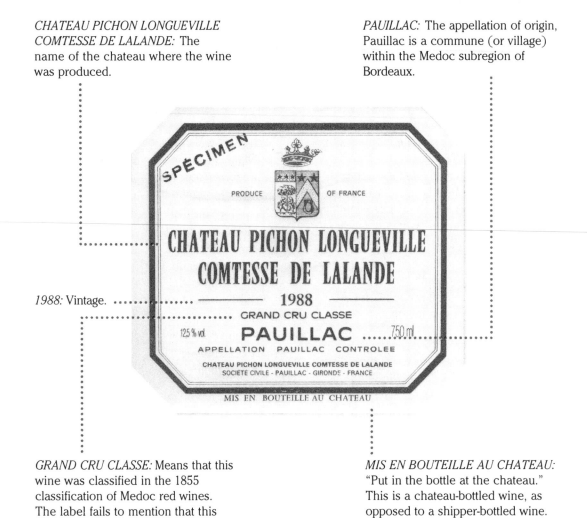

1988: Vintage.

GRAND CRU CLASSE: Means that this wine was classified in the 1855 classification of Medoc red wines. The label fails to mention that this chateau is a second growth, or *Deuxieme cru.*

MIS EN BOUTEILLE AU CHATEAU: "Put in the bottle at the chateau." This is a chateau-bottled wine, as opposed to a shipper-bottled wine.

the highest ranking, and so on down. The highest ranking, *premier cru* ("first growth"), includes only five (originally four) châteaux, one of which (Château Haut-Brion) is actually from neighboring Graves but was included because of its record of excellence. The classified growths of Médoc are ranked first growth, second, third, fourth, and fifth. Below this level are the *cru bourgeois* wines and the *petits châteaux* wines.

The sweet dessert wines of Sauternes were classified at the time of those of Médoc. Other subregions of Bordeaux have since adopted some form of classification. Although such quality classifications may become outdated and no longer reflect reality, they can be a self-fulfilling prophecy—a *premier cru* is expected to be expensive and excellent; therefore, the winemaker can afford to make such a wine, knowing that the market will accept the price.

BURGUNDY (BOURGOGNE)

Burgundy produces three general types of wine:

1. Light, velvety red wine made from Pinot Noir
2. Light, fruity red wine made from Gamay
3. Dry white wine made from Chardonnay

(There are others, but these are the most important.)

Traveling from north to south through the heart of France, you pass through the subregions of Burgundy in sequence:

Chablis—very dry whites
Côte de Nuits—full-bodied Pinot Noir reds, a few whites
Côte de Beaune—lighter Pinot Noir, excellent Chardonnay
Côte Chalonnaise—less expensive Pinot Noir and Chardonnay
Mâcon—Chardonnay whites, including the famous Pouilly-Fuissé
Beaujolais—Gamay reds

The Chablis vineyards are ranked (in descending order of quality) as Chablis Grand Cru, Chablis Premier Cru, Chablis, and Petit Chablis.

The red and white vineyards of the Côte de Nuits and Côte de Beaune (together known as the Côte d'Or) are ranked either Grand Cru, Premier Cru, or no rank at all.

The famous villages of the Côte de Nuits are Nuits-Saint-Georges; Gevrey-Chambertin; Vosne-Romanée; Morey-Saint-Denis; and Chambolle-Musigny. These villages are all famous for their red wines, some of which are fabulously expensive.

Famous villages of the Côte de Beaune (by wine type) are:

Reds
Pernand-Vergelesses
Savigny-les-Beaune
Volnay
Pommard
Beaune
Meursault
Chassagne-Montrachet
Aloxe-Corton

Whites
Puligny-Montrachet
Chassagne-Montrachet
Meursault
Beaune
Aloxe-Corton

Beaujolais may be labeled as Beaujolais, Beaujolais Supérieur (which is 1 percent higher in alcohol than simple Beaujolais), Beaujolais-Villages, or *cru* Beaujolais with a village name. Moulin-á-Vent, Brouilly, and St-Amour are the best known of the *crus*. There are ten such *cru* villages entitled to use their own names. *Cru* Beaujolais is the best of the Beaujolais, but it usually costs less than $15. What a bargain!

RHÔNE

Earthy, gutsy wines, both red and white, are produced along the Rhône River, south of the Burgundy region. The wines of the Rhône are (mercifully) without a ranking system.

Northern Rhône Reds: Big, Syrah-based reds worthy of aging for at least a few years.
Côte Rôtie
Hermitage-Crozes-Hermitage
Cornas
St. Joseph

Northern Rhône Whites: Substantial whites made from Viognier or a blend of Marsanne and Roussane.
Condrieu
Hermitage/Crozes-Hermitage

Southern Rhône Reds: Grenache-based blends (with Syrah, Cinsault, Duriff, Mouvedre, and other grapes).
Côtes-du-Rhône
Gigondas
Châteauneuf-du-Pape

Southern Rhône Whites: Not so common, these big wines are made from Marsanne and Roussane, and are an interesting alternative to Chardonnay.
Côtes-du-Rhône Blanc
Châteauneuf-du-Pape Blanc

Southern Rhône Rosé: Tavel, a dry rosé made primarily from Grenache, is considered by many wine buffs to be the finest rosé in the world.

LOIRE

The vineyards along the largest river in France yield a variety of refreshing (mostly white) wines. Here are the most important ones:
Muscadet—a perfect shellfish wine made from the grape of the same name.
Vouvray—made from the Chenin Blanc grape, Vouvray may be bone-dry (sec), delightfully off dry (demi-sec), or sparkling.
Rosé d'Anjou—an off-dry rosé made mostly from Cabernet Sauvignon and Cabernet Franc.
Pouilly Fumé—straight Sauvignon Blanc in a rich, heady style; the inspiration for California Sauvignon Blancs labeled "Fumé Blanc."
Sancerre—unblended Sauvignon Blanc in a style more acidic than Pouilly Fumé.

FRANCE LABEL—BURGUNDY

MEURSAULT-PERRIERES: Meursault is a commune in the Côte de Beaume subregion of Burgundy; Perrieres is a vineyard ranked *premier cru* (second to *grand cru* in the Burgundy hierarchy).

PREMIER CRU: Second to *grand cru* in the Burgundy hierarchy.

Meursault-Perrières

PREMIER CRU

APPELLATION MEURSAULT 1ᵉʳ CRU CONTROLÉE

Louis Latour

MIS EN BOUTEILLE PAR LOUIS LATOUR

NÉGOCIANT A BEAUNE (COTE-D'OR), FRANCE

LOUIS LATOUR: Producer/shipper (negociant).

MIS EN BOUTEILLE PAR LOUIS LATOUR: Put in the bottle by the negociant, as opposed to domaine or chateau bottled.

ALSACE

Historically, the geographical area of Alsace has belonged to whoever won the most recent war between France and Germany. As such, it is currently part of France but not without considerable German influence in her wines. Late harvest, sweet wines are produced in Alsace.

In this region there is a tradition of varietal labeling: No "cutting" is allowed. If a grape is named, then the content of it must be 100 percent. The term *grand cru* may appear on an Alsace label as an indication that the wine has a minimum alcohol content of 10 or 11 percent (depending on the grape) and meets some perfunctory yield requirements. The varieties used are:

Riesling
Gewürztraminer
Pinot Gris (Fokay Pinot Gris)
Muscat
Sylvaner

A small amount of Pinot Noir (the only red, often used for rosé)

CHAMPAGNE

In order to qualify for the Champagne appellation (according to French *and* EEC law), a sparkling wine must (1) be produced in the Champagne district, (2) be produced from the Chardonnay, Pinot Noir, and/or Pinot Meunier (red) grapes grown there, and

(3) get its bubbles via the *méthode champenoise* (Champagne method.)

The Champagne method is an expensive and labor-intensive means of naturally carbonating a wine. First, wine is made from local grapes. This is no easy feat; the vineyards of Champagne lie so far north that ripeness is an issue in most years. After clarification and a measure of aging, the wine is put into thick Champagne bottles, along with enough yeast and sugar to initiate a second fermentation. It is this second fermentation in the tightly sealed bottle that puts the bubbles in the bubbly—the carbon dioxide cannot escape, so it is dissolved in the wine. The hard work is in removing the dead yeast. After aging the wine with the dead yeast—sometimes for many years, as this adds character to the Champagne—the dead yeast is coaxed into the neck of the bottle by gradually tilting the bottle a little bit each day until it is inverted. The dead yeast is then carefully removed. At this time, the bottle is topped off and adjusted for sweetness. The degree of sweetness appears on the label as:

Natural or Au Sauvage—no added sugar
Brut—very dry, up to 1.5-percent sugar by volume
Extra Dry—up to 2 percent
Dry or Sec—up to 4 percent
Demi-Sec—sweet, up to 8 percent
Doux—very sweet, up to 10 percent

Some other Champagne terms are:

Blanc de Blancs—made only from white grapes, i.e., Chardonnay.

Brut Rosé—pink-colored Champagne. The color comes from the red skins of Pinot Noir and/or Pinot Meunier skins.

Blanc de Noirs—pale sparkling wine from dark-skinned grapes.

Téte de Cuvée—a super-premium Champagne, usually vintage dated.

Vintage—In contrast to the far more common practice of blending wines from different years, vintage Champagne is made from wine from a single harvest. Although most *téte de cuvées* are vintage dated, a year on the bottle doesn't mean that it is superior to a nonvintage bottle.

Sparkling Wine Checklist

1. Pick out a good sparkling wine or Champagne. $10 buys decent bubbly.

2. You want to serve your sparkling wine at about refrigerator temperature.

3. Don't shake the bottle. Don't even handle it roughly.

4. Keep the bottle pointed away from people and other objects you don't want damaged.

5. When you open the bottle you must carefully remove the wire cage, keeping a towel handy in case you feel the cork popping out. Your cork probably won't pop out, so you will need to slowly wiggle it out with a toweled hand. (No, you don't used a corkscrew.) The bottle won't make a pop if you open it right, only a little sigh, and you shouldn't have much, if any, bubble over.

6. In theory, you should let it warm a bit from refrigerator temperature.

7. Glasses and flutes should be filled about two-thirds full. Refill glasses before they are completely empty; this helps keep the wine cool enough to be enjoyed.

8. Keep your opened bottle chilled. You may not own an ice bucket, but you can improvise.

9. If you have a special bubbly stopper or regular cork lying around, and you want to save some for tomorrow, you can store your leftovers in the refrigerator. You will not be able to get the original cork back in the bottle. Most of the pressure dissipates when the bottle is first opened. A regular cork will almost always stay put; by the same token, the bubbles will last only a couple of days if stored in this manner.

Italy

Italian wine is a tough nut to crack. Although the wines of the United States can be explained in relationship to their French counterparts, the wines of Italy cannot. The land we now call Italy has been making wine for four thousand years; however, it was not politically unified within her present borders until the mid-1800s. This land of diverse climates, cultures, and even languages produces a baffling variety of wines.

The wines of Italy rival those of France in variety and, in some cases, quality. Like France, Italy also labels her wines according to geographical origin rather than grape variety (of course, as with France, there are exceptions). Italy is divided politically into twenty regions (eighteen mainland, plus Sicily and Sardinia). The regions of Tuscany, Piedmont, and Veneto produce the majority of the quality Italian wine found in wine shops. Many good wines from other regions are never exported.

The Italian government has officially recognized the traditional wines of Italy (as well as some newcomers) with a system similar to that of France:

1. DOCG (denominazione di origine controllata e garantita) is the highest status conferred on Italian wines.
2. DOC (denominazione di origine controllata) is the next highest level.
3. VdT is a general category for non-DOC/DOCG wines. These initials stand for *vino da tavola*, or table wine.

This system recognizes traditionally outstanding wines and establishes the geographic origin, grape variety or varieties to be used, minimum alcohol content, and aging requirements. For example, Chianti Classico is a recognized DOCG wine. It must be made from (primarily) the Sangiovese grape, have a minimum alcohol content of 12 percent, and come from a particular zone in central Tuscany. With a higher alcohol content (12.5 percent) and three years' aging prior to release, it may be called "Chianti Classico Riserva." It is important to remember that DOC/DOCG status is a guarantee as to where and how the wine is produced; it is not a guarantee as to how it will taste.

The DOC/DOCG laws do not cover all of the good or great wines of Italy. Some of the most expensive

TRENTINO-ALTO ADIGE
VALLE D'AOSTA
FRUILI-VENEZIA GUILIA
VENETO
LOMBARDIA
ASTI
PIEMONTE
EMILIA-ROMAGNA
LIGURIA
MARCHE
TOSCANA
ORVIETO
UMBRIA
ABRUZZO
MOLISE
LAZIO
PUGLIA
CAMPANIA
BASILICATA
CALABRIA
SICILIA

ITALY LABEL

CONTERNO: Producer.

BAROLO RISERVA: Type of wine—specific grape variety (nebbiolo), region of origin, and method of production all assured by DOCG designation.

DENOMINAZIONE DI ORIGINE CONTROLLATA E GARANTITA (DOCG): This designation means that Barolo Riserva is recognized by the Italian government as a traditional wine-type and that this wine meets the standards set forth for this wine-type grape variety, maximum yield, minimum alcohol, aging requirements, etc.

MONFORTINO: A proprietary name used by this producer for its blend of Barolo from several top vineyards. In place of this name you might find a vineyard name on similar bottles.

Although the year is not shown here, it appears on a separate, smaller label on the bottleneck.

wines from Tuscany are the "super-Tuscans," delicious and ageworthy blends of Sangiovese and Cabernet Sauvignon. Also of considerable importance is the production of inexpensive varietal wines for the American market: Chardonnay, Pinot Grigio, Cabernet Sauvignon, Merlot, and Sangiovese. These inexpensive wines compete favorably in their price range with varietals from France, California, and Chile.

The major red grape of the Piedmont region is Nebbiolo. If you encounter an Italian wine with a label written in Italian, Piedmont may be denoted as Piemonte. Nebbiolo is also known in this region as Spanna. Barolo and Barbaresco are the two

most famous Nebbiolo wines from Piedmont. They aren't cheap, but if you like red wine, they are worth the money.

Italy produces a lot of very good red and white wines, many made from grapes most Americans have never heard of. Some of Italy's wines are varietally labeled and some aren't. Rather than present you with a list of Italian-named wines made from grapes you've never heard of like Verdicchio, Vernaccia, and Coda di Volpe, we suggest you find a wine merchant you trust and ask for a tour of his or her store's Italian wines. The following is a comprehensive table of major Italian wine types, not individual wines. Chianti, for example, is a type of wine.

MAJOR ITALIAN WINE TYPES

COLOR	TYPE OF WINE	REGION	GRAPE VARIETIES
Red	Barolo	Piedmont	Nebbiolo
Red	Barbaresco	Piedmont	Nebbiolo
Red	Valpolicella	Veneto	Corvina, Rondinella, and Molinara
Red	Amarone	Veneto	Corvina, Rondinella, and Molinara
Red	Barbera d'Asti	Piedmont	Barbera
Red	Chianti	Tuscany	mostly Sangiovese
Red	Brunello di Montalcino	Tuscany	Brunello (a grape closely related to Sangiovese)
Red	Piave Merlot	Veneto	Merlot
Red	Morellino di Scansano	Tuscany	mostly Sangiovese
Red	Taurasi	Campania	Aglianico and Piedirosso
Red	Salice Salentino	Puglia	Negro Amaro
White	Soave	Veneto	Garganega and Trebbiano
White	Gavi	Piedmont	Cortese
White	Orvieto	Umbria	Trebbiano, Verdello, and Grechetto
White	Greco di Tufo	Campania	Greco and Coda di Volpe

United States

The United States is a big place. The American wine industry began in several different places and exists today in a surprising number of states. The earliest settlers in Virginia found land virtually overrun with vines. These, however, were of a species ill suited to making wine. As a result of some successful exercises in botanical husbandry involving European grapes, the native American grape was tamed.

America's first winery was established in Pennsylvania shortly after the Revolutionary War, and Ohio produced the lion's share of the new nation's wine. Meanwhile, Spanish missionaries began making sacramental wine from European vines in California. California's sun, soil, and cool breezes make for near-ideal conditions for growing European grapevines. The original demand for table wine was created by European immigrants who were accustomed to wine with meals.

The superstar winemakers at the "boutique" wineries have repeatedly demonstrated their ability to produce world-class wines. These wines compare favorably with their French counterparts in power if not finesse, and the *méthode champenoise* sparkling-wine producers offer remarkable value in their California bubbly.

California does not hold a monopoly on American wine— far from it. Many other states make good wine, and most states, in fact, have wineries. Just about every imaginable type of wine is produced somewhere in the United States. But just about all of the *great* North American wines do come from California.

WASHINGTON
IDAHO
OREGON
MINNESOTA
WISCONSIN
NORTH COAST CALIFORNIA
COLORADO
SAN JOAQUIN VALLEY
CENTRAL COAST CALIFORNIA
SOUTH COAST CALIFORNIA
ARIZONA
ARKANSAS
MISSISSIPPI
TEXAS
MICHIGAN
ERIE
OHIO
INDIANA
MISSOURI
KANSAS
ALABAMA
GEORGIA
THE CAROLINAS
CONNECTICUT/ MASSACHUSETTS
FINGER LAKES, N.Y.
HUDSON VALLEY
NORTH FORK, N.Y.
VIRGINIA
PENNSYLVANIA/ MARYLAND/ NEW JERSEY
FLORIDA

The following is a brief list of the major wine variety/area of production combinations in the United States:

Cabernet Sauvignon (or "Meritage" blends of Cabernet Sauvignon, Merlot, and Cabernet Franc):
> Napa Valley
> Sonoma Valley
> Alexander Valley (in Sonoma County)

Chardonnay:
> Napa
> Sonoma
> Santa Barbara

Pinot Noir:
> Carneros (southern Napa/Sonoma)
> Santa Barbara

Sauvignon Blanc:
> Napa
> Sonoma

Bargains from California are getting harder to find because the California wine industry has become so profit-driven that few wines remain underpriced for long. For your money it is hard to beat California jug wine, even those with borrowed European names such as Burgundy, Chablis, Rhine, and Chianti. These are wines for everyday sipping. Your wine dollar is wisely spent on California Champagne-method sparkling wine, especially the copper/pink Blanc de Noirs, also called Brut Rosé.

One distinct advantage that California holds over France is in the production of "fireplace" wines. Wheras French wines, both good and great, are meant to be enjoyed with food, the sunny climate of California brings its grapes to a greater ripeness than most French-grown grapes, which means the wines display greater fruit extracts and lower levels of acidity.

LABEL INFORMATION

American wine labels are required to indicate the geographic origin of the grapes. Generally speaking, exceptional wine will be from very specific areas, perhaps a single vineyard. The more general the area, the less exceptional the wine.

Katherine Vineyard—
> specific vineyard
Santa Maria Valley—
> specific region
Santa Barbara—county
California—state
American—country

MENDOCINO
NORTH COAST
LAKE
SONOMA
NAPA
San Francisco
CENTRAL VALLEY
CENTRAL COAST
Los Angeles
SOUTH COAST

UNITED STATES LABEL

KATHERINE'S VINEYARD: All of the grapes came from this vineyard.

ESTATE BOTTLED: This means that the grapes were grown by the producer.

1995: Vintage year.

CAMBRIA: Producer.

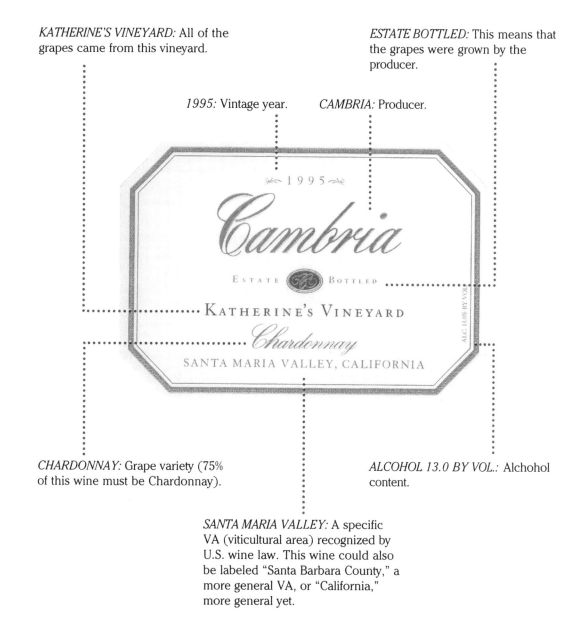

CHARDONNAY: Grape variety (75% of this wine must be Chardonnay).

ALCOHOL 13.0 BY VOL.: Alchohol content.

SANTA MARIA VALLEY: A specific VA (viticultural area) recognized by U.S. wine law. This wine could also be labeled "Santa Barbara County," a more general VA, or "California," more general yet.

Think of it like this: If you reside on Park Avenue, you tell people you live on Park Avenue. If you live in Harlem, you might say you live in Manhattan. If you live in the Bronx, you claim to live in New York City. If you live in northern New Jersey, you live "just outside the City." Get the idea?

VARIETAL LABELING

American wines that indicate a specific grape variety on their label must contain at least 75 percent of that type of grape. This means that inexpensive bottles of premium varietals such as Chardonnay and Merlot are usually "stretched" with less expensive grapes. Several super-premium California red wines are blends of several different grapes. With no one variety above the 75 percent threshold, these wines must be labeled as red table wines. In order to provide an indication of a quality superior to 75 percent pure, the California wine industry coined the term "Meritage" for superior blended wines, both red and white.

Not all California wineries grow grapes; some only buy it, blend it, label it, and sell it. The phrase "produced and bottled by" means that the winery crushed and fermented at least 90 percent of the grapes. The phrases "grown, produced, and bottled by" and "estate bottled" suggest an even more intimate relationship with the wine. On the other hand, "made and bottled by" means that only at least 10 percent of the grapes were crushed and fermented by the winery; the remainder is normally cheap bulk wine. Other phrases with little or no

meaning are "vinted and bottled by" and "cellared and bottled by."

THE PACIFIC NORTHWEST

While any overview of wine production in the United States must focus on California, the wines of the Pacific Northwest cannot be ignored. Quality wines from popular varietal grapes come from Oregon, Washington, and even Idaho. Although these states combined produce far less wine than the state of California, the Pacific Northwest actually enjoys some advantages in wine production over California.

One such advantage is rooted in economics. The wine boom has driven the price of California vineyard acreage sky-high, which in turn has inflated production costs. This is why Washington State Merlot in the $10–15 range is often a better value than similarly priced Californian wine.

Another advantage is the climate. The Yakima and Columbia valleys of Washington are considerably cooler than California's Napa and Sonoma valleys. Cooler temperatures allow red grape varieties to ripen slowly and develop full and complex flavors. The finest red wines of California come from vineyards located in the cooler hills, but Washington State reds have a wide advantage over the red wine produced on California's hotter valley floors.

While California certainly produces enough Chardonnay to go around, Washington excels in the production of "cool climate" white varietals such as Chenin Blanc and Riesling. Similarly, Oregon produces high quality Pinot Noir a difficult-to-grow grape that appreciates Oregon's relatively cool growing season. California wineries, so successful with Cabernet Sauvignon, have struggled for decades with its Pinot Noirs.

Pioneering winemaker David Lett and others recognized the affinity of Pinot Noir for Oregon's cool climate, and today Oregon Pinot Noirs are often described as "Burgundian"—a taste rarely associated with California versions. The highest compliment ever paid to Oregon Pinot Noir comes from the venerable Burgundy wine producer Joseph Drouhin. The Drouhin family considered Oregon Pinot Noir of such high quality that they purchased vineyard land and started producing their own. Today, Domaine Droulin Oregon "cuvee Laurene" is considered by some to be the finest American Pinot Noir ever made.

Pinot Gris is the other success story in Oregon. This grape variety, also grown in Alsace and Italy, grows best in a cool climate. California winemakers have yet to click with this variety, but Oregon Pinot Gris at its best is comparable to the best of Europe's Pinot Gris.

The wines of Idaho are also worthy of mention. Although wine has been produced in the Gem State since the late 1800s (an Idaho wine won a medal at World's Fair in Chicago in 1898), not until the 1970s did Idaho *vinifera* wines, most notably Riesling, reach the market. In addition to Riesling, Gewürztraminer also yields some inexpensive and enjoyable white wines. Much experimentation with various red varieties of wine is going on in Idaho.

One can never forget that California is among the finest wine regions in the world—better than most wine producing *countries*. However, not all grape varieties thrive in its warmth, and the Pacific Northwest with its cooler growing areas compliments California perfectly.

When shopping for wines from Idaho, Oregon, and Washington, look for the varieties that don't thrive in California—Riesling, Pinot Gris, Gewürztraminer, and Pinot Noir. Merlot, which does well in California, does equally well for a little less per bottle in Washington State.

Here are some recommended producers whose wines are worth sampling:

Argyle (Oregon)
Domaine Drouhin (Oregon)
The Eyrie Vineyard (Oregon)
Chateau St. Michelle (Washington)
Hyatt (Washington)
Leonetti (Washington)
The Hogue Cellars (Washington)
Ste. Chapelle (Idaho)

Australia

Australia has been making wine since soon after the first shipload of British settlers arrived in 1788. Geographically isolated, Australia developed her own sophisticated winemaking technology largely independent of that developed in Europe. This factor, along with a combination of intense sunshine and cool breezes, helps to make Australian wines unique. Therefore, a varietal with which you have become familiar, such as Chardonnay or Shiraz (Syrah), will often display different characteristics when produced in Australia—sort of like a jazz combo doing a completely different take on a pop tune.

Blending of premium varietals is common in Australia. One often finds the Chardonnay grape blended with Semillon, and Cabernet Sauvignon blended with Shiraz. This practice pre-dates the wine boom of the 1970s, when varietal wines became so popular. The Aussies knew, as did the Europeans, that when grape varieties are skillfully blended, the whole can be much more than the sum of the parts.

Finally, Australia is a little like California in that all styles of wine are produced there. Dry whites are usually made from Chardonnay or a blend of Chardonnay and Semillon. *Botrytis*-affected Semillon offers us a bargain-basement dessert wine choice that doesn't look at all foolish beside its much more expensive French cousin, Sauternes. A small amount of Sauvignon Blanc is grown. The climate of Australia is well equipped to meet the surging demand for Merlot. The Aussie versions of this prized varietal vary greatly in style, yet most conform to the customer's notion of a low-acid, soft-tannin, easy-to-drink red. Cabernet Sauvignon can be very good, especially for the price. Shiraz can be great, as in Penfold's Hermitage, and is good at any price point.

Inexpensive Shiraz is made in a variety of styles, and some of its wines are quite complex. Because of the warm climate in which Shiraz is produced, the wine shows both fresh-fruit and dried-fruit flavor. Such forward fruit makes Shiraz both a perfect fireplace wine and a worthy match for powerful spices. The combination of Shiraz and

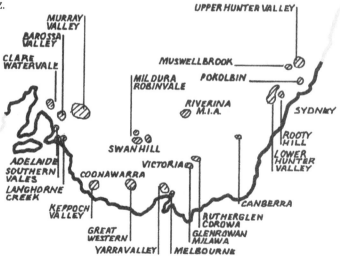

AUSTRALIA LABEL

SHIRAZ CABERNET: Grape varieties used—because neither grape comprises 85% of the wine, the wine does not qualify for varietal labeling and both varieties' proportions are given.

SOUTH EASTERN AUSTRALIA: Region of origin.

LINDEMANS: Producer.

CAWARRA HOMESTEAD: Property where produced.

LINDEMANS

CAWARRA
HOMESTEAD

1993

SOUTH EASTERN AUSTRALIA

SHIRAZ
CABERNET

58% SHIRAZ · 42% CABERNET SAUVIGNON

58% SHIRAZ, 42% CABERNET SAUVIGNON: The blend of grape varieties used.

Cabernet Sauvignon is one of the great bargains in the $8–10 price range. This combo is probably the most frequently found Aussie wine on American shelves. It is versatile, sometimes complex, and usually delicious.

It is fair to say that Australian reds are generally ahead of the whites in terms of the price/quality ratio. But the gap is closing fast. Hunter Valley is becoming the Napa of Australia with its big, ripe Chardonnays. A tendency toward excessive tropical fruit and flabby acid is being corrected by innovative winemaking procedures.

Australia is a big place—its own continent in fact—and it has good weather. Its wines should continue to improve, and it is hoped that its many bargain wines will remain bargains.

Germany

Germany is a country that produces a lot of quality white wine and hardly any red wine of note. The reds that are produced are rarely exported. Germany earns its place among the elite wine-producing countries of the world because of the white wines it produces from the Riesling grape. The overall wine output of Germany is sixth in the world, annually producing about 20 percent as much as France. The Germans are not big wine drinkers either. They drink, per capita, about a third of what the French drink, ranking them twelfth in the world in this statistic.

While Chardonnay-based wines are far more familiar to the American public, Rieslings, especially those from Germany, are just as good. So when people think of German wines, they usually think of Riesling. But Germany has other wines of distinction as well.

German wine has not played a significant role in the United States wine boom, probably for a few different reasons. First of all, California versions of Riesling haven't been that great. Because of this Americans aren't inspired to "go to the source" in the way they have for other grapes. Many consumers who have been hooked by California Chardonnay experiment with the French Chardonnays of Burgundy.

Second, German wines have a reputation for being too sweet. Although many of Germany's wines are less dry than Americans prefer, Germany does make some wonderful dry Riesling. Liebfraumilch, an overrated and somewhat sweet wine, was briefly in vogue in the states in the late 1960s and early '70s. This wine is partly responsible for the misconception that German wine equals sweet wine.

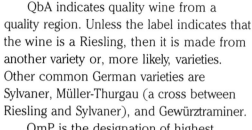

When people look at the indecipherable German wine labels on today's wines, many wonder if they are looking at a Liebfraumilch-type wine. Perhaps if people understood the labels on the bottles, they would be more willing to experiment with German wines.

Here is some help.

Like the other European Union countries, Germany has a government-regulated wine rating system. Of the three levels of quality, the top two are exported to the United States. The levels are:

Tafelwein: Lowest level wine.
Qualitätswein bestimmte Anbaugebiete (QbA): Middle-quality wine
Qualitätswein mit Prädikat (QmP): Highest quality wine

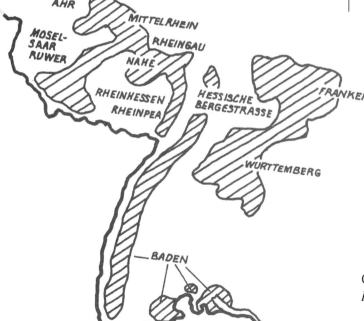

QbA indicates quality wine from a quality region. Unless the label indicates that the wine is a Riesling, then it is made from another variety or, more likely, varieties. Other common German varieties are Sylvaner, Müller-Thurgau (a cross between Riesling and Sylvaner), and Gewürztraminer.

QmP is the designation of highest quality, and QmP wine labels offer more information about the wine. The *Prädikats*, or levels of distinction, indicate the sugar level at harvest. Because Germany's vineyards are so far north, it is difficult to get the grapes to ripen, hence grape sugars are highly prized. Chaptalization, the addition of sugars to increase the alcohol content via fermentation, is not allowed in QmP wines.

These *Prädikats*, or distinctions, are as follows:

Kabinett—normal, fully ripe grapes (9.5 percent minimum potential alcohol).
Spätlese—"late-harvested" grapes, which may produce slightly sweet wine.
Auslese—individually selected, very ripe bunches used to make sweet wine.
Beerenauslese—individually selected, very ripe grapes ("berries") used to make very sweet dessert wine.
Trockenbeerenauslese—individually selected, *Botrytis*-afflicted grapes used to make the sweetest, most expensive German dessert wines.

Look for the word *trocken* on your German wine label as well; this means dry. *Halbtrocken* means half-dry.

GERMANY LABEL—QʙA

MOSEL-SAAR-RUWER: Quality region of origin.

RIESLING: Grape variety.

SCMITT SOHNE: Producer.

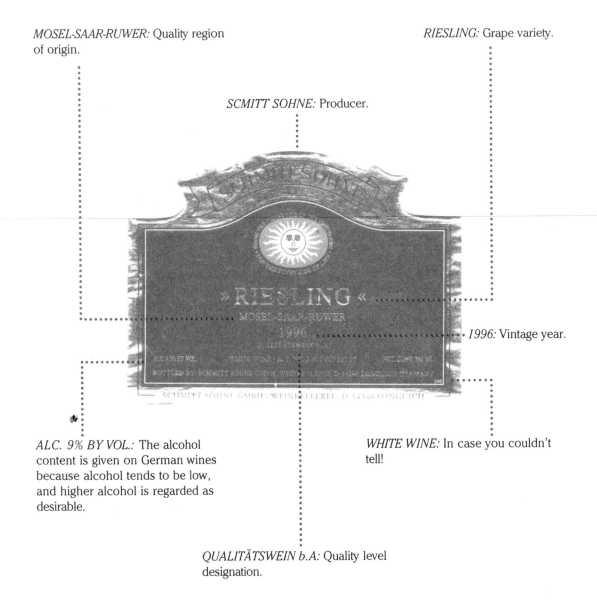

1996: Vintage year.

ALC. 9% BY VOL.: The alcohol content is given on German wines because alcohol tends to be low, and higher alcohol is regarded as desirable.

WHITE WINE: In case you couldn't tell!

QUALITÄTSWEIN b.A: Quality level designation.

GERMANY LABEL—QMP

1991er: Year of harvest; the "er" suffix is a charming Germanism still used on fine wines.

WILLI HAAG: Producer.

BRAUNEBERGER JUFFER: This means that the grapes are primarily from the *Juffer* vineyard in the village of *Brauneberg.*

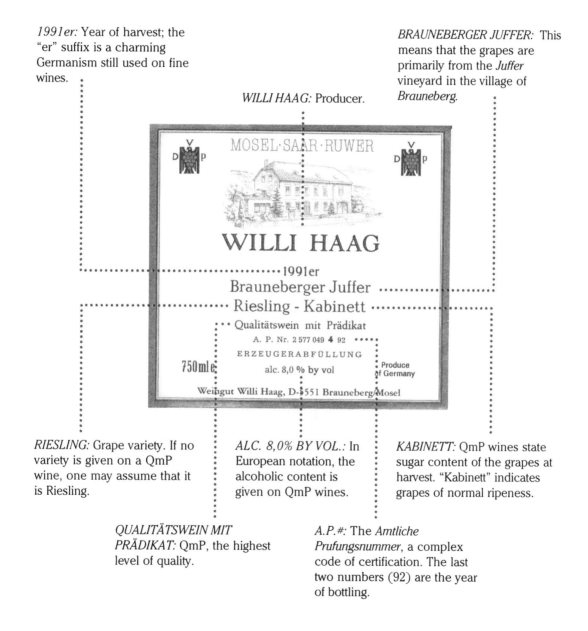

RIESLING: Grape variety. If no variety is given on a QmP wine, one may assume that it is Riesling.

ALC. 8,0% BY VOL.: In European notation, the alcoholic content is given on QmP wines.

KABINETT: QmP wines state sugar content of the grapes at harvest. "Kabinett" indicates grapes of normal ripeness.

QUALITÄTSWEIN MIT PRÄDIKAT: QmP, the highest level of quality.

A.P.#: The *Amtliche Prufungsnummer,* a complex code of certification. The last two numbers (92) are the year of bottling.

In addition, the term *eiswein* may be used in conduction with these *prädikats* if the grapes are crushed after a naturally occurring freeze. By pressing the grapes while frozen, the sugars, acids, and other qualities of the grapes become concentrated. All QmP wines are Riesling unless otherwise indicated on the label. This is the opposite of QbA labeling.

QmP Kabinett and Spätlese wines are as complex and delicious as Chardonnays in the $12–18 price range. A growing trend in German wine is varietal-labeled Riesling QbA wines. At $8–10, these wines represent a very good value and match well with Asian cuisine because their touch of sweetness puts out the spicy fire.

Germany enjoys a healthy sparkling-wine industry. German bubbly, known as Sekt, is quite different from French and California sparkling wines, which are usually made from Chardonnay and Pinot Noir. Sekt is produced from Riesling and other German varieties, and it can be of high quality when produced by the Champagne method.

Of the many wine-producing areas in Germany, the two most outstanding are the Mosel-Saar-Ruwer region (along the Mosel River and its two tributaries), and the three contiguous regions along the Rhine River— Rheingau, Rheinhessen, and Rheinpfaltz. The Riesling grape is the top grape in both areas. Fine Mosel Reisling tends to have mineral and citrus notes, with the classic Riesling floral bouquet. Rhine Riesling is usually richer, with apricot-like fruit. These rival areas distinguish themselves by bottle color—bright green for Mosel wines, brown for Rhines.

Spain

The Spanish wine industry is as old as that of France. The similarities between their wines, however, are few.

The dry table wines of Spain, except for the wines of the Rioja region, are mostly unknown to consumers in this country. Fortunately for Spain, French winemakers fled their own country when *phylloxera* attacked the vineyards of Bordeaux, with many ending up in the Rioja region of Spain. There they taught the locals how to make quality wines from the local grapes, the primary one being the red Tempranillo.

Red Rioja (wine is named after the region in Spain, as in France), is a well-known value, with many good ones selling for under $10. Spain has a tradition of requiring its reserve wines (*reservas* and *gran reservas*) to age in wood barrels for up to ten years. Some people find these wines to be too "woody."

White Rioja does not enjoy the same quality and reputation as the red. It is made from the local Viura grape. However, some are good—dry and oaky are two adjectives that come to mind for these wines.

The Catalonia region, though lesser known than Rioja, produces the bulk of Spain's wines. Penedés, a subregion of Catalonia, may take on a more important role in Spain's wine export business; varietal wines including Merlot and Cabernet are beginning to be produced there.

Spanish sparkling wines, known as Cavas, are a very good value for the American consumer. These come from the Catalonian subregions of Penedés and Conca de Barberá. Almost as much Cava is sold in the United States as French Champagne. Whereas most Cava producers use local grape varieties, which are unknown to people outside of Spain, the top Spanish bubblies are made from Chardonnay. Whenever you are looking to buy a Spanish sparkling wine, look for *méthode champenoise* and "brut" on the label.

It may be Sherry for which Spain's wine industry is most famous. The word "sherry" is an anglicized version of Jerez, the port city from which Sherry is shipped worldwide.

SPAIN LABEL

BERBERANA: Producer.

1988: Vintage year.

RESERVA: Indicates that wine has received additional barrel age—at least three years in barrel and bottle.

RIOJA-Denominacion de Origen Calificada: Rioja is the region, and *Denominacion de Origen Calificada* is the Spanish equivalent of the French AOC or the Italian DOCG designation.

Portugal

Wine grapes have been cultivated in Portugal since the days of the Roman Empire. Extensive trade with England during the Renaissance led to the development and widespread distribution of Portugal's famous fortified wines, Port and Madeira. However, aside from inexpensive Portuguese Rosés (Mateus and Lancers) which enjoyed great popularity in the United States during the Nixon and Ford Administrations, the table wines of Portugal remain a mystery to most Americans. This is true for a few reasons.

There has been no equivalent of neighboring Spain's Rioja in Portugal—no region that has become world famous for inexpensive, high-quality wine. Portuguese winemakers have also refrained from widespread production of the popular grape varieties like Chardonnay and Merlot, which probably would grab an instant market share. Instead, Portuguese winemakers plant varieties barely known outside of Portugal. Finally, the wines of Portugal, aren't fruity enough for the typical American wine drinker. For these reasons, the wines of Portugal occupy very little shelf space in American liquor stores.

But it is for these very reasons that you should give wines from Portugal a try. The wines are different and their producers feel compelled to resist the market forces, which have "Americanized" winemaking all over the world. They are also cheap. A couple of purchases of inexpensive Portuguese wines made from that country's mysterious grape varieties may allow you to uncover an off-beat gem at a very good price. These producers generally follow the European winemaking tradition of producing lighter food wines.

Portugal is divided into several wine-producing regions for table wine production:

Entre Minho e Douro
Douro
Tras os Montes
Beira Alta
Dão
Agueda/Bairrada
Estramadura

Portuguese wine labels will generally give you the name of the region, the predominant grape variety, and the color of the wine. *Tinto* indicates a red wine and *branco* means white.

PORTUGAL LABEL

PERIQUITA: The name of a grape variety, co-opted as a brand-name.

VINHO REGIONAL TERRAS: Region of origin.

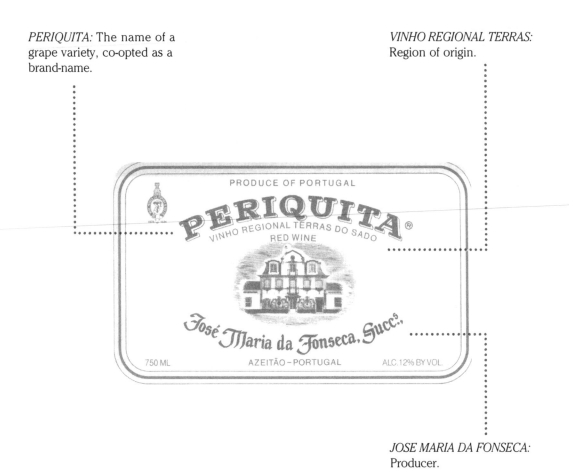

JOSE MARIA DA FONSECA: Producer.

The vintage year appears on a bottleneck label.

The town in which the wine was made may also be noted on the label.

Vinho Verde, which means young wine, is a designation used only for young, acid wine, perhaps *fizzy* from a malolactic fermentation in the bottle. This wine is from the Entre Minho e Douro region.

"Garrafeira" means matured wine, as does "Maduro" and "Reserva".

Some of the grape varieties you are apt to encounter are:

Periquita (red)
Tinta Roriz (red)
Touriga Francesa (red)
Touriga Nacional (red)
Esgana Cao (white)
Verdelho (white)
Arinto (white)

Chile

This 3,000-mile-long nation along the Pacific Coast of South America is rapidly becoming the most important source of inexpensive varietal wines in the world. California wines have steadily increased in price, to the point that a varietally correct $10 bottle of California wine is headed for the endangered species list.

Chile is the big benefactor, producing California-style wines, ripe and fruity. The popular Chardonnay, Merlot, and Cabernet Sauvignon wines have a very loyal following among American consumers looking to hold the line at $6–8 for a bottle of wine. Better Chilean wines costing $10–15 are often excellent values for those wishing to treat themselves and willing to experiment.

Chilean red wines are generally better than the whites. French and American wine people are investing heavily in the Chilean wine industry, so Chile figures to be a growing wine power. It is hoped that it won't outgrow its well-earned reputation for bargain wines.

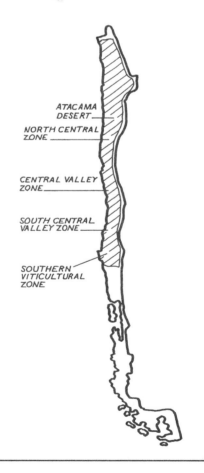

CHILE LABEL

120 SANTA RITA: Brand
name/producer.

1989: Vintage year. Keep in
mind that Southern Hemisphere
wines are picked in the *spring*
of the vintage year, rather than
in the *fall.*

MERLOT: Grape variety. Chile
has yet to make its mark with
anything other than varietal
wines.

South Africa

Fine wine has been produced in South Africa since the 1600s. However, because of politics South Africa was unable to benefit from the wine boom. Although today it is actually politically correct to support South African industry, there is little consumer interest in South African wine. The South African wine industry is now making a concerted effort to gain a share of the international wine market with value pricing, so the country's wines are often a good value.

Chenin Blanc (known in South Africa as Steen) and Chardonnay grapes do well here. The best of these wines are light and crisp, with contrasting elements of fruit and minerals. The whites have a better reputation than the reds, but you would be making a mistake to avoid the reds. The most intriguing red is the Pinotage, a cross of Pinot Noir and Cinsault, a red grape from France's southern Rhône. Shiraz (Syrah) is also produced with some success.

The system of labeling requires that the geographic region of origin be specified on the wine labels. The most notable regions are Swartland, Stellenbosch, and Paarl.

Red or white, the $9–12 wines are fairly priced and can be as good a bargain as Australian wines in the same price range.

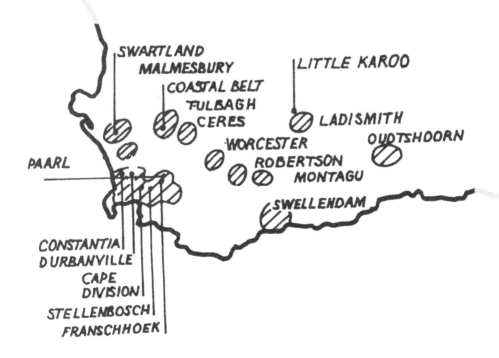

SOUTH AFRICA LABEL

CABERNET SAUVIGNON: Grape variety.

W.O.: May also be written out as "wine of origin." Indicates that the coastal region is the officially recognized region in which this wine was made.

SPRINGBOK: Producer.

RED TABLE WINE: Type of wine.

If the vintage date does not appear on the label itself, it will be on the bottleneck label or the back label.

Canada

Let's be honest. Canada doesn't have a very good climate for growing wine grapes. To make matters worse, the Canadian wine industry, like the United States' wine industry, was crippled by Prohibition and didn't bounce back as quickly or completely.

Generally speaking, Canada grows the hardy French hybrids that can survive harsh winters. Some traditional *vinifera* grapes are also grown. Vineyards exist in southern Ontario and in British Colombia that produce some good inexpensive wines, but the demand for these wines outside of Canada isn't very high.

Although Canadian winemakers are noted for their chutzpah and their wines have some cachet value, wines from neighboring New York and Washington are generally better wines.

It's fun to root for an underdog, and it's fun to serve Canadian wine. Combine both of these activities by turning on the Stanley Cup playoffs, and toast the underdog with a glass of Baco Noir. These red wines are easy to like and won't bust your budget.

SUMMERLAND VERNON KELOWNA PEACHLAND PENTICTON KEREMEOS OLIVER OSOYOOS

HAMILTON TORONTO DETROIT & WINDSOR NIAGARA FALLS ST. CATHARINES BLENHEIM HARROW LEAMINGTON PELEE ISLAND

COUNTRIES at a glance...

	CHEAP REDS	BETTER REDS	GREAT REDS	CHEAP WHITES	BETTER WHITES	GREAT WHITES	CHEAP SPARKLING	BETTER SPARKLING
USA		🍷🍷	🍷🍷	🍷🍷	🍷🍷	🍷	🍷	🍷
Canada	🍷			🍷				
Australia	🍷🍷	🍷	🍷	🍷	🍷			
Germany					🍷🍷	🍷🍷	🍷	
Spain	🍷	🍷		🍷			🍷🍷	🍷
Chile	🍷🍷	🍷			🍷			
South Africa	🍷	🍷		🍷	🍷			
Italy	🍷🍷	🍷🍷	🍷🍷	🍷	🍷		🍷	🍷
France	🍷	🍷🍷	🍷🍷	🍷	🍷🍷	🍷🍷	🍷	🍷🍷

Cheap Reds and Whites: Under $10
Better Reds and Whites: $10–29
Great Reds and Whites: $50 and up

Cheap Sparkling: Under $12
Better Sparkling: $12–29
Great Sparkling: $50 and up*

*France and the United States are the only two countries that make great sparkling wine.

🍷🍷 Extrodinary performance within category

Since countries have a variety of climates and growing regions, many produce good values in wine in almost all categories. If you look hard enough, you can find good values in the *Cheap* and Better categories from all the countries for red, white, and sparkling wines. 🍷🍷 A "double" 🍷🍷 means "especially so."

The Lunatic Fringe

There are some wines on the market that are so out of whack with the mainstream that they deserve special mention. Such wines can be a welcome change of pace.

RETSINA

A favorite of the Greek people, Retsina is a white or rosé wine flavored with pine pitch. This seemingly peculiar practice has ancient historical roots. The earliest winemakers, including the Greeks, often treated clay vessels with pine pitch in order to store wine, and the flavor of pine pitch became accepted over time as a fundamental component of wine.

When glass bottles came into use, pine pitch became unnecessary for storage, but its use continued as a flavoring agent. If this sounds weird, remember that oak evolved as a flavor component in a nearly identical manner. Not coincidentally, this wine goes well with Greek food.

VOUVRAY SEC

The winemakers of Vouvray, located in the Loire region of France, defer to the weather when it comes to winemaking style. In warm, sunny seasons they make the delightfully off-dry white Vouvray demi-sec. After cold and rainy growing seasons, these winemakers turn their grapes into Vouvray sec, which can be the world's most acidic wine. In its driest manifestations, this wine can be excruciatingly tart.

Connoisseurs tend to develop an appreciation for highly acidic white wines, so Vouvray sec has a following. If you want to experience this "acid trip," do not think of drinking Vouvray sec without food. Raw shellfish matches well

ELAPSED BREATHING TIME
13:47

with these sharp wines. Creamy cheeses also go well, providing a pleasing contrast in textures with the wine's acidity.

RIOJA GRAN RESERVA

The finest red wines of the Rioja region in Spain are traditionally aged for up to ten years in oak barrels. Not especially fruity to begin with, Rioja becomes even less so with barrel age. The flavor of oak dominates the wine. Quality Rioja is not thrown out of balance by this flavor component, rather, Rioja Gran Reserva is a very dry, oaky, medium-to-light-bodied red wine with subtle and complex flavors—none of which

are fruit flavors. This wine is especially good with lamb.

AUSTRALIAN CHARDONNAY

The term "fruit driven Chardonnay" applies to many of the Australian versions of this versatile grape. The combination of intense sunlight and cool breezes in Australian vineyards can bring Chardonnay to its fullest possible state of ripeness. Acidity usually diminishes with such full ripeness, making way for a spectrum of obscenely rich fruit flavors—banana, pineapple, peach, coconut, papaya, and fig.

The boldest Australian Chardonnays are high in alcohol, generously treated with oak, and display enough rip-roaring fruit to make your average California Chardonnay seem like spring water. Wine this fruity is very satisfying without food, and somewhat difficult to match with most dishes. Pacific Rim cuisine and seafood that has a natural affinity for fruit, such as shrimp, lobster, swordfish, and shark, do pretty well alongside these massive white wines.

IDAHO WINE

One doesn't normally associate Idaho with fine wine, but neither do your friends. That is precisely why you might want to serve it. Good wine has been made in Idaho for a century. The only winery in Idaho to distribute its wines nationally is Ste. Chapelle of Caldwell, Idaho. Their

Riesling and Gewürztraminer wines are well-made and affordable.

BLACK MUSCAT

This funky, sweet raisin juice is as delicious as it is weird. Black Muscat is unlike any other wine grape. More often used for eating than for winemaking, it nonetheless yields a sweet and spicy wine when grown to full ripeness in California.

It is difficult to imagine this wine with food. Black Muscat is a perfect "fireplace wine" and makes a good low-alcohol alternative to Port. Two California versions to look for come from Rosenblum Cellars and Andrew Quady.

OLD VINE REDS

Grapevines first produce useful grapes in their fifth year and reliably yield grapes for another fifteen or so. Middle age then sets in, and the yields diminish. It is a common practice for volume-oriented growers to uproot and replace when their grape production begins to tail off. Some growers, however, maintain vines that are many decades old and are richly rewarded (in quality) for doing so. Although old vines yield relatively few grapes, "old vine" wines usually have more complex and concentrated flavors than wines of the same variety from younger vines.

"Old Vines" Zinfandels are fairly common in California, and a few "Old Vines" Petite Sirahs are also available. Both varieties offer up peppery, concentrated wines, and are a cost-effective alternative to high-priced California Cabernet Sauvignon wines. There are even a few white wines whose labels boast of old vines, but these are rare. Some well-known California producers of old-vine reds include Rodney Strong, Rosenblum, and Cline for Zinfandel, and Lolonis, which makes "Orpheus" Petite Sirah from old vines.

You can also find some French Red Burgundy wines with a "Vieilles Vignes" (old vines) designation on the label. Perhaps the most famous of these is Domaine Ponsot Clos de la Roche Vieilles Vignes, which sells for over $100 a bottle.

ALSACE GEWÜRZTRAMINER

As the true personality of this quirky grape is laid bare on the therapy couch of Alsatian soil, we learn that Gewürztraminer is the Dennis Rodman of *vitis vinifera*. Its in-your-face aromas and unsubtle flavors of lychee, rose pedal, and grapefruit rind overwhelm the senses and make it the most easily recognizable variety of wine. Cheese and crackers, and other bland foods, do okay with it, but in general, it is difficult to match with food. Notable exceptions are sausage and sauerkraut which have a regional affinity with Gewürztraminer.

Pacific Northwest versions of the variety tend to be more accessible and somewhat sweeter than Alsatians which are Gewürztraminer in its purest form. Some well-known Alsatian producers are Domaine Zind Humbrecht, Zimbach, Domaine Weinbach, and Hugel.

C H A P T E R 7

BUYING WINE

BOTTLED BY ADAMS MEDIA

NET CONTENTS: THIRTY-FOUR PAGES

PRODUCT OF USA

Retail Wine Shopping

Unless you set out for the wine store with a specific bottle of wine in mind, you will have to make a buying decision based on limited information. Your goal is to bring home a wine you will like, at a price you feel comfortable with. In the end you may end up with a bottle you've had in the past because this was the most informed selection you could make.

Although every wine store is unique, it is possible to make some useful generalizations that might help you decide which store you should shop. There are big stores; there are little stores; and there are stores in between. In most states, the big store can take advantage of huge-quantity discounts at the wholesale level. The bigger the store or chain, the bigger the discounts it is apt to receive. However, this doesn't necessarily mean big stores are better for all of the people all of the time.

The second variable is expertise. "Wine geeks" cost more money to employ than unskilled stock clerks. The greater the level of expertise in a store, the higher the labor cost. Wine stores (of any size) with excellent service generally cannot afford to offer much of its stock at rock-bottom prices.

So we have two variables—size and expertise. Every store is different, but we can get some sense of the retail wine-buying experience from these four hypothetical store types:

1. Small store with expertise
2. Small store without expertise
3. Big store with expertise
4. Big store without expertise

SMALL STORE WITH EXPERTISE

This store might well be a hobby, or at least a labor of love, for a semiretired big shot from the wine industry or for a corporate fast-track dropout. Chances are that there won't be a bad bottle of wine in the store. The proprietor has probably tasted and personally selected them all. Need advice? This is the best place to get it. Stores like this do well in college towns, because college professors like to soak up all the free wine information available and talk wine with their colleagues.

The downside to such a place is that a staple item such as Kendall-Jackson Chardonnay will be far more expensive in this type of store than in any other. This boutique has far less purchasing power than the big stores and doesn't make it on volume.

SMALL STORE WITHOUT EXPERTISE

The wines in stores like this are often limited to huge brands such as Gallo, Fetzer, Kendall-Jackson (hopefully), and the like.

And why not? With all the money such wineries invest in advertising, plus their name recognition, these wines sell themselves. The prices aren't cheap, but they may be cheap for a store this size. The selection is usually going to be disappointing at such a store.

However, some of these stores may have had some expertise at one time. Sometimes such expertise is asked to leave in order to keep the store from going bankrupt from its excellent and costly wine inventory that doesn't move fast enough. This means a bargain, buried in the bargain bin, could be a real treasure that the remaining staff did not know enough to mark up as it aged. Browse this type of store very carefully the first time you go there.

In states where wine may be sold in food stores, the small store without expertise might be a convenience store. Here you are looking for something you know is drinkable. Such wines seem to taste great when purchased in the middle of nowhere five minutes before closing.

BIG STORE WITH EXPERTISE

At first glance, this type of store might look like a discount store, since the twenty-case floor stacks are evidence of considerable purchasing power. Upon further inspection you see a lot of wines from remote regions of the world, maybe even from Lebanon or Idaho. There may also be a

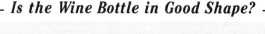

Is the Wine Bottle in Good Shape?

When you buy a bottle of wine, you don't want to buy damaged goods. Since there are no tires to kick, you need to use other tests.

1. Is the bottle filled up? This used to be more of an issue in the less industrial days of wine bottling. See how high the wine is in the neck of the wine bottle compared to other bottles. There is no need to pay the same for less.

2. Feel the cork through the plastic wrapper on the top of the bottle. The cork shouldn't feel pushed in or out. The top of the cork should be close to flush with the top of the bottle. Cork movement can be indicative of a bad cork or a wine that has been exposed to temperature extremes.

3. Hold the bottle up to the light. Is it clear or murky? Only in an older wine is it okay to see sediment. Wine from the same "batch" should be the same color. If you can't figure out which color is the right color, buy a different wine.

Before you buy wine at a store, you should be convinced that the store is kept at cool temperatures twenty-four hours a day. You also don't want to buy wines that are stored in a place where they get a lot of light or are exposed to a radiator.

small army of neatly dressed clerks assisting customers and offering expertise. Here you have a high labor cost, and at least part of the inventory isn't jumping off the shelves.

This big store with expertise is a good place to find wines that you can't find anywhere else, such as:

Older wines, particularly red Bordeaux and Port

Hard-to-find Champagne, such as Blanc de Noirs or Brut Rosé

A good selection of Alsace and German wines

Wines from countries that don't export much wine

An expensive wine that no one has heard of

The perfect gift for a knowledgeable wine buff

BIG STORE WITHOUT EXPERTISE

This store has truly strong purchasing power. They buy single brands of liquor by the trailerload, and their wholesalers jump whenever anyone from such a store calls to place an order. Such a store can buy for less and afford a lesser markup on their inventory (30–40 percent, rather than 50–60 percent), because of the volume of business they do. Some of the wines at such a store sell at prices below what the smaller stores pay *wholesale* for the same wines. The wine-buying public flocks to these stores to take advantage of the great prices and good selection.

Big stores without expertise might not have as esoteric a selection as the big stores with expertise, but if you are looking for popular wine driven by national advertising dollars (such as Moët et Chandon White Star Champagne; Kendall-Jackson Chardonnay; Meridian Chardonnay; Georges Duboeuf Beaujolais-Villages; Fetzer varietal wines; and Glen Ellen varietal wines) this is where you should be going, especially if you are going to be buying in bulk.

ANATOMY OF A WINE STORE

With the preceding information you should be able to size up the stores in your area and know when to shop where. Now it's time for a tour of the typical wine store. Except for the smaller store, they often have a similar layout.

The jug wall is a selection of easy-to-reach, inexpensive jug wines, usually near the store entrance. The Californians are all there—Gallo, Inglenook, Almaden—with the old names: Burgundy, Chablis, etc. These wines take up quite a bit of the store because they sell, and the bottles are big, holding up to 4 liters. The small store with expertise isn't likely to carry these wines because they mostly avoid head-to-head price comparisons with bigger stores, also known as "getting beat up."

Continuing along the wall near the California jug wines, you will see imported jug wines and the lesser fighting varietals. These two types are usually sold in the 1.5-liter bottle, and like California jug wines, they jump off the shelves. This is where the wine money is for most liquor stores.

The middle of the floor in a typical wine store is filled with racks of 750-ml bottles on their sides in metal racks. They are arranged by country, then maybe by region (depending on the country and size of the store), color, and variety. California wines, however, may not be near the rest of the United States wines (if there are any). They also aren't likely to be broken down by region.

Then ends of racks are usually occupied by "floor stacks" or "end caps." These are popular wines bought and sold in high volume. These wines may be terrific bargains if they are "rock-and-roll-items"—major brands that sell so fast that the store can afford to mark them up less. In a large store without expertise, a rock-and-roll item such as a Moët Champagne might be offered for only pennies over cost in order to attract customers into the store.

Another explanation for an end cap is quite the opposite. The store may have bought the wine at a deep discount and is marking it up as much as 80 percent, bringing it back to the standard retail price. They want to sell a lot of these and make a lot on each bottle. In either case, the store wants you to buy a wine from the end cap, which makes sense because these wines are readily accessible to customers.

Unless you are in a store with expertise, how can you get information about the wines? Can you trust the little "shelf talkers"

taped to the racks? Probably not, since they are likely to be composed by the wholesaler or the wineries themselves. These are hardly objective sources of information. A shelf talker in a store with expertise may be pointing to a wine worth buying, when written by someone from the store. (You may see the store logo on the card.) It is quite likely that the store bought a lot of a good wine, and they want to move the wine and make you a satisfied customer.

Assuming you can't get any good information from a store worker or display, here are some good tips:

Know a Grape: If you like Sauvignon Blanc but can't find your favorite bottle, you may want to try a bottle from a different producer.

Know a Region: If the Cabernet you like is from Alexander Valley, California, try a different Cabernet from that same region. Climate and soil, *terroir*, play a big part in winemaking.

Know a Producer: If you like Pride Mountain Merlot, you may like Pride Mountain Cabernet Sauvignon, since the two wines are made by the same person, or at least with the same philosophy.

If you have enough interest in wine that you've made it this far into the book, then you owe it to yourself to attend a free wine tasting, which are often held at wine stores. Certainly, tasting a wine without having first to buy it is a worthwhile opportunity.

Cheap Wine

Everybody needs cheap wine at some point in their lives. Maybe you're saving your money to buy something more significant than wine; maybe you're making Sangria, for which good fruit juice is a better investment than good wine; or maybe you're hosting an art opening. Whatever the reason, you want to get a lot for a little.

It is foolish to spend a lot on wine for such occasions as a barbecue or picnic, just as it is also foolish to bring a lesser wine to a dinner table where very good food is being served. Rosés are considered to be a good choice for informal occasions (and not so good a choice for semiformal and formal meals).

As you learn about wine, and your $7-a-bottle palette becomes a $12-a-bottle palette, it becomes very difficult to slum it. Why? Because you know what your cheaper wines are missing. Yet money is a reality that most of us can't afford to ignore all the time. You need to search for a $7 wine that reminds you of a $12 bottle, or one that simply tastes really good; both are out there.

If you are having a cocktail party, you should serve both a red and a white wine. Chilean wine is your cheapest option for a low-cost varietal wine (as opposed to a generic jug wine). Australia may be the best choice for one or two more dollars per bottle, assuming you want to spend the money. The Australians like to blend grapes at the low end of the price spectrum, and the result is usually better than the sum of the parts. They have two winning formulas, one red and one white. The red blend is the Shiraz/Cabernet Sauvignon blend. The white blend is the Semillon/Chardonnay blend. The Shiraz/Cabernet wines tend to be blended at about a 50/50 ratio, whereas whites tend to be around 70/30 Semillon. Both are great values and will impress anyone who understands wine at your cocktail party.

Another good cocktail party red/white pairing is Spanish Rioja—red and white. Rioja is less fruity than the Australian wines. This makes it better with food, for some people's tastes, but you may find it lacking if you aren't serving munchies.

When you go to a wine store, choosing a $6–$8 bottle can be very tricky. In this range you run the risk of buying a wine you don't like at all. Although the choices we listed above are usually safe, you will probably be confronted with more than one of each type of wine in that price range.

Fortunately, it is in the wine merchant's interest to give you good advice. It will make you more likely to return to his store for wine, and more likely to want to drink more wine in the future.

If you are making a wine drink such as Sangria, you are probably going to make a lot of it. Sangria has juice, spirits, sugar, and other ingredients, so you won't be able to tell good from bad wine. You need California jug wine, and a lot of it. Gallo, Inglenook, and Almaden are three good sources for red and white jug wines.

If you are having a reception and you want to serve cheap wine, but jug wine just isn't good enough, you have some tough choices. Jug whites are easier to enjoy than jug reds. You could spend more money on your red wines, or, if you have access to some clean, empty carafes or even old wine bottles, you could be a little inventive. If you have patience and a couple of empty bottles or containers, you can mix yourself a lot of "starving artist" wine. We have found that if you take some decent jug wine and add to it the right bottle of $10 wine, the jug wine gets much better. We have found that a 750-ml bottle can perk up a magnum (1500 ml) of lesser wine.

Hints for success: Avoid varietal jug wines, the worst of the "fighting varietals" category. A magnum of $7 Merlot isn't the answer. California jug wines often contain a lot of Zinfandel (red Zinfandel, not white), although a generic red won't mention any grape variety on its label. Because of this, we recommend your good bottle be an honest Zinfandel ($8–10). Even if the jug wine isn't Zinfandel based, Zinfandel is a very strong grape and will be able to exert its influence better than most other varieties. Similarly, if you want to "fortify" a white jug wine, try a California Chardonnay; those tend to have a lot of fruity flavor too.

Cheese makes almost all wines taste better, and this is especially true for cheap wine. So if you are serving wine at your reception, make sure you have cheese and crackers, not M&M's and pretzels.

Vintage 1992

TYRRELL'S WINES

NIL MAGNUM NISI BONUM

LONG FLAT RED

South Eastern Australia Table Wine - Alcohol 12.5% by Volume

Produced by Tyrrell's Vineyards Pty Ltd
Pokolbin, Hunter Valley, Australia

PRODUCT OF AUSTRALIA

750 ml

Tyrrell's Long Flat Red: A Case Study in Good Cheap Wine

If you buy enough wine, you are bound to stumble upon an inexpensive wine you consider to be one of the world's best kept secrets. You buy bottle after bottle and get to know every nuance of the wine. You even get to know how the wine will taste the next day.

For us that bottle is Tyrrell's Long Flat Red. This is a $7 bottle of wine that comes from Australia made from Cabernet Sauvignon, Shiraz, and Malbec grapes. We first tasted the 1994 vintage in December of 1995. Southern Hemisphere wines are generally six months older than Northern Hemisphere wines, as the grapes are usually harvested in March rather than October.

The wine was a little over a year and a half old and tasted very smooth. But what amazed us the most was how much better the wine tasted a day after we opened it. We didn't even take any steps to preserve the leftovers. We drank what we wanted, put the cork back in the bottle, put the bottle on the kitchen table, and went to bed.

If you become a wine person, you will understand our need to tell all our friends about this wine. We'd even buy them a bottle so they could see how great it was. Some friends liked the wine more that others, and no one seemed as excited as we were. This is probably because it was our discovery, and we took pride in the wine as if we had grown the grapes ourselves.

The story doesn't end here.

One day in the late spring of 1996 we showed up at the liquor store only to find the 1994 vintage had been exhausted and the 1995 bottles were now on the shelves. Of course we had to try it. When we did, we didn't like it. We then went to other stores searching for 1994's, but there weren't any to be had. So the Long Flat Red chapter in our lives seemed closed.

Nine months after rejecting the 1995 vintage, we went back and bought another bottle. Why? We were curious to remember what it was about the wine that we didn't like. When we tasted the wine, it was like the 1994 vintage we remembered so well. Evidently the wine had had time to age. The wine that was released fifteen months after harvest improved dramatically with nine more months in the bottle. We then stocked up on the 1995's knowing the 1996's would soon be on the shelves.

When you start going into various wine and liquor stores just to check out the wine selection, strange things are bound to happen. Two weeks after rediscovering the 1995 vintage, we stumbled upon a little liquor store that had six 1992 bottles. We bought them all except for the one whose yellow label had been turned white by prolonged exposure to direct sunlight.

However, this was fools gold. After trying two disappointing bottles, we realized that all the bottles had been subjected to improper storage, and we returned the remaining unopened bottles for a refund.

The Safest Wines to Buy

Although this book attempts to demystify wine, there are way too many wine-buying options and wine-making parameters to make buying wine a no-brainer. Even if you find a wine you like, when stock of that vintage runs out you may be searching for a new wine. Many wines taste different from vintage to vintage.

If you buy wines with labels printed in English and the grape variety or varieties in the wine are denoted, you will at least know a few things about your potential purchase, like what the heck you're buying. Not only will you have some idea of what you are buying, but after you drink the wine you can look at the bottle and know what type of wine you just did or didn't enjoy.

Because Australia and California have good grape-growing weather most years, and wine from both places is labeled in nothing but English, buying wines from these two countries is the best place for wine beginners to start. But don't get the impression these wines are better than wines from other regions.

If you are buying California jug wines, they are going to be the same every year. These wines get a bad rap from wine snobs. If you need a lot of wine, these large commercial wines are an excellent choice. But chances are, if you are reading this book, you want your tastes to be able to branch out into less familiar territory.

Australian red wines that are exported to North America may be the safest red-wine bet around. These wines tend to be accessible without being overly simple. The white wines from Australia, especially the blends of Semillon and Chardonnay, tend to be crowd pleasers. Straight Chardonnay is a fairly safe bet, although some versions could be considered too fruity for the dinner table.

Again, since the wine's grape variety or varieties are printed on the label, it will be easy to reproduce a positive Australian wine experience, even if you can't find the same bottle the next time you buy wine in a store or order it in a restaurant. Australia exports a lot of good, easy-to-drink, inexpensive red and white wines, and keeps things easy for consumers, since they don't seem to export many bad bottles.

Chardonnays from large California producers that sell in the $10–$13 range are a very safe bet. Chardonnay is an easy grape to grow in the California climate. The big producers have the formula down pat. They grow some Chardonnay grapes; they buy some other Chardonnay grapes from other vineyards; they have a goal—their Chardonnay formula; and they always reach that goal.

Beaujolais Nouveau ("new wine" from the French region of Beaujolais) is an easy red wine to buy. Although the label doesn't say so, all of this wine comes from the

Gamay grape. It is meant to be consumed right away, so you won't have to worry that the wine you are buying is too young. All of its producers make Beaujolais in a light, simple, fruity, good-with-food style. These wines are also consistent from year to year. Best of all, they are cheap: Good ones can be had for $7. The very best, the *cru* Beaujolais, sell for under $15. This is a terrific red wine to serve to people who think they only like white wine.

Pinot Gris (or Pinot Grigio, as it is called in Italy) is a white wine that is very easy to drink and to match with food. Powerfully spiced foods can overwhelm this somewhat timid wine, but it goes well with a wide variety of pastas, seafood, and lighter chicken dishes.

Another good way to get a good wine is by sticking with producers whose wines are generally good and widely available. This may be the best way to venture into European wines. Reliable European producers include Louis Latour (France), Ruffino (Italy), and Montecillo (Spain).

Consistently Good Red Wines ($10 and under)

Beaujolais-Villages—Louis Jadot (France) $9
Zinfandel—Rosenblum (California) $10
Pinot Noir—Firesteed (Oregon) $9
Shiraz—Hardy's Nottage Hill (Australia) $8
Shiraz—Lindemans Bin 50 (Australia) $10
Merlot—Dulong (France) $8
Cabernet Sauvignon—Dunnewood (California). $10
Cabernet Sauvignon—Santa Rita (Chile). $7
Chianti—Castello di Gabbiano (Italy). $10
Chianti—Castello di Quercetto (Italy). $10
Rioja—Bodegas Monticillo (Spain) $9

Risky Wine Purchases

What can go wrong when you buy a bottle of wine?

You can buy wine that is just plain lousy. Some wines, like some movies, just shouldn't have been made. This is one of the best reasons for keeping a couple of auxiliary bottles around the house at all times.

Other wines may deserve to have been made, but like some movies, you just don't like them. If you have no idea what you like and/or have no idea what you are buying, you may end up with a good wine that you happen not to like.

If you are buying wine to be consumed with a meal, you can get into trouble with the "right wine at the wrong time" syndrome. The concept of buying *the* right wine is a silly one. When painting your house, you may look at a hundred color samples and pick *the* right one, but the wine-buying scenario is very different. There is a good chance you have never tasted the wine you are thinking of buying. If you have, you may not have had it with the food you are planning on serving. Even if you have had the identical wine with the dish you are planning on cooking, the ingredients in the food you are making can vary. Onions can vary in intensity, as can garlic and lemon juice. Not all medium-rare steaks are cooked alike.

However, our concern is wrong wines. If you are selecting a wine for four people to enjoy with dinner, you really only have one objective—pleasing everyone. If you are selecting a wine for your own enjoyment, you have a much easier task and no one to apologize to if your wine choice doesn't work out.

So, what is the most likely scenario for buying a bad wine? Wines that are inexpensive or that have a label that boasts of a popular grape variety can often be bad wines. If a bottle of Chardonnay or Cabernet Sauvignon were of high quality, it wouldn't sell for $6. You are much better off trying a nonvarietal wine or a "lesser" variety at the low end of the price spectrum.

Some wines are quirky. Gewürztraminer is a white-wine grape grown in Germany and Alsace (France), and elsewhere it produces white wines that are frequently too sweet for most Americans. Even for people who like some Gewürztraminers, many are apt to be too sweet. Any wine that is noticeably off-dry is risky unless you, and anyone else expected to drink the wine, have had it before and enjoyed it. Gewürztraminer is an interesting grape variety worth exploring, but you probably should do some scouting before buying some for others to drink.

Zinfandel has a lot of fruit and a lot of body. Some of these wines are too overpowering for many people. However, once you get to know a Zinfandel or two you like, you will find it matches well with a variety of hearty meals.

Now, if you have an idea of what wine grape varieties you like, buying a European wine can be difficult without a pocket guide or knowledgeable salesperson to guide you. If you find you like California Pinot Noir and

are thinking of trying a French Pinot, you won't usually find the words "Pinot Noir" on the bottles of French wines you see at the liquor store. You need to develop an understanding of the cross-relationship between California varietals and French wine regions. Cheat sheets are allowed.

If you are buying wine for people other than yourself, especially wine to be consumed with meals, don't be daring. Stick with the rules, unless you know that your group doesn't like red or white wine.

Older wines are difficult to buy. Some wines fade when they are aged too long; other older wines are still too young. You may see a fifteen-year-old bottle of wine that could easily be five years too young or five years too old.

Consistently Good White Wines ($10 and under)

Sauvignon Blanc—Kronendaal (South Africa) $6
Sauvignon Blanc—Canyon Road (California) $8
Chardonnay—Monterey (California). $7
Saint-Véran—Louis Latour (France) (It's Chardonnay!) $10
Chardonnay—Meridien (California) $10
Semillon/Chardonnay—Penfolds Koonunga Hill (Australia) $8
Pinot Grigio—Mezza Corona (Italy). $10
Riesling—Bernkasteler Kurfurstlay Kabinett (Germany). $9
Riesling—Schmitt Soehne (Germany) $7
Muscadet—Marcel Martin (France) $8

Buying Wine for the Nonconnoisseur

If you are buying wine for a person who has only a casual interest in wine, chances are that person is going to drink the wine with a meal. Your goal is to buy a wine that is easy to like.

If you are buying wine for someone who likes white wine and who likes things that are familiar, then a California Chardonnay is a good choice. The wine is probably going to taste good, assuming you don't look for the cheapest California Chardonnay in the store. Also, there is nothing more familiar to the casual white-wine drinker than "California" and "Chardonnay." If there is a knowledgeable salesperson in the store, ask for a bottle that isn't too acidic or oaky; a $12 Chardonnay from California is a very safe bet.

If you want to give something a little less conventional in the white-wine area, an Italian Pinot Grigio costing $10–12 is a good choice for a lighter white wine. These wines are excellent with food. The Semillon/Chardonnay blends from Australia are also usually very good and fairly priced at $8–10. You could also track down a bottle of wine from your home state. The majority of states have a commercial wine industry that produces accessible wines, although they tend to be a couple of dollars overpriced.

When it comes to red wine, there is no sure thing equivalent to the white California Chardonnays. If you are trying to buy a red wine for a person who wants something familiar, you might try a Chianti from Italy, which matches very well with food. Chianti, thanks in part to the American jug wine named Chianti, has a lot of name recognition. Although decent $8 bottles are out there, you may want to improve your odds of getting a good bottle and spend $10.

If you want to buy a red wine for someone adventurous, your choices are vast. A Canadian Baco Noir is a very drinkable red wine. It's quite compatible with food but boring without it. A price of $8–10 will usually get you a good-tasting, unassuming Canadian red. French Beaujolais (Nouveau or not) wines from the Gamay grape are easy to buy ($8–10) and easy to drink. Many of the Beaujolais Nouveaus also come with a festive wine label.

Although it sounds ridiculous, you could buy a red wine with an interesting or funny label and/or name. There are a lot of bottles for $10 and under to choose from in this category. If you buy a nonvarietal U.S. table wine, you are probably going to end up with a middle-of-the-road safe wine. If the person to whom you are giving the wine really doesn't know one grape from another, packaging may be the thing to look for.

For the Grateful Dead fan there are at least two California wines with names and labels inspired by the Grateful Dead, or at least targeting Grateful Dead fans. Look for Dead Red "Space Your Face" red table unwine (non-alcoholic) and Grateful Red, a Pinot Noir. These wines are crafted to be accessible—like the music? Expect to spend between $10 and $15 for such a wine: not cheap, but less than a ticket to a 1990s Dead Show.

Marilyn Merlot pairs a hot varietal with a popular icon, who appears in living color on the label. At $20, this wine may be worth more to you unopened.

If you are interested in spending upwards of $20 for a red, a California, celebrity-free Pinot Noir may be your best option. These wines are rich and fruity, and easily appreciated by wine novices and veterans alike.

Buying Wine for the Connoisseur

If you are going to buy wine as a gift for a connoisseur, and you are not a connoisseur, you have a couple of good options. If the gift is for someone who takes pride in his or her roots, try to buy a good bottle from the homeland. (Let's hope that the homeland isn't France or Italy.) Good bottles of wine are produced in many countries around the world. Good wines from Israel, New Zealand, Canada, and Switzerland, to name a few, are definitely out there. South Africa is not the only country in Africa that produces wine. Morocco, Algeria, and even Egypt make wine. Such purchases may require some research, but a knowledgeable wine salesperson, or possibly the Internet, can point you in the right direction. A $20–30 bottle is apt be good, and spending any more for a wine of unknown quality is foolish.

Another approach is to buy a "best-of type" with a reasonable price tag. The best wines from the famous regions of the world are going to cost you a couple of hundred dollars. However, the best wines from Chile, Oregon, or the underappreciated Alsace region of France will cost you far less. For example, $30 will buy you an excellent Riesling from Alsace. The premium French *cru* Beaujolais wines won't kill you financially. These wines are especially good for people who live in warm climates or who entertain a lot.

Buying a magnum (double-sized bottle) of good wine is another offbeat but sensible idea. The wine itself may not wow the connoisseur, but these bottles look impressive at any dinner table. Expect to spend $35–50 for a magnum capable of impressing a connoisseur.

Wine for People Who Don't Like Wine

What qualities in wine do some people find objectionable? Three, usually—acidity, tannin, and alcohol.

Wine is the most acidic beverage we consume. The acids in wine are balanced in part by its fruit and sugar. In dry wines, those with little or no residual sugar, the acidity can be overwhelming for a non-wine person. Acidic wines are often described as "food wines," mainly because they can be best appreciated with food already in your mouth. Starches such as bread, rice, or pasta provide balance to the acidity.

So, the answer is to find wines low in acidity. Most American rosés fit into this category, as do Australian Chardonnays. French Beaujolais (made from Gamay grapes) is the red wine that is most likely to be acceptable to a person who doesn't like the acidity of wine.

For those who dislike the strong taste of alcohol, there are two wonderful types of wine to enjoy. Moscato d'Asti is a low-alcohol, slightly sparkling wine from Northern Italy. At 5.5 percent alcohol, half that of normal wine, its subtle floral components shine through. Only slightly higher in alcohol is late-harvest, somewhat sweet German Riesling, which can be exquisitely rich (and a somewhat expensive gift for someone who claims not to like wine).

Red Wine for People Who Don't Like Red Wine

Don't waste big bucks on red wine for someone who claims to hate it. There are many people who enjoy white wine who, after tasting a few reds, give up on the genre. Cheaper red wines tend to be more offensive than cheaper whites. Since most people start off drinking inexpensive wine, it makes sense that a lot of them write off red wine during their formative wine-drinking years.

Look for low-tannin wines. Beaujolais, from the southern Burgundy region of France, is a fruity, crowd-pleasing, gulping wine. This Gamay-based wine may be the strongest argument against red-wine prejudice. Australian blends of Cabernet Sauvignon and Shiraz show enough raisiny fruit to put the tannin in its place for under $12. For $11–15, California Pinot Noir, thick with glycerine and unctuous fruit, converts many a red-wine skeptic. Rioja from Spain is another option.

If tannin isn't the problem, then maybe it's a yearning for fruit. California Pinot Noir is the fruitiest incarnation of the varietal. Red Zinfandel is also very fruity, but it may be too tannic to convince someone that red wine deserves another chance. If you choose a Pinot Noir, look for the rich and fruity Pinots that come from California, especially those from the Carneros and Santa Barbara regions. French Pinot Noir and those from Oregon and Washington tend to be more austere as they have less ripe fruit flavor.

White Wine for People Who Don't Like White Wine

This one is difficult. If they say they don't like white wine, then they probably don't like typical California Chardonnay. White wine that is served chilled and that lacks tannin is generally a less complicated beverage, which, for many red-wine drinkers, translates into boring. Imagine trying to convince someone who thinks fishing is boring that it isn't.

There are many directions to take:

1. Try good French Chardonnay—white Burgundy is less fruity and more acidic (in a good, thirst-quenching way) than most California and Australian Chardonnay.

2. Go weird with Viognier, the Rhône white with a personality so different from Chardonnay as to be unrecognizable to a Chardonnay drinker. Viognier is growing in popularity with California winemakers.

3. Gewürztraminer, the Dennis Rodman of white grapes, is certainly worth a shot.

4. Best of all options may be a decent French Alsace or German Riesling. Less pungent than Gewürztraminer, Riesling is more flowery than fruity—again, different enough from Chardonnay that it is worth a try.

Experimentation

Like any pursuit, the study of wine requires experimentation: finding out what is what, and what your likes and dislikes are. However, since you can't do computer simulations in your research, and your research costs money and would take a lot of time to do correctly, you will probably need to make some compromises in your research techniques.

If wine is a new interest, your first goal is probably to find one wine you like. Do you like red better than white, or vice versa? Most people have a preference. Let's say you think you like red wine better. Now what?

Unfortunately, money is the first issue that you need to address. How much are you willing to spend on a bottle of wine? If you have a friend or spouse with whom you are going to do your experimenting, that saves money. It also saves time, as you can go through bottles twice as fast. If you can get a group of four people together, you can tackle two to four bottles at a time. Remember, each of you can bring some leftover wine home. You can then report to each other on which leftover improved the next day and which didn't.

Another way to save research time and money is to go to a wine tasting. A lot of wine stores have tastings on Saturday afternoons. At such a tasting, you may have the chance to sample a few wines, after which you may want to buy bottle of a wine you liked. It is a good idea to patronize such a store. Developing a relationship with a knowledgeable wine salesperson is a very good idea for any wine drinker, regardless of how much one knows about wine or spends on a bottle. These people taste a lot of wines you haven't tasted and can save you from many mediocre wines.

Anyway, let's assume you are willing to spend $8 on a bottle. Now what?

First, you need to realize that you won't be able to taste all types of wine for $8. Red Zinfandel, which grows almost exclusively in California, doesn't come that cheap. If you find a bottle, you probably won't want to drink it. It is difficult, but not impossible, to purchase an Italian Nebbiolo for that price. Chianti from Italy, made from the Sangiovese grape, can be found for $8. You can try some good Syrah from Australia, South Africa, or France. Red wines from Spain's Rioja region, made primarily from Tempranillo, are very affordable; at $8, you will find yourself a level or two up from the bottom. Chile also produces a wide variety of wines at bargain prices.

Decide on a grape variety, rather than region, to study. Try at least three different wines from a single grape variety before drawing any definitive conclusions about your preference. Wines from any grape can be made in many different styles. If you have a wine person who can help you select a diverse grouping of good wines within a variety, your experiments will be more enjoyable and your findings more accurate.

For $5–7 you can find wines you like, especially nonvarietals, but it is difficult to judge varietals at this price because the quality just isn't there. At this price level, you should be looking for the nonvarietal gems that most stores offer.

Your experimentation with wine may last a week or a lifetime. Along the way you should be able to come up with at least one grape variety you consistently enjoy. If you are buying a wine from a grape variety you usually like, chances are good that you are buying a wine you are going to enjoy.

No matter what your price range is, it is easy to go through streaks of bad luck buying wine. Not that the wines will necessarily taste bad, but you will find them to be disappointing, which often translates to boring. When this happens, it may be time to return to an old favorite.

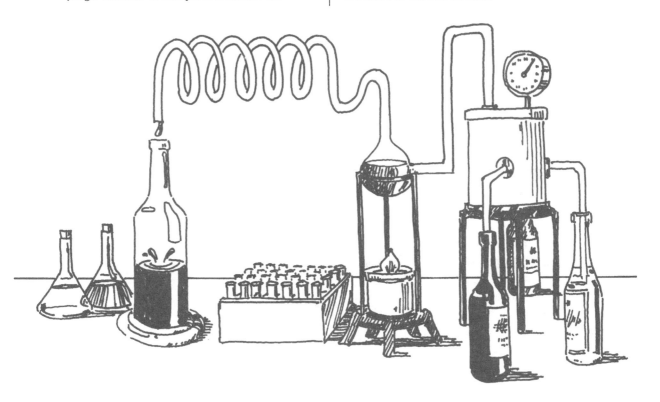

Keeping Track of What You Like

If you drink wine, you want to remember whether or not you liked it. This allows you to repeat a good wine experience and avoid a bad one. If you are like most people, including the know-it-alls who wrote this book, you think you can remember what you liked and didn't like without writing anything down. This system doesn't work. If you write one sentence about each wine you try, you will learn what your preferences are and avoid unnecessary disappointments. This is a good use for your home computer.

If *grape* equaled *wine*, then record keeping probably wouldn't be necessary. However, the equation is *grape + grape quality + soil + climate + winemaker + oak = wine.*

What happens to a lot of people is that they drink a bottle of a certain type of wine that they like, such as an Australian Shiraz, then think they have found *the* red wine for them. They may, over time, come to realize that they really only like one Australian Shiraz out of every three or four they try. Without record keeping, it may take a while to figure this out. Worst of all, it is easy to forget which ones you actually liked. The Australian Shiraz you like may actually be crafted in a style that is more common in France's Syrahs, less fruity and more tannic.

By keeping track of the wines you consume, you will discover what wines you need to try. If you have had ten California Chardonnays and never had a white wine from Italy, then you owe it to yourself to try an Italian Pinot Grigio.

If you have a wine that is really good and you want to remember what it is when you go to the wine store the next time, then you need to make sure that information is with you when you go. This means you want your short list of favorite wines to be in your wallet at all times, just like your driver's license. If you carry an address book with you at all times, you could write your wine list there. You could use the space for *Q* names to store your white wines and the *X*'s to store your favorite red wines, or you could keep one list and record the red wines you like in red ink.

Don't add a wine to your special list until you've had it twice. For every wine you like twice, there will be five wines that you like a lot more the first time you drink them. This phenomenon seems to happen quite a bit to new wine drinkers.

The Wine Journal

We have included a sample of a wine tasting journal. This journal includes a place to stick the label from the bottle. Removing a wine label isn't that difficult. First, empty the contents of the bottle. Then, fill up a large kettle or pot with hot water, add a small amount of soap and the empty wine bottle. Let the bottle soak for several hours (or overnight). In the morning, the label will peel right off. If this method only yields partial success, a butter knife is a good tool for getting the rest of the label off the bottle.

You will then need to let the label dry. It is best if you let it dry on a surface that touches only a small portion of the label, like a dish rack. This will help keep the label from adhering to another surface. It the label does get stuck, water will take it right off the surface, but your label will be wet again.

NAME OF WINE _____

VINTAGE YEAR _____

VINTNER _____

REGION AND COUNTRY _____

PRICE _____

WHERE TASTED _____

FOOD SERVED WITH _____

_____

COLOR _____

AROMA _____

TASTE _____

COMMENTS _____

_____

Place label here.

NAME OF WINE _____

VINTAGE YEAR _____

VINTNER _____

REGION AND COUNTRY _____

PRICE _____

WHERE TASTED _____

FOOD SERVED WITH _____

_____

COLOR _____

AROMA _____

TASTE _____

COMMENTS _____

_____

_____

Place label here.

NAME OF WINE _____

VINTAGE YEAR _____

VINTNER _____

REGION AND COUNTRY _____

PRICE _____

WHERE TASTED _____

FOOD SERVED WITH _____

_____

COLOR _____

AROMA _____

TASTE _____

COMMENTS _____

_____

_____

Place label here.

NAME OF WINE _____

VINTAGE YEAR _____

VINTNER _____

REGION AND COUNTRY _____

PRICE _____

WHERE TASTED _____

FOOD SERVED WITH _____

_____

COLOR _____

AROMA _____

TASTE _____

COMMENTS _____

_____

_____

Place label here.

NAME OF WINE _____

VINTAGE YEAR _____

VINTNER _____

REGION AND COUNTRY _____

PRICE _____

WHERE TASTED _____

FOOD SERVED WITH _____

_____

COLOR _____

AROMA _____

TASTE _____

COMMENTS _____

_____

_____

Place label here.

NAME OF WINE _____

VINTAGE YEAR _____

VINTNER _____

REGION AND COUNTRY _____

PRICE _____

WHERE TASTED _____

FOOD SERVED WITH _____

_____

COLOR _____

AROMA _____

TASTE _____

COMMENTS _____

_____

_____

Place label here.

NAME OF WINE _____

VINTAGE YEAR _____

VINTNER _____

REGION AND COUNTRY _____

PRICE _____

WHERE TASTED _____

FOOD SERVED WITH _____

_____

COLOR _____

AROMA _____

TASTE _____

COMMENTS _____

_____

_____

Place label here.

NAME OF WINE _____

VINTAGE YEAR _____

VINTNER _____

REGION AND COUNTRY _____

PRICE _____

WHERE TASTED _____

FOOD SERVED WITH _____

_____

COLOR _____

AROMA _____

TASTE _____

COMMENTS _____

_____

_____

Place label here.

NAME OF WINE _____

VINTAGE YEAR _____

VINTNER _____

REGION AND COUNTRY _____

PRICE _____

WHERE TASTED _____

FOOD SERVED WITH _____

_____

COLOR _____

AROMA _____

TASTE _____

COMMENTS _____

_____

_____

Place label here.

NAME OF WINE _____

VINTAGE YEAR _____

VINTNER _____

REGION AND COUNTRY _____

PRICE _____

WHERE TASTED _____

FOOD SERVED WITH _____

_____

COLOR _____

AROMA _____

TASTE _____

COMMENTS _____

_____

_____

Place label here.

NAME OF WINE _____

VINTAGE YEAR _____

VINTNER _____

REGION AND COUNTRY _____

PRICE _____

WHERE TASTED _____

FOOD SERVED WITH _____

_____

COLOR _____

AROMA _____

TASTE _____

COMMENTS _____

_____

_____

Place label here.

NAME OF WINE _____

VINTAGE YEAR _____

VINTNER _____

REGION AND COUNTRY _____

PRICE _____

WHERE TASTED _____

FOOD SERVED WITH _____

_____

COLOR _____

AROMA _____

TASTE _____

COMMENTS _____

_____

_____

Place label here.

NAME OF WINE _____

VINTAGE YEAR _____

VINTNER _____

REGION AND COUNTRY _____

PRICE _____

WHERE TASTED _____

FOOD SERVED WITH _____

_____

COLOR _____

AROMA _____

TASTE _____

COMMENTS _____

_____

_____

Place label here.

Wine Tasting (Rather than Wine Drinking)

Drinking wine is easy; tasting wine requires following a fairly standard set of procedures.

Professional tasters prefer a day-lit, odor-free room with white walls and tabletops to allow for optimum viewing of a wine's color without anything visually stimulating enough to distract one from the wine. Normal people enjoy tasting wine with friends at a dinner table and don't worry about the distractions of food smells and other niceties.

No matter where you conduct your tasting, make sure your wines are served at the right temperature. This is critical! Wines served too cold can't really be tasted. Those served too warm will seem out of balance. By this we mean a warm white wine may seem too sweet, while a warm red wine is apt to taste too acidic or alcoholic.

Because different people come to a tasting with different tasting experiences, they will describe the same wine differently, even if it is registering the same in each person's brain. If one person usually drinks Cabernet Sauvignon and another usually drinks a softer wine like Merlot, then they are apt to differ in opinion on whether a particular wine is tannic. So it's an inexact science, but an enjoyable one.

Remember that tasting is not a test—your subjective response is more important than any "right answers." The bottom line is: Wine that tastes good to you is good wine.

Below is the basic six-step process of wine tasting.

1. *Look at a Wine:* Judging a wine's color allows you to make some assessment about how old a wine is and how heavy a wine might feel in your mouth. Young red wines are close to purple in color. Over time, they pass through red toward brown. White wines start off in various shades of clear and they head toward a straw color.

   Different wines have different colors. Cabernet Sauvignon is darker by nature than Sangiovese. Also, the riper the harvested grape, the more color it adds to a wine.

   Judging density of color is where the strong light source and white background come in to play. Clear, clean glasses are also essential. Thickness of color usually indicates a richness, fruitiness, and/or heaviness. Thickness is best judged toward the edges of the wine as it sits in the glass. Glasses are tipped to a 45° angle to create a large edge of wine against the side of the glass. This means you don't want your glass much more than a quarter full during a critical tasting. The proper way to hold any wine glass is by the stem.

This will keep smudges off the bowl so you can see your wine better and not influence its temperature with the warmth of your hand.

2. *Swirl the wine in the glass:* Swirling will help expose a wine to more oxygen, which could be a goal of the taster eager to taste a wine right out of the bottle, but is usually done to release aromas. Swirling is another reason to conservatively fill your wine glass. The tears of wine that slowly run down the side of the bowl after the swirling stops will evaporate quickly and release concentrated aromas.

   The easiest way to swirl a glass full of wine is to leave the base of the glass on the table. If you swirl your glass somewhat vigorously, you will create an invisible tornado of aromas that lift up and out of your wine glass.

3. *Smell the wine:* This is where all hell can break loose. Cries of "tar," "elder-berries," "coconut," "coffee," "tobacco," and so on, are apt to be uttered at a tasting. This may be the most difficult aspect of a tasting for the novice to swallow. The best way to smell a wine is to stick your nose into the glass. There is no getting around this. If you aren't in a social setting that will support this type of behavior, at least bring the glass very close to your nose. Sticking your nose into the glass right after you swirl it will allow you to catch the updraft of

Wine Tips for People on a Date (Even If It's with Your Spouse or Mom)

1. Red wine can temporarily stain your teeth, although it brushes right off.

2. If you have plans to do something after dinner, you should consider drinking lower-alcohol wine. There is a big difference between 11 percent and 14 percent. German white wines are usually low in alcohol.

3. No jug wines or screwcaps, unless you are looking to end a relationship.

4. Don't overspend, as it can intimidate the other person and make you appear to be pompous and/or insecure.

5. Always ask the other person if they would like more wine before pouring it into their glass.

6. When pouring wine, always pour yours last.

7. Don't feel the need to finish the bottle.

the little tornado of aroma you have created.

It will take you a while before you believe your nose. When you walk near a coffee shop and you smell something that reminds you of what coffee smells like, you conclude you are smelling coffee. When you stick your nose into a wine glass, you may have a difficult time convincing yourself that you are indeed smelling a wine aroma. Our olfactory sense is our strongest sense and it has the best memory, but most of us don't use it very much in our daily lives.

4. *Taste It:* Finally, the moment even a neophyte can understand. You may not taste everything the wine veteran claims to taste, but if you listen to what more experienced wine drinkers say about a wine, your mind and your mouth will begin to sense what they are talking about. With time, you will be able to experience and understand the many flavors of wine as well as its important components such as acidity and tannin.

It is important to let the wine linger in your mouth for at least ten seconds; otherwise, you aren't really tasting it. It's important to roll the wine around your mouth with your tongue, exposing it to as much of your mouth as possible. Serious tasters will open their lips a bit and inhale into their mouths while wine rests on the tongue. This encourages vaporization, which releases aroma and flavor.

5. *Swallow or Spit:* If you are at a dinner table, you are probably not going to be spitting out your experiments. However, if you go to a tasting where you sample a lot of wine, you are going to want to spit out most of the wines you try. Of course it is easier to judge a wine's aftertaste, known as its "finish," when you swallow it rather than spitting it into a bucket.

6. *Make a Note—Written or Mental:* If you are at a serious tasting, most people will be making written notes on the wines they are tasting. If you are at a dinner table or friend's living room, you might not want to pull out a notebook, but you should make a permanent mental note of a wine you really like. Then, back at home, write your notes in this book.

OBVIOUSLY A 1983 DOM DE CHEVALIER BORDEAUX FROM THE REGION OF THE UPPER GARONNE

Buying Wine in a Restaurant

The more you learn about wine, the more painfully aware you become of the prices of wine in restaurants. If you enjoy going to restaurants and want to enjoy wine when you are there, consider the following:

Food is often marked up more than wine.

Good restaurants usually mark up food 2 1/2 times, in other words, a $20 entree would cost the restaurant $8. While some restaurants mark up wine as much, most charge around double their cost for midrange wines. It is true that the restaurant adds expertise and convenience to the raw ingredients of your entree. Insist on the same with your wine—proper temperature, sparkling clean and appropriate glassware, and proper, attentive service.

If nobody bought wine, there would be fewer restaurants.

Most restaurants need wine sales to survive. If you like a particular restaurant, your wine purchases will help keep it there.

You can send it back

. . . within reason. If a wine has gone bad, has suffered from a spoiled cork (commonly referred to as "corked"), has turned sour, or smells rotten, any restaurant should gladly take it back. If a wine steward or waiter has enthusiastically recommended a wine and you don't like it, you should be allowed to return it. But, if you simply don't like a wine, step back a bit. Do others at your table agree? Have you tasted it without food? If so, taste it with a well-chewed piece of bread in your mouth. Wine is meant to be tasted with food. Might it need to breathe? If you aren't sure, ask the waiter to pour some wine into a glass, and let it breathe for a few minutes. If you still just don't like it, a good restaurant will probably try to keep you happy, especially if you are a regular customer. It is best not to make a habit of this practice. By the way, most wines sent back in restaurants go back to the supplier, thus relieving the restaurant of the cost. The exception to this is older wine.

Older wine

Let's say you order a twenty-year-old Bordeaux. This wine may have been in the restaurant's cellar for fifteen years. For $100 a bottle you have a right to expect good, solid wine. However, can you send it back if, while showing no flaws, it fails to provide the expected religious experience? Probably, but you should consider that the price of older wine often reflects its scarcity rather than its intrinsic value. You pay a premium for the opportunity to enjoy wine on your twentieth anniversary from, say, the year of your marriage. So, be thoughtful about returning such wines—the restaurant will probably have to eat the cost of the bottle (which, when they bought it, might have been surprisingly little money).

How Wines Go Bad

Red wine. If the fruit vanishes and the color fades, it's too old. A brown color or a vinegary taste indicates improper storage.

White wine. If it's brown colored or tastes burnt, it is too old or was improperly stored.

Either wine can be "corked"—when the cork is partially dissolved into the wine by biological activity.

Sparkling wine. No fizz indicates improper storage or a wine that is too old.

Wine by the Glass Is Usually a Rip-Off

The markup on bottles of wine is far less than the markup on mixed drinks. Many customers now order a glass of wine in place of that initial cocktail, so smart restaurant operators make sure that they make the same money on that drink and mark up wine by the glass accordingly. A better value is premium wine by the glass, a category in which the markup is more in line with the wine program than with the martini program. These premium wines by the glass are a convenient service for those who can't agree on a bottle or don't want to drink that much.

Know the Price Structure

In a retail store, you can calculate the price of wines very easily. In most cases the wine costs about 50 percent over wholesale. After a few shopping trips, you will know what the most commonly sold wines in your area cost on the wholesale level.

Good restaurants often mark up more expensive wines at a lower percentage than their inexpensive choices. This encourages customers to "trade up" for better value.

The Magic Rule

In a good restaurant with fairly priced food and wine, wine as good as the food will cost about twice the price of the average entree.

Know Your Comfort Level

Everyone who buys wine develops a price point in their mind beyond which they are not comfortable, for fear that they will not appreciate a wine's value. This point goes up the more you learn about wine.

Enjoying Wine with Your Dinner

Just as at home, in a restaurant you have some control over the enjoyment of your wine. Is this white too cold? Let it warm up on the table and in the glass, and taste the hidden flavors as they emerge. Is the red too warm? Your server should cool it for you in ice water for five minutes or so. Your server should be pouring it for you—in proper glassware, never more than half full—though it's okay to pour it yourself. Don't drink it all before the food arrives (unless you're planning to buy another bottle, of course).

Wines for People with Too Much Money*

"Let's start with a toast, dear . . ."
> . . . Louis Roederer Cryistal Rosé Champagne is about $100/bottle.

"Care for Chardonnay?"
> . . . Le Montrachet from Domaine de la Romanée-Conti will set you back $700/bottle.

"How about Merlot . . ."
> . . . Château Le Pin, from Pomerol (in Bordeaux), is released at about $400/bottle.

". . . Or maybe an elegant little Burgundy?"
> The wine from the Romanée-Conti vineyard, the most precious holding of Domaine de la Romanée-Conti, is also released at about $400/bottle.

"At least California is still a bargain . . ."
> This is the most expensive Cabernet Sauvignon is Caymus Special Select, at about $100/bottle.

". . . The wife here has a sweet tooth . . ."
> For dessert, try Domaine Zind Humbrecht Sélection des Grains Nobles ("SGN") Tokay Rangen "Clos St. Urbain" Grand Cru. This gem will cost you about $200 for a *half bottle*.

These prices are for NEW wines. You can pay tens of thousands of dollars for older wines. Get the idea? Wine is like anything else—cars, watches, clothes. . . . You are limited only by your budget and your sanity.

* Prices listed are retail and subject to availability.

The Wine Ritual

You ordered the wine, and you are shown the label. Is it the right year? If you ordered a "reserve," make sure it is not a lesser bottling from the same producer. So far, so good. Tell the server to keep the cork, unless you collect corks; it is of no use to you once you have verified that it hasn't rotted during its years in the bottle. Do taste the wine while the server is there. Any problem should be addressed immediately. Your server should then pour wine for everyone at the table.

Tipping on Wine

Many people treat tipping on wine as a separate issue. There's no need to. One might argue that the same effort applies to serving a $100 bottle as a $20 bottle, and, therefore, one need not tip a full 15 percent on the more expensive wine. (However, the same reasoning, if applied to tipping on an expensive entree versus tipping on a cup of soup, would be foolish). Save the math problems for another time and just tip on the whole bill, with maybe an extra $5-10 to the wine steward (or server) for an especially enjoyable recommendation.

An alternative tipping strategy is to tip 20 percent on your food and 10–15 percent on your restaurant wine purchases.

The Bottom Line

If you enjoy drinking wine with dinner, it may make more sense to go out for dinner less often and then indulge yourself on those occasions. Or, you may prefer to go out for dinner as often as possible and order only a glass of wine, rather than incur the expense of a whole bottle.

CHAPTER 8

WINE AND FOOD

BOTTLED BY ADAMS MEDIA

NET CONTENTS: TWENTY-TWO PAGES

PRODUCT OF USA

Food and wine have always been a great combination at the dinner table. Meals featuring wine have come to symbolize good times. Here is a partial list of reasons, past and present, why people enjoy wine and food together:

1. Few beverage options existed when wine became part of food culture centuries ago.
2. Pure drinking water has not always been widely available.
3. With its high acidity and other properties, wine assists in the digestion of food.
4. Certain wines are so delicious with certain foods that they seem made for each other, enhancing each other and your enjoyment.
5. When a meal is served as a celebration or holiday feast, the alcohol in wine raises everyone's spirits.
6. When an intimate meal is enjoyed by a couple, wine seems to enhance the intimacy.
7. Water is boring.
8. If you don't drink anything when you eat, the food might get stuck.

You can probably think of other good reasons for matching wine with food. Of course, just as you can enjoy food without wine, you can enjoy many wines without food. Sweet wines, wines naturally low in alcohol, and low-acid wines are easy to enjoy alone. Rich, chewy wines may be too much flavor for your taste at the dinner table. If you like such wines, you'll want to drink them at other times. Drinking a favorite wine alone is always pleasurable without food.

Matching Food and Wine

Since food and wine are so enjoyable together, it should be a fairly simple matter to match them. Unfortunately, it is doubtful that any dining ritual has caused more needless anxiety than that of choosing the "correct" wine for dinner. What a shame! We're talking about two very enjoyable things—good food and good wine. Unless you make a fundamental error and choose a pairing that results in an unpleasant chemical reaction in your mouth, an error that is 100 percent avoidable, you can't go wrong. With a little effort and thought, you can pair wine and food so that they make each other taste better!

Many people are familiar with the old, well-established rule of food/wine pairing—"White wine with fish, red wine with meat." While this rule is not as valid as it once was (we'll show you why), the reasoning behind it is sound and deserves examination.

Think of a nice, fresh fillet of sole, neatly grilled. Most of us who enjoy fish would welcome a squeeze of fresh lemon on it. Why? The acid in the lemon "cuts" the intrinsic fish flavor without overpowering it. Thus white wine, with its more apparent acidity and less powerful flavors, would be more appropriate for sole than red wine.

Imagine a roast beef with delicious gravy made from onions and pan drippings. The assertive flavor of the gravy matches in magnitude the flavor of the beef, as would a rich red wine. Just as onion gravy would overwhelm the fillet of sole, so would most red wines. And just as a squeeze of lemon would be lost on the roast beef, so too would most white wines. If only it were that simple.

Chef August Escoffier (1846–1935) is widely regarded as the father of French cuisine. French cuisine, in turn, is the mother lode of fine cookery in Western civilization. Thus, for many decades it was a truism that the finest restaurant in any American city was a French-inspired restaurant with a menu that could have been written by Escoffier himself. The accompaniments and sauces for each entree of the *repertoire classique* were thoughtfully dictated by Escoffier in his authoritative culinary writings. Matching a wine to the meal was relatively straightforward; the French wine list covered all the bases.

Although the teachings of Escoffier are still relevant today, he lived, cooked, and wrote in a time before reliable refrigeration and easy transportation. The world of fine cookery has evolved accordingly. Where

French restaurants once reigned supreme, we now find Thai, Brazilian, Northern Italian, and Moroccan restaurants of equal stature. But perhaps Escoffier's most enduring gift is the ability of French cuisine to adopt and incorporate such varying influences. If he were alive today, he might stumble upon a "fusion" restaurant that blends many international influences, often on the same plate. If it were thoughtfully and competently prepared, Escoffier would undoubtedly approve . . . But he might have trouble choosing a wine.

Among the many changes in fine cookery since Escoffier's time, the increasing complexity of food is the most troublesome for matching wine with food. Here are some guidelines (not rules) that will help.

1. Don't dwell on color

There are enough other factors to consider; the color will take care of itself. For instance, chicken dishes can be prepared to match well with any wine, depending on the ingredients. Lighter reds and strong whites can survive most food pairings.

2. Match strengths

Powerfully flavored dishes require wines of equal fortitude. *Example:* Herb-crusted leg of lamb or garlicky ratatouille match well with a strongly flavored wine, usually red.

Delicate dishes need delicate wine. *Example:* Simply prepared white fish (like sole) need a gentle wine, usually white.

3. Opposites attract

Example: The spicy cuisine of the Pacific Rim needs a light, sweet wine to extinguish the fire. Rich cream or butter sauces are well matched with an acidic, "cutting wine."

4. Regional affinity

In Europe it is a truism that regional cooking goes best with the local wine. Since gastronomy and oenology evolved side by side, it stands to reason that food and wine derived from the same soil and served on the same dinner table have an underlying affinity.

5. Simple wine with complex food

This would solve the hypothetical dilemma of Escoffier in a "fusion" restaurant. Pair this food with a varietal not inclined to great complexity—Pinot Blanc (among whites) and Merlot (among reds) come to mind.

6. Complex wine with simple food

The best way to showcase a fabulously complex (and expensive) wine is to pair it with a simple, yet delicious, background dish. *Examples:* A super-premium Cabernet Sauvignon with plain grilled steak or a great white Burgundy (Chardonnay) with plain broiled fish.

7. Match price

A $50 Chianti would be wasted on a pizza, but a carefully prepared dinner deserves an equally special wine.

8. Sparkling wine still goes with almost anything

Because the bubbles make up for the lightness of flavor, sparkling wine can be perfectly fine with traditional red-wine dishes.

9. And so does Rosé

Wine snobs are quick to dismiss rosé. If it tastes good, drink it. Although it is not really "right" with any food, it isn't really "wrong" either, unless, of course, you don't like rosé.

10. Match wine to the occasion

The above-mentioned rosé is frequently mentioned as a "picnic wine." Informal gatherings call for informal wine. Save the haughty bottles for three-fork dinner parties and/or pompous relatives.

11. Serving red wine with fish

As long as the acid level is high and the tannins are barely noticeable, red wine is fine with most seafood. Here are some suggestions:

Simple Chianti or other Sangiovese-based Italian wine

Certain Pinot Noirs—Côte de Beaune, Chalonnais, Oregon, lighter California

Beaujolais or other Gamay-based wines

Lighter versions of Merlot (or Merlot blends)—Saint-Emilion (Bordeaux) is especially good.

Rioja, from Spain—Though not high in acid, these Tempranillo-based wines are versatile and inoffensive.

12. White wine with beef

Certain whites are big enough to stand up to charred sirloin and other beef dishes. Consider high-alcohol and well-oaked California or Australian Chardonnay. Viognier-based whites are up for the challenge as well. This offbeat varietal can be one of the most pleasant surprises of the wine world.

13. Serve cheaper wines with cheese

The fat in cheese makes wine taste better. This makes cheese an important ingredient at receptions at which large quantities of inexpensive wine are served.

14. Fruit and wine don't match

Most fruits are acidic, and so are most wines. Fruit acids can throw a good wine out of balance.

15. Wine and chocolate don't match

And they never will, although it's fun to try!

You don't need to match!

So you love sole and you love Cabernet Sauvignon . . . Fine! Have them together. A sip of water and a nibble of bread will smooth the transition from one to the other. Beware, however, of serving wine with known wine-killers—artichokes, eggs, avocados, peanuts, asparagus, and chili peppers. These are among the most troublesome food ingredients, as they react negatively with any wine in your mouth. Sturdy Chardonnay is as good a wine as any to serve with a known wine-killer. Riesling can coexist with hot and spicy flavors that obliterate most wines, but it is certainly a shotgun wedding at best, with painfully spicy food.

White Wine with Red Meat (Anti-Match #1)

So you all want steak and white wine . . . a sommelier's nightmare? Not really. There are some big, strapping Chardonnays from California's Sonoma and Napa regions that could climb in the ring with just about any dish and hold their own. The secret is wood, an important component of any big California Chardonnay. Ripe Chardonnay fruit, high alcohol, and a glycerine-charged body benefit from new-oak aging, which seems to unify these powerful components while adding further complexity. Australian and Santa Barbara Chardonnays also qualify but are likely to show more fruit than wood. Big French Chardonnays from the Côte de Beaune are a possibility, but their higher acidity and more subtle charms may be lost on red meat.

If you are less interested in the wine than the food, any subtle white wine can be served. However, the wine's flavors won't be easily noticed.

Red Wine with Fish (Anti-Match #2)

This is a hip way to break the rules, especially with something like a tuna or swordfish steak. Look for high-acid, low-tannin wines—Italian reds tend to be versatile, as are Pinot Noirs from Oregon and Burgundy. California Pinot Noir is probably going to be too fruity. Rioja may be okay with fish. French Saint-Emilion, in which Merlot usually predominates, is a light take on a fruity grape and a decent match with fish. European wines are crafted to be food friendly. This is good to remember when you are trying to make an unorthodox food/wine match like fish with red wine.

If you end up with a red that is powerfully flavored, you are going to end up missing most of the fish's flavor. If you have a wine that is too strong for your fish or any meal, put it aside and drink it after you finish your food. The better the fish, the more you'll want to preserve the food experience.

As a general rule, fish that is grilled takes on a charred flavor that makes it more compatible with red wines than white. It stands to reason that the fish we usually grill are quite flavorful to begin with—salmon, tuna, swordfish, and shark.

Wine and Food Matches

RED MEAT DISHES

Chili con carne	Beaujolais (an easy-drinking red); Zinfandel (a red to stand up to your chili)
Grilled steak	Cabernet Sauvignon (an ultimate match); Shiraz/Syrah (a good choice at a better price)
Hamburger	Any red wine you like that is inexpensive
Roast beef	Pinot Noir and Merlot (softer reds than for your grilled steak). If you are wild about Cabernet Sauvignon, then have a Cabernet from Bordeaux.
Steak au poivre (Steak with black peppercorn sauce)	BIG REDS!—Zinfandel from California and Rhône reds are perfect
Tenderloin	Same as for roast beef: Pinot Noir and Merlot are the best choices.

OTHER MEAT DISHES

Chicken (roasted)	Almost any wine you like—this is a very versatile dish.
Chicken (highly seasoned)	Chenin Blanc and Riesling
Duck/Goose/ Game birds	Pinot Blanc or Viognier (whites); Pinot Noir or Merlot (reds)
Ham	Rosé; California Pinot Noir; demi-sec Vouvray; Gewürztraminer
Lamb (simple)	Cabernet (especially from Bordeaux); Rioja red from Spain

OTHER MEAT DISHES

Lamb (with herbs and garlic)	The herbs and garlic are going to cut into your ability to taste the wine. Try a big red (a steak au poivre wine). And go easy on the garlic.
Pork	An Italian or Spanish red; any white you like
Sausage	Gewürtztraminer or an ordinary red
Turkey	Rosé; any white you like; a very light red
Veal	California Chardonnay is perfect
Venison (deer)	A big red wine—Cabernet, Nebbiolo, Syrah, or Zinfandel will do

SEAFOOD DISHES

Anything with a cream sauce	White Burgundy (clean, crisp Chardonnay)
Lobster	Champagne; dry Riesling; white Burgundy
Oysters	Muscadet, a French white, is ideal with oysters; Chablis (dry French Chardonnay) or Champagne
Salmon	Sauvignon Blanc
Shrimp	Light and dry white wine
Swordfish	White wine
Tuna	Versatile like chicken; anything but a big red is okay. A light red is probably the ideal match.
White fish (sole, etc.)	Sauvignon Blanc, light Chardonnay

PASTA DISHES

Red sauce	Chianti or other Sangiovese-based red
Vegetables	Pinot Grigio; light red
White sauce	Pinot Grigio

INDIAN & ASIAN CUISINE	These food cultures developed without wine, except for rice wine (saké). Beer is often a better match. German Riesling and inexpensive sparkling wines are your best wine choices, or Beaujolais if your wine has to be red.
PIZZA	Rioja red, Italian red, Canadian red, any red—unless you like white, then any white. After all, pizza is *the* no-fuss food. Don't spend a lot of money on this match.
VEGETARIAN DISHES	Red beans and darker starches and vegetables go with red wine. Lighter and greener foods go better with white wine. Petite Sirah is quite good with hearty vegetable dishes like vegetarian chili.

SNACKS

Bread	Everything goes with bread.
Caviar	Champagne and money; Vodka and money
Cheese: rich and creamy (i.e., Brie, Camembert)	Sauternes or an off-dry Riesling
Cheese: goat, and feta	A Spanish or Italian red, although most wines, red or white, go okay.
Cheese: other	Whatever wine you want. Cheese makes cheap wine taste better!
Fruit	Not a good match with wine. Grapes especially are very bad with wine.
Pâté	Gewürztraminer or light red
Rich pâté (i.e., foie gras)	Sauternes or an off-dry Riesling
Salty snacks	Something cheap. Remember to quench your thirst with water, not wine.

A Few Notes on Drinking Wine Without Food

We call wines that we drink without food "fireplace" wines, although neither of us has a fireplace. If you like wine and you're not hungry, you can either wait until you have an appetite again, or just enjoy a glass of wine on its own. If you buy wine to be enjoyed without food, keep the following in mind.

Low-acid wine is better

High-acid wines need food to show well. The unmitigated acidity of many classic food wines are such that they cannot be enjoyed alone. Remember, acidity helps quench a thirst and cuts through the starch and fleshiness of food. A fruity Pinot Noir or Chardonnay from California will certainly go well solo, as will an Australian Chardonnay or Shiraz/Cabernet blend.

Have your white wine a bit warmer than usual

Good white wine is best at 45–50°F (8–10°C), which is warmer than your refrigerator. Without food to focus on, you can ponder the complexities of a good white wine, which reveal themselves more at warmer temperatures. If you open a bottle and let it warm over time, you can observe the wine at different temperatures. Try a white you know you like, and learn its secrets.

Have your red wine a little cooler than usual

A slight chill takes the edge off the acidity and makes the wine more soothing on the tongue. Any red is easier to take served cooler, although not quite as easy to taste.

Avoid big, tannic wines

Unless you are a huge fan of tannin, a lot of tannin will be more overbearing without food. Save that special Cabernet for the dinner table, or at least the cheese and crackers table.

Sweetness is okay

If you have always avoided anything but dry wines, do yourself a favor and try an off-dry wine for a change. German Riesling, Vouvray demi-sec, and California Gewürztraminers, Rieslings, and rosés are all wines that don't require food in order to show their best qualities.

Now is the time to try a fortified wine

Dry or sweet, light or dark, you can't go wrong. Remember that the fortified wines—Port, Sherry, Madeira, and Marsala—are fortified with alcohol, so you will be sipping, not gulping.

Sweeter and sparkling

Off-dry Champagnes and sparkling wines that don't go well at the dinner table are quite enjoyable without food. The fruity and well-made Blanc de Noirs from California are an affordable way to try some not-so-dry bubbly.

Cooking with Wine

Many French or French-inspired recipes call for wine as an ingredient. Just as food and wine have a wonderful affinity at the table, so too in the kitchen. There is an adage about this (source unknown): Cook with the best, drink the rest. Well, there are a lot of adages out there, and we find this one to be silly. The wine you cook with needs to be drinkable but certainly not great. Here's a common sense rule: If you wouldn't drink it, don't cook with it. This rules out the overpriced, denatured "cooking wine" found in supermarkets next to the Worcestershire sauce.

Restaurants sometimes use the name of a wine on the menu in order to market a dish. You may see "Pinot Noir Sauce" or "Champagne Beurre Blanc" in the menu description. This is unreliable. If the wines used in these recipes were that great, the restaurant would be serving them by the glass, not by the ladle. Some swank restaurant might actually say "Dom Pérignon Sauce" on its specials menu, but chances are that such a wine was opened in error the night before. Always consider the "cachet value" factor when encountering anything wine related at a restaurant.

Good chefs know how to choose good quality, cost-effective wines for cooking. Here is a list of frequently called-for wines for cooking, and some tips for choosing them.

Dry White Wine

Look for simple, fruity table wines—Chardonnay or Sauvignon Blanc from the "fighting varietal" band of wines. Avoid sharp, acidic wines, excessively woody wines, and sweet wines—all of these qualities become more concentrated during cooking.

Dry Red Wine

Again, fruity and simple table wines are the way to go. Pinot Noir and Zinfandel are good choices. Pinot Noir is almost always low in tannin. You must choose your Zinfandel more carefully; look for a lighter-bodied Zinfandel.

Sherry

True Spanish Sherry adds considerable character when called for in a recipe. Avoid very dry fino Sherry and sweet cream Sherry. The safest choice is Amontillado, a light-amber-colored, medium-bodied Sherry.

Port

Ruby port, the least expensive type of Port, is probably the best for cooking. It is fruity and sweet, and will retain its color better than the more expensive Port types. Port is powerful stuff and should be used in modest amounts in dishes. In addition to Ruby Ports from Portugal, Australian "Ports" tend to have a nutty sweetness reminiscent of Sherry that works very well in cooking.

Madeira

There are no substitutes when a recipe calls for Madeira. Madeira is a key component of France's rich Sauce Périgourdine: a sinful concoction of foie gras, truffles, and demi-glace. Madeira sauces have a particular affinity for beef, game, and mushroom dishes. For cooking, a medium-bodied Bual or a full-bodied, sweet Malmsey Madeira are best.

Marsala

This Sicilian fortified wine is a staple in southern Italian cooking. The label on a Marsala bottle will indicate whether it is dry or sweet. For cooking, the sweet style, with its richer flavor, is the better choice.

Vermouth

Always use white vermouth when cooking. The intense complex flavor of vermouth enhances many light seafood dishes. Good-quality white vermouth is widely available from Italy, France, and California.

Brandy

It is worth splurging for a relatively inexpensive Cognac of the "V.S." grade when a recipe calls for brandy. Cognac offers reliable and intense flavors and because "nip"-sized bottles of brandy (as well as other spirits that may be called for in a recipe) are readily available, this ingredient won't cost you a fortune.

Sparkling Wine

When you cook any sparkling wine, you will eliminate its primary qualities—bubbles and alcohol. In most cases, Champagne as an ingredient is useful for its cachet value only. However, a simple beurre blanc sauce can benefit from the two remaining qualities of good Champagne—high acidity and yeast flavor. A good way to impress your dinner guests is to cook with the same bubbly that you will be serving with the dish. Most recipes call for only a quarter of a bottle of sparkling wine. You can then reseal your bottle with a special Champagne bottle stopper or a regular wine cork reinforced with the original wire cage. Serve it with dinner and accept the accolades you receive from your guests with the proper amount of modesty.

Pale Californian, Champagne-method sparkling wines are a good choice for cooking. These tend to have a tad more fruit than their French counterparts, which makes them a bit more of a vocal ingredient in the kitchen.

Recipes

RED WINE MARINARA SAUCE

For 16 ounces of pasta

1 teaspoon olive oil
1-1/2 cups onions, finely chopped
1 red bell pepper, finely chopped
1/2 cup thinly sliced mushrooms
3 cloves garlic, minced
1 tablespoon dried basil
1 teaspoon dried oregano
One 15-ounce can tomato sauce
One 6-ounce can tomato paste
1 tablespoon soy sauce
1/2 cup dry red wine

Heat the oil in a skillet over medium heat. Add the onions and cook, stirring, until transparent. Stir in the pepper, mushrooms, garlic, basil, and oregano. Continue to cook until the ingredients are soft.

Add the tomato sauce, tomato paste, soy sauce, and red wine, and continue to cook over medium heat, stirring frequently, until the sauce just boils and then thickens.

Serve hot over drained cooked pasta.

RED CLAM SAUCE

For 16 ounces of pasta

4 dozen small littleneck clams, well
*   scrubbed and rinsed*
1/4 cup olive oil plus 1 tablespoon for
*   the clams*
1 teaspoon finely chopped garlic
1 tablespoon chopped flat-leaf parsley
1/3 cup dry white wine
2 cups canned whole tomatoes, with
*   the juice, or 1 pound fresh*
*   tomatoes, peeled, seeded, and*
*   chopped*
1 tablespoon tomato paste
Salt and freshly ground pepper to taste

Place the scrubbed clams with the 1 tablespoon olive oil in a large pot over high heat. Cover and steam until the clams open, about 5 minutes. Remove from the heat and cool. Pour the liquid through a strainer lined with a paper towel to catch any sand. Reserve the cooking broth. The clams can remain in the shells or be removed and returned to the liquid at this point.

Cook the garlic in 1/4 cup olive oil in a large saucepan until softened. Stir in the parsley. Pour in the wine and cook until the liquid is reduced by half. Add the tomatoes and the paste. Stir well to combine, then add 1/2 cup of the clam liquid. Add salt and freshly ground pepper to taste. Simmer for 15 minutes, or until the sauce thickens. Add the clams; heat through quickly, being careful not to overcook. Remove the pan from the heat.

Add drained cooked pasta to the pan and toss well.

WHITE CLAM SAUCE

For 16 ounces of pasta

*4 dozen small littleneck clams, well
   scrubbed
1/4 cup virgin olive oil plus a
   tablespoon for the clams
2 cloves garlic, finely chopped
1/4 cup dry white wine
Salt and freshly ground pepper to taste
1/8 teaspoon dried hot red pepper
   flakes
1/4 cup chopped flat-leaf parsley
2 tablespoons unsalted butter*

Place the scrubbed clams with the
1 tablespoon olive oil in a large pot over
high heat. Cover and steam until the clams
open, about 5 minutes. Remove from the
heat. Pour the liquid through a strainer lined
with a paper towel to catch any sand.
Reserve the clam broth. *Note:* The clams
can remain in the shells or be removed and
returned to the liquid at this point.

Heat the garlic in the 1/4 cup olive oil
in a large saucepan until softened. Pour in
the white wine and cook about 1 minute,
until the alcohol has evaporated. Add
1/4 cup of the clam liquid and salt to taste.
Simmer 2 minutes to blend. Add the clams,
and sprinkle in the pepper flakes and
parsley. Heat through quickly and remove
from heat. Swirl in the butter.

Add drained cooked pasta to the pan
and toss well.

Heat the sauce, and add the pasta to
the pan to finish cooking. When the pasta is
al dente and most of the sauce has been
incorporated, swirl in the butter.

SHRIMP SOUP

Serves 4

*2 tablespoons unsalted butter
3/4 cup finely chopped onion
1/2 cup chopped carrot
1/2 cup chopped celery
1/2 teaspoon dried thyme
1 small bay leaf, crumbled
1/2 pound medium shrimp, peeled
   and deveined
4 cups chicken stock
1/2 cup dry white wine
1/2 cup shells
1/4 cup half-and-half
Salt and freshly ground pepper
   to taste
2 tablespoons chopped parsley*

In a large soup pot, heat the butter over
medium heat. Add the onion, carrot, celery,
thyme, and bay leaf and sauté until softened. Add the shrimp and sauté quickly
until just pink. Add the chicken stock, bring
to a boil, and simmer 20 minutes. Add the
wine, bring to a boil, reduce heat, and
simmer 10 minutes.

Meanwhile, in a medium saucepan,
bring at least 2 quarts of water to a boil.
Add 1 teaspoon salt. Add the shells and stir
to prevent sticking. Cook until al dente.
Drain and stir into the soup.

Remove the soup from the heat. Stir
in the half-and-half, add salt and fresh
pepper to taste, and return the pan to the
heat to rewarm. Do not let boil. When
heated through, sprinkle with the parsley
and serve.

RATATOUILLE
Serves 4

2/3 cup olive oil
2 red onions, cut into medium dice
4 cloves garlic, chopped
1 tablespoon each dried oregano, basil,
    and thyme
1 teaspoon dried hot red pepper flakes
1 large eggplant, cut into small dice
1/4 cup balsamic vinegar
1/3 cup dry red wine
One 28-ounce can Italian plum toma-
    toes, with juice, diced
1 medium zucchini, cut into small dice
1 red bell pepper, cut into medium dice
1 green bell pepper, cut into medium
    dice
1/2 pound mushrooms, chopped fine
2 tablespoons unsalted butter
Salt and freshly ground pepper
    to taste
4 large firm tomatoes

In a large saucepan, heat the olive oil
over medium heat. Add the red onions,
garlic, herbs, and red pepper flakes and
cook until the onions are soft. Add the eggplant, and cook briefly over high heat, stirring constantly. Add balsamic vinegar and
red wine, stir, reduce heat, and simmer until
the eggplant is tender but not soft. Add the
tomatoes, zucchini, peppers, and mushrooms and simmer over low heat until the
vegetables are tender, about 10 minutes.
Swirl in the butter. Add salt and pepper to
taste. The mixture should be fairly thick. Set
aside and cool.

CHICKEN LASAGNA
Serves 10

12 lasagna noodles, uncooked
2 tablespoons olive oil, plus additional,
    if necessary
1 pound boneless, skinless chicken
    breasts, diced
3 cups sliced fresh mushrooms
1 cup thinly sliced carrots
1/2 cup sliced onions
1 cup frozen green peas, thawed and
    well drained
1 teaspoon thyme
1/2 cup unsalted butter
1/2 cup flour
3-1/2 cups milk
1/2 cup dry sherry
1/2 teaspoon salt
1/4 teaspoon cayenne pepper
One 12-ounce container low-fat ricotta
    cheese
2 cups grated part-skim mozzarella
    cheese

Preheat the oven to 350°.
    In a large, deep skillet, heat the oil over
medium heat, add the chicken, and sauté
until cooked through. Remove with a slotted
spoon, drain on paper towels, and reserve.
    Add a bit more oil to the skillet, if nec-
essary. Add the mushrooms and cook briefly.
Add the onion and mushrooms and sauté
until softened. Set aside.
    In a large saucepan, melt the butter over
medium heat. Blend in the flour with a
wooden spoon to make a loose paste. Cook
over low heat until light golden color.

Gradually add the milk, stirring with a wire whisk until blended. Stir in the sherry, bring to a boil over medium heat, and cook for 5 minutes, or until thickened, stirring constantly. Stir in the salt and cayenne. Reserve 1 cup of the sauce, set aside.

In a bowl, combine the ricotta and 1 cup of the mozzarella.

Bring at least 4 quarts of water to a rolling boil. Add 1 tablespoon of salt. Add noodles and stir to separate. Cook only until flexible, not until done. Drain by pouring off hot water and adding cold. As the cool noodles slide into the colander, remove them to a kitchen towel to drain.

Spread 1 cup sauce over the bottom of a 13-by-9-by-2-inch baking dish. Arrange 4 lasagna noodles (3 lengthwise, 1 crosswise) over the sauce. Top with half of the ricotta mixture, half of the chicken mixture, and half of the remaining sauce. Repeat the layer. Top with the 4 remaining lasagna noodles. Spread 1 cup sauce over the last complete layer of lasagna, being sure to cover the lasagna completely.

Cover the dish with foil and bake for 1 hour. Remove the pan from the oven, uncover, and sprinkle with the remaining cup of mozzarella. Bake 5 minutes, uncovered. Remove from oven, cover, and allow to rest for 15 minutes before cutting into squares for serving.

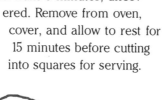

TURKEY AND BROCCOLI IN A CREAM SAUCE
Serves 4

> *5 cups broccoli florets (from about 1 large head)*
> *1/4 cup olive oil*
> *2 tablespoons chopped garlic*
> *1 pound turkey breast, skin removed and cut into 1/2-inch-thick strips*
> *1 cup dry white wine*
> *1 cup chicken stock*
> *1 cup heavy cream*
> *1/2 cup freshly grated Parmesan cheese*

In a large pot, bring at least 4 quarts of water to a rolling boil. Add 1 tablespoon salt. Add the broccoli and blanch it for about 3 minutes. Remove with slotted spoon to a bowl of cold water. Let stand briefly, drain, and return to bowl.

In a large, deep skillet, heat the oil over medium heat. Add the garlic and turkey and sauté until the turkey is just cooked through and tender. Using a slotted spoon, transfer the turkey to the bowl with the broccoli.

Add the wine, stock, and cream to the skillet, bring to a boil, and cook until thickened slightly, about 8 minutes. Add the broccoli and turkey, and cheese to the sauce and toss until heated through and evenly coated. Serve over pasta.

ZITI WITH HEARTY LAMB SAUCE
Serves 4 to 6

1 tablespoon olive or vegetable oil
3/4 pound lean ground lamb
2 cloves garlic, finely chopped
1 onion, finely chopped
1/2 teaspoon dried rosemary
1 cup canned crushed tomatoes
1-1/2 cups dry red wine
1 pinch of ground nutmeg
1 pinch of ground cloves
Salt and freshly ground pepper to taste
1 pound ziti
1/3 cup freshly grated Parmesan cheese

In a large, deep skillet, heat the oil in a medium saucepan over medium-high heat. Add the lamb, breaking it up with a wooden spoon, and garlic and cook until the meat begins to brown, about 3 minutes. Add the onion and rosemary and cook briefly. Add the crushed tomatoes, wine, nutmeg, and cloves. Bring to a boil and reduce to simmer. Add salt and pepper to taste. Cook, uncovered, until the lamb is tender, about 20 minutes.

Check the lamb occasionally to make sure there is enough liquid to cover it. If not, add a small amount of water.

Meanwhile, in a large pot, bring at least 4 quarts of water to a rolling boil. Add 1 tablespoon salt. Add the pasta, stir to separate, and cook until al dente. Drain. Stir half the Parmesan into the lamb sauce. Add the pasta, toss well, and heat through over low heat. Transfer to a warm platter, sprinkle with the remaining cheese, and serve.

CANNELLONI WITH SALMON AND TOMATO CREAM SAUCE
Serves 6

One 10-ounce package frozen, chopped spinach, thawed and drained
One 16-ounce container ricotta cheese
1-1/2 pounds salmon fillet
1 cup dry white wine
1/2 cup chicken stock
2 cloves garlic, sliced
Salt and ground pepper to taste
4 tablespoons unsalted butter
2 medium tomatoes, peeled, seeded, and chopped
2 cups medium cream
2 tablespoons tomato paste
1 pound fresh pasta sheets or 1 package cannelloni (12 pieces)
1 egg, lightly beaten
1/4 cup freshly grated Parmesan cheese
Note: Pasta sheets can be bought in stores where fresh pasta is sold.

Place the salmon in a large skillet. Pour the wine and chicken stock over the fish and add the garlic slices. Bring the liquid to a boil over high heat. Reduce heat to a simmer and cover. Poach the salmon until pale pink and just cooked through. Cool. Break up the salmon into flakes. There should be about 2 cups.

To make the filling: In a large bowl, combine the spinach, ricotta, and salmon. Salt and pepper to taste. Set aside.

To make the sauce: Melt the butter over medium heat. Add the tomato and sauté 1 minute. Add the cream and tomato paste, stir, and bring to a boil. Reduce the heat and simmer until the liquid is reduced by one-third. Set aside.

To make the cannelloni: Preheat the oven to 350°. Lightly grease a baking dish. Cut the pasta sheets into twelve 5 x 6-inch rectangles. Brush with egg. Place fish filling on the longer edge.

Roll and overlap the edges, placing seam side down on the baking dish. Pour tomato sauce over and sprinkle with Parmesan.

Note: If using dried cannelloni, cook them in boiling, salted water until less than al dente. Drain and fill.

Bake 20 to 30 minutes until the sauce is bubbling and the cheese golden. Serve.

GREEK PASTITSIO
Serves 6

> *1 pound lasagna noodles*
> *2 tablespoons olive oil*
> *2 pounds ground lamb*
> *1/2 cup chopped parsley*
> *1 onion, chopped*
> *5 cloves garlic, minced*
> *1/2 teaspoon ground cinnamon*
> *One 8-ounce can tomato sauce*
> *1/2 cup red wine*
> *1/4 cup butter, at room temperature, cut into pieces*
> *3 eggs, beaten*
> *1 cup freshly grated Parmesan cheese*
> *4 cups béchamel sauce (see Chapter 4), flavored with a pinch of ground cinnamon*

Preheat the oven to 350°.

In a large, deep skillet, heat the oil over medium heat. Add the lamb and brown, breaking it up with a wooden spoon, about 5 minutes. Add the onion and garlic and sauté until softened, about 3 minutes. Drain.

Add the parsley, cinnamon, tomato sauce, and wine. Let simmer over medium-low heat for 30 minutes.

In a large pot, bring at least 4 quarts of water to a rolling boil. Add 1 tablespoon salt. Place the noodles in the boiling water carefully, sliding them down gently into the water and stirring to prevent them from sticking to each other or to the pot. Cook until not quite al dente. They will cook further when baked. Drain and quickly transfer to a large bowl. Add butter, eggs, and 1/2 cup of the Parmesan, and toss well.

Place half of the noodles in the bottom of a large casserole dish. Top with the meat sauce, and cover with the rest of the noodles. Pour the béchamel evenly over the top. Top evenly with cheese. Bake until top is golden and bubbling, almost 1 hour.

WINE FONDUE

> *1 cup butter*
> *1 cup all-purpose flour*
> *4 cups milk*
> *2 cups Chablis*
> *2 teaspoons chicken flavored bouillon powder*
> *Pieces of chedder cheese, thinly sliced, about 1-1/2 pounds*

Melt the butter in a large saucepan. Stir in the flour; cook for several minutes over low heat. Add the bouillon, milk, and Chablis; stir frequently until mixture thickens. Stir in cheese until melted and smooth. (Use more or less cheese, according to your own taste.) Transfer to a fondue pot; keep warm.

Serve with slices of bread and raw vegetables.

Dinner Party Hints

1. Don't invite people you don't like.
2. Serve two to three different wines, at least one red and one white.
3. If you are serving to a younger crowd, having two-thirds of a bottle of wine per person is a good amount. Older people tend to want to drink less. The longer the event lasts, the more wine people will want to drink.
4. If you are asking guests to bring wine, you should offer them some advice on what to bring. This will help you guide people toward wine that goes with what you are serving. The less a guest knows about wine, the more specific your suggestion should be.
5. Don't force a food/wine pairing. Wine does not go readily with soup, salad, or fruit.

A dinner party usually begins with guests trickling into your home. Rather than having the early arrivals sitting on your sofa twiddling their thumbs and complimenting you on how dust free the corners of your rooms are, you should have a predinner stand-up course of wine and wine-friendly snacks. If your guests are apt to be standing, these snacks should require only a single hand, since the other is reserved for wine.

When planning a small dinner party with guests who are usually punctual, you need not have a stand-up course.

Because some people are *red-wine-only people* and some others are *white- wine-only people*, you will want to offer both at all times. A sparkling wine is a good stand-up-course wine. Offering sparkling wine with sparkling water as the alternative during this course is probably okay too.

At the dinner table each guest should, in a perfect world, be given two glasses. Having a nonidentical pair of glasses is preferable for keeping track of what is in what glass. Don't dictate what a guest should drink. You may think the white goes with the first sit-down course and the red with the main course, but some of your guests may not want to see things that way.

If you don't have a stand-up course, be daring and serve a dessert wine for dessert. Because such a wine is sweet, it is best served alone. Offer coffee and tea after the dessert wine to help rouse your guests from what has become hours of eating and drinking. Don't let people drive drunk or overly drowsy.

Wine Drinks

MIXED DRINKS WITH WINE

There is no substitute for a wine that you truly enjoy, but there is a place for wine as an ingredient in a mixed drink. Combine wine with the bubble of sparkling water for a refreshment with less overall alcohol content. Combine the flavor enhancement of a liqueur or fruit juice for a change of pace. These are light-hearted drinks with unpretentious ingredients and flexible proportions. That's what makes them so appealing.

MULLED WINE

6 oz.	red wine
splash of	brandy
1 tbs.	fine sugar
splash of	lemon juice
2 whole	cloves
1 dash	cinnamon

Combine ingredients in a saucepan and heat to simmer. Do not boil. Stir well. Pour into a coffee mug.

SANGRIA

1 bottle	dry red wine
2 oz.	Triple Sec
1 oz.	brandy
2 oz.	orange juice
1 oz.	lemon juice or juice of 1/2 lemon

1/4 cup	fine sugar
10 oz.	club soda
	chilled orange and lemon slices

Chill all ingredients together except club soda for at least one hour. Before serving, pour into a pitcher or punch bowl over ice and add club soda. Makes approximately 10 servings.

WHITE OR RED WINE COOLER

4 oz.	wine
2 oz.	pineapple juice
2 oz.	club soda or sparkling water
	wedge of lemon or lime

Pour wine, juice, and soda over ice into a large wine glass. Stir gently. Garnish with a full wedge.

RED OR WHITE WINE SPRITZER

4 oz.	wine
2 oz.	club soda or sparkling water
	wedge of lemon or lime

Pour wine over ice into a large wine glass. Add club soda. Stir gently. Garnish with a full wedge.

KIR

| 1/2 oz. | crème de cassis (or to taste) |
| | 4 oz. dry white wine |

Pour the cassis into a large wine glass. Add the wine. Do not stir. The cassis is meant to be at the bottom so the drink gets sweeter as it diminishes. More white wine can then be added if desired. Serve with a lemon twist.

BISHOP

4 oz.	red wine
2 oz.	orange juice
1 oz.	lemon juice or juice of 1/2 lemon
1 tsp.	fine sugar

Pour juices and sugar into a mixing glass nearly filled with ice. Stir. Strain into a highball glass over ice. Fill with red wine. Garnish with a fruit slice.

VALENTINE

4 oz.	Beaujolais
1 tsp.	cranberry liqueur
2 oz.	cranberry juice

Combine ingredients in a shaker half filled with ice. Shake well. Strain into a wine glass.

MIMOSA

| 3 oz. | chilled champagne |
| 3 oz. | orange juice |

Combine in a champagne flute or white wine glass. Stir gently.

How to Ruin Your Wine-Drinking Experience

1. Serve your wine at the wrong temperature. Reds should be slightly cooled; whites and sparkling wines should be cold, but not too cold.

2. Brush your teeth and rinse your mouth with mouthwash prior to drinking wine. The acidity of the wine will be very noticeable in this situation.

3. Serve wine in a non-wine glass. There is no reason for this. Sure the wine in theory will taste about the same, but part of the wine experience will be lost. Wine glasses encourage us to sip.

4. Break the cork when trying to remove it from your wine bottle. This is very easy to do with a cheap corkscrew.

5. Drink too much wine and get drunk and/or fall asleep.

6. Drink wine with someone you don't like or someone who talks too much about too little.

7. Drink your good wine after having too much bad wine.

8. Start drinking wine late at night to help ensure a hangover.

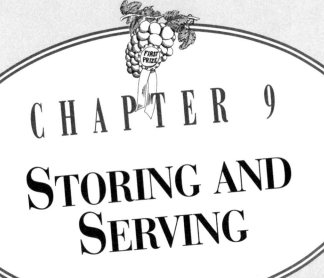

C H A P T E R 9

STORING AND SERVING

BOTTLED BY ADAMS MEDIA

NET CONTENTS: TWENTY-FOUR PAGES

PRODUCT OF USA

Wine Bottles and the Metric System

When you go to the liquor store, you buy beer by the ounce and wine by the milli-liter. This is dictated by U.S. federal law. There are 12 ounces in your standard bottle or can of beer. Whether it originates from the United States or elsewhere in the world, a standard bottle of wine has a standard size of 750 ml or three-quarters of a liter.

This means a bottle of wine is three-quarters' the size of a 1-liter (33.6-ounce) bottle of Coke. That equals 25.2 American ounces. So a bottle of wine is a sip bigger than two bottles of beer. Rip off? Fear not, the alcohol contained in a bottle of wine is about the same as five 12-ounce beers, although this ratio does vary quite a bit dependng on the specific beer and wine. Wine also comes in quarter bottles, half bottles, and magnums (double-sized bottles). These less popular sizes contain 187.5 ml, 375 ml, and 1500 ml (1.5 liters).

Dessert wines often come in half bottles, as they tend to be sweet, alcoholic, and drunk in moderation and only on special occasions. Most decent wine stores have a small section of half bottles of regular wine. These are good when you don't want a lot of wine, and don't want to worry about saving what is left over.

The magnum is used to sell large quantities of wine. Champagne is often promoted in magnums, in double magnums, and in even larger sizes. A wine bottle that is triple magnum, six regular-size bottles' worth of wine, is a Rehoboam; a double magnum, or 4 bottles of Champagne is called a Jeroboam.

There are many cheap wines sold in magnums, but there are also some very good wines available in this size. A good wine in a magnum-sized bottle makes a great impression on any dinner table. Anything larger than a magnum, regardless of what it's called, isn't practical.

Speaking of practical, if you want to christen your new yacht with a bottle of Champagne, you need to order a special bottle. Huh? The carbonation in sparkling wines puts so much pressure on the bottle that they are made with extra thick glass so as not to break from internal pressure—or from a collision with the side of your new yacht.

The quarter bottle mainly gets used to provide individual servings in bars and on airplanes, and as a free sample size.

Aging and Storing

Wine needs to be aged. Everyone takes this to be a truth, even people who don't drink wine. Wine happens to be one of the few agricultural products that can improve with age. If you think back to the time when people didn't have refrigerators and freezers, you'll realize how important this quality really is.

The fact that wine could be bottled and stored (aged) was a primary reason why it was aged. Since wines could age over a period of years, and wines from different years could be aging in the same cellar, the wine's vintage year became of consequence. Because weather is such an important factor in the growing of grapes and it varies from year to year (especially when you consider that the growing season is nearly six months long), each year's wines vary.

Whether a particular year was a good or a great year for a certain wine may not be known until two or more years after the harvest, when people start drinking some of the bottles from that harvest. However, generally favorable weather during a growing season usually ensures a good year for winemaking. It does not, however, guarantee a great year.

Most red wines and almost all whites do not benefit from more than four years of aging. This is because a winemaker cannot usually make a bottle of wine that tastes good after only two or three years and also will be able to evolve into something even better a decade later. Few products are manufactured with the intent that they will be sold ten months later, never mind ten years later.

Wine that is produced with its components in a drinkable balance doesn't need to be aged much at all. Wines with bolder components need one or more years to allow the components to mellow. However, wines can be, and some are, made in such a way that they will be unapproachable for a decade. These are rare and expensive wines that are crafted with great skill and aimed at a small audience. Most of these wines are red, and much of the aging process involves the relationship between fruitiness and tannin. The truly ageworthy wines are made from the noble-red varieties: Cabernet Sauvignon, Nebbiolo, Sangiovese, Syrah, and, to a lesser extent, Pinot Noir and Merlot.

WELL I GUESS IT'S ABOUT READY.

WARNING! WARNING! SPORTS ANALOGY AHEAD!

Let's take a look at the evolution of an expensive and ageworthy red wine as if it were a major-league baseball pitcher whose career is broken down into four phases.

1. The wine is tasted by experts right out of the barrel when it is produced. Praise emanates. "Powerful tannin, overwhelming fruit, great length," they say. "What power! What potential!" A young pitcher comes up from the minor leagues with a 98-mph fastball, with a penchant for throwing an occasional wild pitch. The sportscasters exclaim, "What power! What potential!"

2. The wine goes into its dormant phase. Roaring fruit subsides and becomes masked by the tannin. The flavors are out of balance. The pitcher injures his arm, develops a drug or alcohol problem, and ends up back in the minor leagues.

3. Given time, the wine reemerges from its slumber with mature fruit flavors of tobacco, cedar, figs, etc.—well worth the wait and the price. The pitcher successfully completes a drug rehabilitation program, discovers religion, and eventually returns to the major leagues with off-speed pitches and pinpoint control. He becomes a twenty-game winner.

4. The wine loses its redeeming qualities. The fruit and tannin are gone. It tastes like weak tea. Because it's

from a great year, it has cachet value on a wine list; it's worth more unopened than opened. The pitcher fills stadiums, especially when the team is on the road. However, the home crowd knows the pitcher is washed up and prefers he stay in the bullpen.

Any wine you choose to put away should be kept away from light and, ideally, in the range of 48°F–58°F/9°C–15°C degrees. Keeping a typical wine at 70°F/21°C for six months isn't going to be much of a problem.

If a wine is stored in a warm environment, it matures too quickly; in too cool an environment it will mature too slowly. If your home gets warm in the summer and you do not have air conditioning, it is probably a good idea to drink any good wines you have been saving.

If you are storing wine, lay each bottle on its side; this keeps the cork moist. Whether you are saving a wine for a month or a decade, it is always a good idea to do this. Cork will contract if it is allowed to dry, possibly allowing air to get into the bottle.

It would probably never occur to you to shake your wine bottle, but if it does, don't do it. Some wine experts have made an observation, although unconfirmed by scientists, that vibrations adversely affect wine. This doesn't mean you should carry an expensive wine home from the liquor store with the gentleness with which one carries a newborn baby, but if you dream of building a wine cellar someday, don't buy a house next to railroad tracks.

Serving Temperature

Sparkling wine should be served chilled, possibly with an ice bucket to keep it chilled. White wine should be chilled, but not ice cold. Most wines are allowed to warm up from a stay in a refrigerator for a little while before being served. Red wine should be served a little cooler than normal room temperature.

Unless you own a wine thermometer, the notion of serving a wine at a specific temperature is silly. If you are serving white wine, chances are you have been refrigerating it. Unless your home has a temperature around 63°F/17°C, you will need to manipulate the temperature of every bottle of wine, using the air in your refrigerator (or freezer!), the air in your home, and possibly ice, if you are drinking sparkling wine.

To chill a wine you put it in the refrigerator. To warm it, you take it out. Where you live, what season it is, and how you regulate the temperature in your house determines how warm your home is. On a hot summer night, in a city apartment or restaurant that doesn't have air conditioning, you may find yourself and your wine sitting in an 86°F/30°C room.

General rules of thumb regarding serving temperature allow most people to enjoy wine without needing to be both a physicist and a meteorologist.

- You can drop the temperature of a warm full bottle of wine roughly 4°F/2°C every

ten minutes it sits in your refrigerator. You can chill it about twice as quickly if you put the bottle in your freezer. The fastest way to chill wine is in a mixture of ice and water. Add salt to the water if you are in a *real* hurry.

- If you are taking a bottle of white wine from your refrigerator, you can raise its temperature in a cool room roughly 4°F/2°C every ten minutes, more quickly if you pour some into a glass. If you are in a very warm room, figure it will warm at twice that speed.

- You can manipulate the temperature of wine bottles with warm and cold water faster than with warm and cold air. However, guessing the temperature of such water is iffy, especially a warm-water temperature. If you are drinking an ordinary wine or are in a hurry, you may want to consider placing your wine bottle in a pot or pan of warm or cool water. After all, it's only wine.

- Using the freezer: A bottle of white wine will go from normal room temperature to drinking temperature in forty to forty-five minutes if you put it in your freezer. This is about half the time it takes via the refrigerator.

Now let's build some guidelines on this math.

Red Wine

You want to drink this at about 64°F/18°C. If you are drinking a red of questionable quality with bad elements you might want to numb a bit, or a Beaujolais (good or bad), serve it at 60°F/15°C.

If your home is at 70°F/21°C, then you want to put your wine in the refrigerator for fifteen minutes. If it is at 86°F/30°C, then you should keep your wine in the refrigerator for about forty minutes to bring it down to 64°F/18°C.

White Wine

You want to drink white wines at about 48°F/9°C. If it is a really expensive white wine, you will want to taste it more, and you should serve it at 58°F/14°C. Let's assume your refrigerator is at 42°F/6°C. This is cool for a refrigerator, but not uncommon in this era of good home appliances. We'll also assume you didn't spend $100 for your bottle of white wine and would like to drink it at 48°F/9°C.

To get your white wine warmed up to drink, figure that it will warm at 4°F/2°C every ten minutes if your home is at 70°F/21°C, and twice that speed if it is at 86°F/30°C. So take it out fifteen minutes before serving, or eight minutes prior in a very warm setting.

Sparkling Wine

This should be served at about 42°F/6°C (about the temperature of your refrigerator). It's probably ideal a tad warmer, but unless you are drinking in a very cold room, it will warm up fairly quickly. So if you plan on taking your bottle out of your refrigerator for any length of time, you will want an ice bucket around. Warm sparkling wine is anything but festive.

Sherry

Light Sherry should be served like a white wine. Sweeter, darker Sherries should be served like red wine—even normal room temperature is okay.

Port, Marsala, and Madeira

Same as red wine.

Dessert Wines

Same as white wine.

Trial and error will help you perfect the timing for the temperature in your home, refrigerator, and freezer, but the guidelines above are a good place to start. Even if you get the serving temperature thing perfected, you'll always need to deal with the fact that wine warms up every minute it sits in your glass.

Letting Wine Breathe

What is breathing? It is exposing wine to air, aerating it. Oxygen is the element in the air that affects wine. White wines don't seem to react right away to oxygen, so when we talk about letting a wine breathe, we are talking about a red wine. If this were a chemistry book, we would be explaining a set of complex reactions and processes. Let's stick to how the air changes the flavor of wine.

Practically all wine is crafted in a way that causes it to evolve over time. If this were not the case, then we'd be buying and drinking month-old wine like we buy month-old beer (if we're lucky). A large part of the evolution is the mellowing of the wine. Tannins and acids are the components that most need to mellow. Without sufficient exposure to oxygen, wines can taste harsh. Eventually, as the tannins and/or acids fade a bit, the fruit begins to exert itself and the wine's components become more balanced. After too much exposure, wine—especially red wine—begins to taste like vinegar. This is caused by the development of acetic acid.

A Zinfandel, Cabernet Sauvignon, Shiraz/Syrah, or Nebbiolo may need to breathe for an hour or more, depending on how the wine was made and how mature it is. Equally important are the personal tastes of the people who will be drinking the wine. Some people like to taste wines right out of the bottle and experience the evolution over time. A Beaujolais Nouveau doesn't need to breathe much. This makes sense, as it is crafted not to evolve but to be drunk just weeks after harvest.

Generally speaking, all red wines taste better ten minutes after you open the bottle and pour it into the glass. Just taking the cork out and leaving the wine in the bottle is ineffective, since so little of the wine is exposed to air. Let your wine breathe in a glass. Wines that are still before their peak when the cork is removed may taste much better after half an hour or more in a glass.

Letting your wine breathe doesn't have to be a controlled scientific experiment. It is interesting merely to observe how bad some good wines may taste when you first open the bottle. Just keep in mind that a red wine will probably be better (and unlikely to be worse) after ten minutes of aeration. A white wine may also benefit from some air and is unlikely to taste worse. Some wines actually taste better the next day. We've had some $6 bottles of red wine that tasted like $12 bottles the next day. It's important to note that these wines were in a recorked bottle and not left out for a day in a wine glass.

If you ever have an expensive bottle of wine fifteen or more years old, you don't want to give it much air time. These wines can change drastically literally from minute to minute. Because a lot of the mellowing has already been done by sitting in the bottle for years, these wines may run out of gas an hour after the bottle is opened. However, that can be an incredible hour, in which a seemingly static bottle of liquid changes dramatically. Don't bother saving part of an old wine for the next day unless you want to experiment: It will probably be dead.

$50 Bottles of Wine That Are Worth the Money

1. *Château Pichon-Lalande (Pauillac, France).* These wines are delicious, ageworthy Cabernet Sauvignon–based blend.
2. *Louis Jadot Gevrey Chambertin (France).* This is a large, reliable producer of Red Burgundy, which is, of course, Pinot Noir–based. The Clos St.-Jacques version of this stuff costs more than the regular version, which is good enough to impress you and anyone else you might want to impress.
3. *Mumm Renée Lalou Champagne.* If you've read this book, you know this stuff comes from Champagne, France.
4. *Chablis Grand Cru Les Clos.* This is simple, elegant, excellent French Chardonnay.
5. *Silver Oak Cabernet Sauvignon from California.* These bottles are tough to find, tougher not to like.
6. *Penfold's Cabernet Sauvignon Bin 707.* This is a great wine from Australia.
7. *Domaine Zind Humbrecht (Alsace, France).* This is a single-vineyard Grand Cru-Riesling and Gewürztraminer.
8. *Château Raymond Lafon Sauternes (France).* A full bottle of this is delicious dessert wine is an expensive bargain.
9. *Château Smith-Haut-Lafitte Blanc (France, again).* This is the finest Sauvignon Blanc–based wine in this price range!
10. *Beaune Clos de Mouche from Joseph Drouhlin (France, again!).* A bottle of this is as good as any California Chardonnay, especially with food.

Wine Glasses

All wine glasses have stems that connect the base to the bowl or cone of the glass. It is proper etiquette to hold the stem of the glass. This keeps your hand from heating the wine and it keeps fingerprints off the bowl.

There are three main styles of wine glasses: all-purpose white-wine glasses, large bulbous glasses for red wine, and a third style for sparkling wine, a flute, which is tall and very slender.

There are many wine-glass styles to investigate at upscale wine shops and housewares stores, but sticking to the three styles makes the most sense for most people. There are even wine glasses for individual grapes. The Burgundy glass, theoretically, is designed for the enjoyment of Pinot Noir wines that come from Burgundy.

If you don't own any decent wine glasses, get a set of the all-purpose glasses. The Burgundy glass has a bulbous bowl, some more wide than tall, on a stem that is used almost exclusively for red wines. Burgundy-style glasses look sharp but are less practical than white-wine glasses. White wine shouldn't be served in a Burgundy glass, but the all-purpose white-wine glass is perfectly fine for red wines.

If you entertain guests, or yourself for that matter, and you like red wine, it is nice to have a set of both the all-purpose and the larger red glasses. This allows you to serve two different wines without there being any confusion about which glass holds which wine. The better wine goes in the bigger glass.

Wine glasses come in different sizes. It is possible to buy a glass that holds 16 ounces or more. A good-sized glass holds 12 ounces, and you probably don't want to buy a glass that holds less than 10 ounces. We recommend your everyday glass be an all-purpose one that holds about 10 ounces. Larger glasses do add an exclamation point to a festive occasion and are a good way to go when choosing a second set, but they are a bit ostentatious and more likely to get broken.

Stay away from odd colors or shapes for your wine glasses. Wine is meant to be looked at through clear glass and to flow out of your glass smoothly without nooks and crannies to negotiate.

Wine glasses do break. Because you are going to lose some glasses over time, you should buy glasses that are easy to replace and that you can afford to break on occasion.

Don't serve wine in plastic glasses or cups. If you are having a large reception, you can rent wine glasses for the occasion, usually at a reasonable price. It adds a little class to the occasion, regardless of the wine in the glass.

SPARKLING WINE   CHAMPAGNE FLUTE   WHITE WINE   RED WINE

Pouring Wine

Is this something you really need to worry about? No, but there are a couple of things to remember. If you work at a restaurant you have quite a few things to keep in mind.

When pouring, it is polite to serve yourself last.

You shouldn't fill a wine glass more than half full; one-third is considered optimum. The fuller the glass, the more difficult it is to swirl your wine, which people do in order to smell the aromas in the wine and thus enhance their enjoyment. Even if the people at your table aren't big wine sniffers, don't fill the glass up past half way. By not overfilling the glass you can see if your wine is viscous and leaves legs (tears) on the glass.

You probably always want to pour 5 or 6 ounces, regardless of the size of the glass. When pouring non-sparkling wine, aim for the center of the glass; it's not going to bubble up. Sparkling wine should be poured slowly and against the side of the glass so it doesn't bubble over.

When you have poured enough, give the glass bottle a slight twist as you lift it upright, which helps prevent a drop or two from dribbling down the side of the bottle.

If you are *serving* wine by the bottle in a restaurant, you will first be expected to present the bottle to your customers before opening it. You are supposed to make the presentation to the person who is most likely to be paying for the wine, usually the person who ordered the wine. This ritual is to show the customer you are serving the wine that was ordered. Most restaurants have a wine-serving policy that may even include how you hold the bottle when pouring it.

Some wine bottles have a touch of sediment that tends to emerge from the bottle when it is almost empty. This is because the sediment is heavier than the wine. If you are drinking a red wine more than a few years old, the chance of there being sediment increases.

Sediment isn't going to kill you, but you are apt to be surprised when you see it in the bottom of your wine glass. Sediment will make your wine cloudy and can adversely affect the flavor of it. A simple rule of thumb is to avoid trying to get every last drop out of a bottle of wine (especially a red) by turning the bottle vertical when pouring the last of it into a glass.

If you see some sediment in your wine glass, there's no need to worry. Chances are that most of it will end up at the bottom of the glass.

Affordable Wines Worth Aging

Sauternes (France) Dessert Wine from the Bordeaux subregion of Sauternes. A good producer is Château Raymond Lafon; there are also others. Age for a long time, but play it safe and pull the cork before its twenty-fifth birthday. *Cost: $25 half bottle*

Petites Châteaux, (the plural of Petite Château). These are lesser châteaux of Bordeaux (France), with good red blends, usually of Cabernet Sauvignon, Cabernet Franc, and Merlot. Age for 4–5 years. *Cost $8–16*

Moulin-a-Vent (France). This is one of the ten premier villages for Beaujolais. Age for 4–5 years. *Cost: $10–15*

Riesling from Alsace (France). Purchase wines from one of these top producers: Trimbach, Hugel, or Domain Zind Humbrecht. Age for 4–5 years. *Cost: $15–30*

White Burgundy (France), a Chardonnay-based wine. Look for wines produced by Joseph Drouhlin, Louis Latour, and Domaine Laflaive's Bourgogne Blanc. Age for 5–10 years. *Cost: $20–40*

Chianti (Italy). Buy Sangiovese-based reds from Castello di Ama or Ruffino. Age for 5–10 years. *Cost: $10-20*

Vintage Port (Portugal). A port with a vintage year is one made from grapes from a particularly good harvest. Prices vary widely on these. Half bottles are available. Unless you are immortal, you'll have a difficult time overaging one of these. Two reliable producers in this category are Dow and Croft. *Cost $15 and up*

Chateauneuf-du-Pape (France—both a place and a wine name). These are red wines based on any number of thirteen grape varieties of various combinations and percentages. They are a perfect example of why the French are less interested in grape variety than place of origin. These are very good wines and can be aged a long time. Two top producers are Vieux Télégraphe and Beaucastel. *Cost: $16–30*

The Right Cabernet Sauvignon. This, the premier red-wine grape, is meant to be aged. Ask a wine person whose judgment you trust for a suggestion for a Cabernet worth aging. Tell him how long you are willing to wait and how much you are willing to spend.

Decanting

Decanting is not an everyday necessity for any wine drinker. Many wine drinkers go a lifetime without needing to decant any wine.

Decanting is the process of pouring wine from its bottle into a carafe or a decanter. The main purpose of this is to leave the sediment behind. Sediment can be a problem with older red wines, especially Ports. If you are serving such a wine, you need to consider a few things.

Let the wine sit upright for a couple of days. When you serve the wine, you should pour it slowly out of the bottle, so as not to disturb the sediment that has settled to the bottom. You will need a bright light, candle, or flashlight to shine through the bottle to monitor the sediment as it drifts toward the neck of the bottle.

Decanting also aerates the wine. If you are decanting a Port, aeration isn't a big deal. But if you are serving an old, red table wine, the clock is ticking. These wines generally don't last long after opening before their fragile components begin to fade.

If you don't have a decanter, you can either pour your wine slowly and carefully, which will leave much of the sediment behind, or pour it into an old but clean wine bottle. Having a steady hand is always important when decanting, and it becomes that much more important if you try to decant from bottle to bottle. Some people choose not to bother with decanting and deal with the sediment on a glass-by-glass basis. This approach is okay if the amount of sediment doesn't detract from your enjoyment.

A "quick and dirty" method of decanting wine is to filter it through a cheesecloth or a coffee filter. This is foolproof, although purists might protest the wine's touching a foreign object.

Sometimes it is desirable to decant a young wine solely for aeration. This should be done quickly, almost violently, to expose as much wine to as much air as possible. Let the wine rest for about an hour before serving. This method will make young reds, especially California Cabernet Sauvignons from top producers, more enjoyable.

If you've invested in a wine that will need decanting, it is hoped that you will have remembered to invest in a decanter, or at least saved a wide-mouth carafe and its top for the occasion.

Cork

The usual way to keep air, more precisely oxygen, out of an unopened bottle of wine is with a cylindrical piece of cork. Cork expands in the neck of the bottle and provides an airtight seal, unless the cork dries out. If an unopened bottle of wine is left in a very cold place, the cork can be forced out of the bottle. Rotten and shrunken (dried-out) corks are the two most common cork maladies.

It is the interaction of oxygen with wine (letting the wine breathe) that causes the wine to evolve. You don't want this to happen until you are ready to open your bottle of wine.

When you buy a wine, feel the cork through the plastic or lead wrapper on the top of the bottle. Make sure the top of the cork is about level with the top of the bottle. If it isn't, get a different bottle. If you bring a wine home and remove the cap to find a cork whose top is moldy, you should probably return the wine.

Probably the best way to keep air out is with a screw (twist-off) cap. If you drink carbonated soft drinks, you know the twist-off cap is effective in keeping air out of bottles. However, the twist-off cap has come to symbolize cheap, and to some people undrinkable, wine. Switzerland, ever practical, often uses screwcaps on many of the wine bottles. Few of these are exported.

Unlike screw caps, corks may have imperfections that can cause a wine to go bad in the bottle. An imperfect seal allows oxygen to interact with the wine, prematurely aging it. A portion of the cork may disintegrate into the wine, causing it to have an unwanted corky flavor.

It is a good idea to have a couple of good corks from bottles already consumed lying around your kitchen in case you encounter a cork problem. A broken or brittle cork should be replaced with a better one if you recork your wine. Eventually, old corks will reexpand and won't fit in a wine bottle, so replace your saved corks with newer ones from time to time.

If you keep empty half bottles around for storing leftovers (see the "Saving Leftovers" section), you should keep your spare corks in these bottles. Not only will your corks stay slim, but the inside of these bottles won't collect dust.

Corkscrews

Corkscrews are used for removing the cork from the bottle. They are not used to open sparkling wines; this would be both dangerous and unnecessary, as the pressure behind the cork will help you to remove it and perhaps send it flying. Believe it or not, there are actually organizations for corkscrew collectors. These folks buy, sell, and trade rare and/or expensive corkscrews, have newsletters, etc. But let's talk about the corkscrews that people actually use to open a bottle of wine.

Worm (or Auger)

This is found on some jackknives; you just never knew what to call it. The worm and a handle (the jackknife doubles as the handle) doesn't work very well. Do not buy one of these things. The worm, however, is the main part of most corkscrews. Unless you are using the butler's corkscrew (see below), you will need to bore your way into a cork before you can pull it out of the bottle. Sometimes plastic versions of these are given away as promotional items. *Cost: Free–$3*

Screwpull

This device is considered to be the most effective and practical corkscrew. It is designed to ensure that the worm bores straight into the cork. All you do is put the screwpull in position on the bottle and start turning the handle. At first you are boring the worm into the cork. Then, when the worm is deep enough in the cork, you suddenly find that your turning of the handle is pulling the cork out of the bottle. It seems like magic, until you use one and figure out how this clever device works. (*Hint:* The cork "rides up" the thin, teflon-coated worm.) *Cost: $18–25 (for a good one)*

Winged Corkscrew

This is the metal corkscrew with wings, and a bottle-cap opener at the end of the handle. Some people don't like these because they don't have control of the direction of the worm as it bores into the cork. However, once you are comfortable with this type of corkscrew, your success rate will be very high. Also, having a bottle-cap opener on your corkscrew is a nice convenience.

To use a winged corkscrew you align the worm perpendicular to the top of the cork. Then you start twisting the handle while keeping the corkscrew as vertical as you can. The hand you use to steady the bottle should be positioned so as not to impede the wings that lift as the worm bores into the cork. When the wings get to the 11- and 1-o'clock position, you stop turning the handle and, instead, press the wings down. This brings the cork up and out of the bottle. Ideally, the cork will still be in one piece. If the cork doesn't come all the way out of the bottle, you will be able to yank it out of the bottle while holding the corkscrew. *Cost: $5–10*

Waiter's Corkscrew

This corkscrew has a little knife on it to cut the wrapper off the top of the bottle before removing the cork. This is a nice feature, but the mechanics of getting the cork out of the bottle leave a lot to be desired. However, practice makes near perfect. The worm is manually turned into the center of the cork. A swinging arm attached to the corkscrew is then placed on the lip of the bottle. This provides leverage so that the wine server may pull up on the other end of the corkscrew and thus pull the cork out. If you don't plan on working in a restaurant, don't buy this type of corkscrew; spring for a screwpull. *Cost: $8–16*

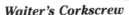

Butler's Corkscrew

Also known as the "Ah-So" corkscrew, this style is the only one that doesn't use a worm to bore through the cork. You slide the two prongs down the sides of the cork, and then twist and pull the cork out of the bottle. One of the prongs is longer than the other, and you need to get this one between the cork and the edge of the bottle before positioning the other prong. This is not an easy device to use without a lot of practice. However, for people who buy a lot of old wines whose corks may have deteriorated a bit over the years, this device is the best way to get a bad cork out of a bottle in one piece. *Cost: $10–12*

Port Tongs

The fanciest and most dramatic device for opening bottles is a set of "port tongs." As the name implies, this contraption is designed for opening very old port bottles whose corks have disintegrated. The tongs are heated red-hot in a fireplace and then closed around the neck of the bottle. This heats the glass in a narrow band just below the cork so that, when brushed with a feather that has been dipped in cold water, the glass neck neatly cracks. The top of the bottle and the crumbly cork are then removed and the port is decanted. *Expect to pay over $100 for a pair (if you can find them).*

Champagne

As we mentioned earlier, a champagne bottle does not require any type of corkscrew to remove its cork. It should, however, be opened with the same caution used in handling a dangerous weapon. Imagine the bottle as a gun and your finger as the safety catch. Always keep a thumb or finger over the cork. First remove the foil and wire, with your thumb hovering over the cork. Then point the bottle at a 45° angle away from everybody. Grip the cork firmly in one hand and pull with the other. Never turn the cork. As the internal pressure loosens the cork, continue to hold it firmly.

Saving Leftovers

Leftover wine is an issue that stirs controversy. Products have been made to keep leftover wine "fresh." These devices either pump out the air in the bottle or replace the air with inert gases. The goal is to keep oxygen away from leftover wine in the bottle. The effectiveness of these products varies from study to study.

Restaurants that serve premium wines by the glass must sometimes choose between serving a questionable wine and throwing it away. White wine, kept chilled, keeps well, but a red wine that was opened a day or two ago may no longer be worth drinking.

If you open an old bottle of red wine, it is best drunk within an hour or two before it loses the qualities that made it worth aging all those years in the first place. Leftovers from these wines aren't worth saving. Fortified wines and dessert wines, on the other hand, will last quite a while without much effort.

The question is, how does one best save table wine for future consumption?

PLAN 1

The easiest and, in our opinion, best thing to do is the following. Get yourself a half bottle of wine. Drink it. Enjoy it. Save the bottle and the cork. Clean the bottle by rinsing the inside with hot water a couple of times. Let it dry; then put the cork back into the empty bottle.

You now have a surrogate half bottle for future wines. When you open a bottle of wine that you know you won't finish, it's time to use your half bottle.

Step 1. Open the new bottle.
Step 2. Pour half of its contents immediately into the half bottle. Fill it high into the neck, leaving little or no room between the top of the wine and where the bottom of the cork will be.

Step 3. Cork the half bottle.

Step 4. Refrigerate it (optional for red wines).

You now have a half bottle of wine that received very little exposure to oxygen and is not receiving much, if any, in its new home. This will preserve many red wines, especially young ones, for up to two weeks. If you refrigerate the bottle, the wine will last longer. Because wines vary and room temperatures vary, the ability of your wine to hold out in its new home will vary.

What does refrigeration do? It slows down the biological activity going on in the wine. Oxidation is the biological activity that turns wine to vinegar.

Half bottles, for the most part, are shorter than full bottles and fit better standing up in refrigerators, even on a door shelf.

Note that the bottle that stores your leftovers doesn't need to be a wine bottle. You can use a soda bottle or even a ketchup bottle. If your bottle is clear glass, then it is easier to inspect it for cleanliness on the inside. Green or clear-glass half bottles are preferable to brown; it is difficult to see the wine level as you pour into a brown bottle.

If you have saved a red wine, you will need to remember to remove the wine from the refrigerator forty-five minutes before you plan to drink it. A half bottle of wine will warm up somewhat more quickly than a full bottle.

If you end up drinking some of the leftover wine from the half bottle that day or on a subsequent day, it is a good idea to refrigerate your red because there will now be oxygen in your bottle.

PLAN 2

Recork and refrigerate leftover wine in its original bottle. The sooner after opening, the better.

No matter what you do to save your wine, you don't have to lay the bottle on its side. In fact, this is a bad idea because the wine may be able to sneak past the cork, causing a mess and a loss of wine.

All of this fuss is unnecessary for preserving inexpensive jug wine. The process of pasteurization, usually used on such wines, kills everything in the wine that can make it go bad.

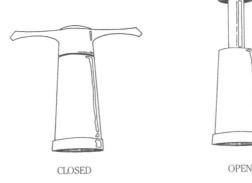

This wine vacuum pulls air out of a open wine bottle to preserve leftover wine.

CLOSED   OPEN

Saving Sparkling Wine

If you drink sparkling wine more than twice a year, and you find yourself having some left over, you might want to invest in a sparkling-wine bottle stopper (shown at right). This little device does a good job of retaining the carbonation. A regular wine cork also works, although unless you secure it with the original metal cage from the sparkling wine bottle (or aluminum foil), it can pop out. When saved properly, sparkling-wine leftovers will keep pretty well for a day or two.

Or, you can always make the following mixed drinks with your leftover champagne or sparkling wine.

CHAMPAGNE COCKTAIL

1 tsp.	fine sugar
3 dashes	bitters
6 oz.	champagne, chilled

Dissolve sugar in bitters in the bottom of a champagne flute. Add champagne. Stir. Top with a lemon twist.

MIMOSA

3 oz.	chilled champagne
3 oz.	orange juice

Combine in a champagne flute or white wine glass. Stir gently.

MIDORI MIMOSA

2 oz.	Midori
1 tsp.	lime juice
4 oz.	champagne, chilled

Combine in a champagne flute or white wine glass. Stir gently.

BELLINI

2 oz.	peach nectar
1/2 oz.	lemon juice
	chilled champagne

Pour juices into a champagne flute. Stir. Fill with champagne. Stir gently.

CHAMPAGNE MINT

1/2 oz.	green crème de menthe
	chilled champagne to fill

Pour crème de menthe into a champagne flute. Add champagne. Stir gently.

CHAMPAGNE CHARISMA

2 oz.	champagne, chilled
1 oz.	Vodka
1/2 oz.	peach-flavored brandy
1 oz.	cranberry juice
1–2 scoops	raspberry sherbet

Combine all ingredients except champagne in a blender. Blend well. Pour into a large red-wine goblet. Add champagne. Stir.

CHAMPAGNE FIZZ OR DIAMOND FIZZ

2 oz.	gin
1 oz.	lemon juice or juice of 1/2 lemon
1 tsp.	sugar
4 oz.	champagne

Combine gin, lemon juice, and sugar in a shaker half filled with ice. Shake well. Strain into a highball glass over ice. Add champagne. Stir gently.

BUCK'S FIZZ

5 oz.	champagne, chilled
1/2 oz.	Triple Sec
1 oz.	orange juice
1/2 tsp.	grenadine

Pour champagne, Triple Sec, and orange juice into a champagne flute. Add grenadine. Stir. Garnish with an orange slice.

SCOTCH ROYALE

1-1/2 oz.	scotch
1 tsp.	fine sugar
dash	bitters
	chilled champagne to fill

Dissolve sugar in bitters and scotch in a champagne flute. Fill with champagne. Stir gently.

KIR ROYALE

1 oz.	crème de cassis
	chilled champagne to fill

Pour ingredients into a champagne flute or wine glass. Stir gently.

Cleaning Wine Glasses

There are different approaches to the goal of having a truly clean wine glass. By clean we mean no dust, no odor, no visible or invisible caked-on liquids from previously contained beverages, and the curveball—no soap residue.

If you choose to run your glasses through a dishwasher, you then must clean the glasses by hand using hot water to remove soap residue, which you may or may not be able to see or smell.

If you clean your glasses by hand using dish soap and water, the same thing must be done. When you clean your glasses by hand, you can better regulate the amount of soap you use. Less is better.

Your third option is to use no soap at all. A thorough cleaning is possible using only hot water, clean fingers and maybe a sponge that has no soap on it. This is the method we use.

If you don't own many glasses or you're lazy or just don't care, you may use a wine glass for other beverages like juice or water. This is okay. We do it, and many other people do it too. A wine glass has an elegant functional shape, and it is difficult to resist the urge to use it when it is the most convenient glass and you want some juice, water, or other liquid refreshment.

Wine Stains

This isn't a fun topic, because a good piece of clothing or a carpet may be at stake and there is no sure answer. Red-wine stains are tougher to remove than white-wine stains.

Salt and water is the best home recipe for removing wine stains. We have used both hot and cool water with salt and had some success. If you have a piece of clothing that you can remove right away, you might want to try to clean it yourself with salt and cool water if the label reads *dry clean only*. Do this your own risk to the fabric, but not all dry-clean-only fabrics are as delicate as their labels suggest. We suggest you use about

ten ounces of water with two table-spoons of salt, less salt for better fabrics.

On cotton, a lot of hot water poured from a foot away onto a wine stain primed with salt works pretty well, even when this is done the next day.

If you spill wine onto a carpet or rug you can use salt and water. Cool water is safer, so if you have an expensive carpet or rug, restrict these efforts to cool water and conservative amounts of salt.

We have also heard that white wine poured onto a red-wine stain can be effective in neutralizing the staining elements in red wine. We make no promises with this solution.

Bottle Shapes

The French didn't invent wine, nor did they perfect it. They did, however, define the standards to which all other wines are held. As such, French wines have served as role models for California wines. It is a tribute to the primacy of France that her regional bottle shapes are imitated in California in order to indicate the intended style of the wine.

In the Bordeaux region of France, Merlot and Cabernet Sauvignon are the dominant red varieties, whereas Sauvignon Blanc and Semillon are used to make white wine. Thus in California, the easily recognizable Bordeaux bottle shape, with its full, rounded shoulders, is normally used for these varietals. A variation of this classic shape is tapered to a narrower width at the base,

making the bottle both prettier to look at and more difficult to stack.

The wine producers in the Burgundy region use the more common, slope-shouldered shape for both reds and whites. Accordingly, the California versions of the Burgundian varieties—Chardonnay, Pinot Noir, and Gamay—are offered in Burgundy bottles. A similarly shaped bottle is used in the Loire region of France where, among other wines, Pouilly Fumé is produced. Pouilly Fumé is a dry, "smoky" rendition of Sauvignon Blanc and is the stylistic prototype for California Fumé Blanc. The California producers, led by Robert Mondavi, distinguish their Fumé Blanc from their herbaceous, Bordeaux-like Sauvignon Blanc by bottling the former in a Loire

SHERRY RED & WHITE BURGUNDY CLARET GERMAN WINE CHAMPAGNE LOIRE VALLEY CHIANTI

(Burgundy) bottle and the latter in a Bordeaux bottle.

Another variation of the versatile Burgundy bottle is used in the Rhône valley, for both red and white wines. Though not widely produced in California, the white varieties of the Rhône region—Viognier, Marsanne, and Rousanne—are generally packaged in Rhône (Burgundy) bottles.

California does produce a fair amount of varietal Syrah, the grape of the great northern Rhône reds, Côte Rôtie, and Hermitage. Here too the bottle shape follows suit. Before Syrah there was a plethora of similarly packaged Petite Sirah originating in California. This varietal was originally mistaken for the noble Syrah, but it has now been tentatively identified as the Duriff grape, one of the thirteen grape varietals allowed in Châteauneuf-du-Pape. Despite its popularity, Châteauneuf-du-Pape has no equivalent in California. Apparently there is no market for a powerful blend of Syrah, Grenache, Duriff, and the rest. The Châteauneuf bottle, though, is worth mentioning here—it is a Burgundy shape impressively embossed with a "badge" just above the label. This package alone might coax a California vintner to offer a version of it.

The wines of Alsace, nearly all white, are sold in tall, slender bottles nearly identical to those in neighboring Germany. Thus, the varieties of Alsace, primarily Riesling and Gewürztraminer, are sold in similar bottles by California producers. Germany has a long tradition of wine making. Her two major fine-wine-producing areas lie along the rivers Rhine and Mosel. In order to better distin-

guish between these approximately equal rivals, the Mosel-Saar-Ruwer bottles are bright green, whereas the Rhine bottles are brown. These two regions agree on the nobility of the Riesling grape, which is used for the finest wines of each. California vintners usually use brown bottles for their Rieslings, perhaps to indicate the Rhine-like richness achieved in the California sun.

The bottles used for Champagne require an important structural consideration: They must be able to withstand six atmospheres of pressure. Thick and sturdy glass is therefore required, as is a protruding "lip" around which the wire basket may be secured. Other than those differences, the classic Champagne bottle is just another variation of the ubiquitous Burgundy shape. However, the bottles used for tête de cuvée, the super-premium Champagnes, are usually different. The relatively squat bottle used for Dom Pérignon and others in the highest price range has historical roots in the Champagne region. It is likely that the long, thin neck associated with this shape made easier the hand-disgorging (removal) of the dead yeast, a labor-intensive process used today only for these fabulously expensive premium Champagnes (for lesser Champagnes it is usually done by machine). The tête de cuvée Champagne bottle type is increasingly used for cheap sparkling wine. The premium California sparkling-wine makers, many of which are sister companies to Champagne firms, tend to use the standard Champagne bottle.

Although California producers consistently use French regional bottle shapes, Italy and Spain usually use the two basic shapes, those of Bordeaux and Burgundy, with no apparent pattern. Whereas the wines of Rioja are usually offered in a Bordeaux bottle, perhaps as a nod to their oenological mentors, they are sold in the Burgundy shape as well. Chianti, the flagship wine of Tuscany, has a split personality: The better wines are sold in Bordeaux bottles, while many of the cheap versions come to market in a straw-clad centerpiece of a bottle. The latter is becoming harder to find as the Tuscan standards of quality steadily improve. Barolo and Barbaresco, the twin pillars of Piedmont, are sold in either the Bordeaux or Burgundy shapes, with no apparent pattern.

Just as there are "wines from the edge," there are bottle shapes so far out of the mainstream that they merit mention. The Italian wine Pescovino is sold in a fish-shaped bottle—the better, perhaps, to suggest an appropriate food pairing. Portuguese rosé was popular early in the wine boom, and Mateus and Lancers,

the two most popular, come to our shores in bottles far more distinctive than the wines within.

As a result of intense marketing efforts, some new trends have emerged. Brilliant blue bottles, usually used for Riesling or other light wines, certainly stand out in the store. Kendall-Jackson uses a slope-necked, "sexier" bottle that is a variant of the Burgundy shape. Unlike the Burgundy shape, however, little thought seems to have been given to the center of gravity of this new shape, and cellarmasters and retailers find it infuriatingly unstackable in standard bins. The carnage of accidentally broken bottles will undoubtedly grow as this shape proliferates. Sillier yet is the "collar" now appearing at the top of many bottles. This protrusion is there supposedly to prevent drips. The bottles still drip, however, and they are more difficult to open with standard corkscrews.

AHHHH!

C H A P T E R   1 0

U.S. WINE VACATIONS

BOTTLED BY ADAMS MEDIA

NET CONTENTS: THIRTY-THREE PAGES

PRODUCT OF USA

Wineries and vineyards make great vacation destinations, or even day trips to incorporate into a vacation. Wineries are usually located in and around rural, farming areas. The fields offer breathtaking vistas and a chance to escape from the city, either by bike, by car, or on foot. Some wineries have gotten so marketing savvy that they have opened award-winning restaurants right on the premises.

A typical winery might offer a tour of the facilities that covers the wine-making process particular to that location. Tours usually run about an hour in length and are often followed by wine tastings. Emphasis here is on the word *tasting*: Wineries are not in the business of giving away the profits. You'll probably receive a quarter of a glass or less of any wine for tasting, athough a typical tasting might cover two to six varieties, depending on what is being sold. However, if you are planning to visit several wineries in an area, make sure to appoint a designated driver, and give yourself some resting time between wineries to truly enjoy the day.

These tastings can be complimentary, but not always. Often, there is a nominal fee for each glass poured. The wineries encourage you to buy bottles of the wine you have tasted, but you shouldn't feel pressured to buy. Wineries realize that you are spreading word of their wine just by telling your friends you went to the winery. However, many wineries generate the majority of their sales from these visits, so if you sample something you truly love—buy it.

You might not be able to find it back home in your local liquor store.

The most obvious wine-lovers' destination in the U.S. is California—Napa Valley, Sonoma, or the South Central Coast all offer spectacular scenery and the chance to taste some truly wonderful wines. However, as wineries are cropping up all over the country, we've also included some alternative destinations you might want to consider.

Reliable Producers of Wines Costing $7–$10

1. C. K. Mondavi, California, USA . . . . Reds and Whites
2. Monterey Vineyard, California, USA. . . . . Reds and Whites
3. Columbia Crest, Washington, USA. . . . . Reds and Whites
4. Hardy's, Australia . . . . Reds and Whites
5. Rosemount, Australia. . . . . Reds and Whites
6. Springbok, South Africa . . . . Reds and Whites
7. Concha y Toro, Chile . . . . Reds and Whites
8. Walnut Crest, Chile. . . . . Reds and Whites
9. Georges Duboeuf, France . . . . Reds and Whites
10. Rene Barbier, Spain. . . . . Reds and Whites
11. Monticello, Spain . . . . Reds
12. Mezza Corona, Italy. . . . . Reds and Whites

Note: Although wines change year to year, especially inexpensive ones, the big producers strive for consistency. This list won't fail you at a wine shop or at a restaurant. The authors are, of course, biased toward producers whose wines we have had and liked, and don't claim to have collectively tried more than a thousand wines in any given year.

Finger Lakes Wine Tour

There are five Finger Lakes in western New York State and surrounding three of them is the home of a burgeoning wine industry. This area has been producing wines and wine grapes for over one hundred years. Currently, there are fifty-two wineries in the region, and each one is unique and special in its own way.

The best part about visiting the wineries surrounding the Finger Lakes is the breathtaking scenery and general lack of commercialism of the area. Unlike Napa Valley or Sonoma, New York State wineries are decidedly less popular and, so, less frequently visited. Therefore, you'll never find yourself waiting in traffic or waiting at a tasting. You might be pressed to buy a glass or two at the wineries to cover the cost of the tasting, but the overall experience is surely worth the price of admission.

It is fairly easy to get to and around the Finger Lakes. You can fly into Rochester, New York, which is a forty-five-minute drive from wine country. If you are traveling by car from southern points, choose communities like Ithaca or Watkins Glen as a home base. Both locations offer a wide variety of lodgings, and a surprisingly diverse spectrum of restaurants. Consider staying in a cozy bed and breakfast during your trip (Call the Finger Lakes B&B Association for reservations: 1-800-695-5590); there are several hotel/motel travel accommodations as well. Call ahead for reservations in the popular summer and fall months. You'll also be able to get a calendar of events specific to the wineries and vineyards.

While you cannot possibly visit all of these wineries in a week, we've listed them in a variety of tours. Each involves traveling around or near one of the lakes. The wineries are listed in an order in which you can best visit them.

THE WINERIES

Cayuga Lake, New York
Swedish Hill Vineyard and Winery
4565 Route 414
Romulus 14541
(315) 549-8326
Open daily; call for tour hours.

Lakeshore Winery
5132 Route 89
Romulus 14541
(315) 549-7075
Open daily 10:30–5:00 from April to November. Call for tour hours.

Knapp Vineyards Winery & Restaurant
2770 County Road 128
Romulus 14541
(607) 869-9271
Open Monday to Saturday, 10 a.m. to 5:30 p.m.; Sunday, 12 to 5 p.m. Tours daily at 1:00 p.m.

Cayuga Ridge Estate Winery
6800 Route 89, at Elm Beach
Ovid 14521
(607) 869-5158.
*Open from May until November Noon
to 5:00 p.m.. Tours daily at 2:30 p.m..*

Hosmer Winery
6999 Route 89
Ovid 14521
(607) 869-3393
*Open daily from April to December.
Call for tour hours.*

Lucas Vineyards
3862 County Road 150
Interlaken 14847
(607) 532-4825
*Open Monday to Saturday, 10:30 a.m.
to 5:30 p.m.; Sunday, 12 to 5:30 p.m.*

Americana Vineyards Winery
4367 East Covert Road
Interlaken 14847
(607) 387-6801
*Open Daily May through October. Call
for tour hours.*

Six Mile Creek Vineyard
1553 Slaterville Road (Route 79 east)
Ithaca 14850
(607) 272-WINE
Open daily from Noon to 5:30 p.m.

King Ferry Winery-Treleaven
658 Lake Road
King Ferry 13081
(315) 364-5100
*Open Monday to Saturday, 10 a.m. to
5 p.m.; Sunday, 12 to 5 p.m.*

Keuka Lake, New York
Hunt Country Vineyards
4201 Italy Hill Road
Branchport 14418
(315) 595-2812
*Open daily, tours and tastings. Call for
tour hours.*

**Dr. Konstantin Frank's Vinifera
Wine Cellars**
9749 Middle Road
Hammondsport 14840
(607) 868-4884
*Open Monday to Saturday, 9 a.m. to
5 p.m.; Sunday, 12 to 5 p.m.*

Heron Hill Vineyards
9249 County Route 76
Hammondsport 14840
(607) 868-4241
*Open daily, tours and tastings. Call for
tour hours.*

Bully Hill Vineyards
8843 Greyton H. Taylor Memorial Drive
Hammondsport 14840
(607) 868-3610
*Monday through
Saturday 9 to 5,
Sundays 12 to 5 p.m.*

**Olde Germania
Wine Cellars**
8299 Pleasant Valley
Road
Hammondsport 14840
(607) 569-2218
*Open April through December Monday
through Saturday 10 to 5; Sundays
12 to 5.*

McGregor Vineyard Winery
5503 Dutch Street
Dundee 14837
(607) 292-6929
Open daily, call for tour hours.

Keuka Overlook Wine Cellars
5777 Old Bath/Gardner Road
Dundee 14837
(607) 292-6877
Open June through November, Friday to Sunday, 11 to 5.

Barrington Cellars Buzzard Crest Vineyards
2690 Gray Road
Penn Yan 14527
(315) 536-9686
Open May through October, Friday through Mondays 11 to 5.

Keuka Spring Vineyards
273 East Lake Road (Route 54)
Penn Yan 14527
(315) 536-3147
Hours change seasonally, call ahead for availability.

Seneca Lake, New York
Fox Run Vineyards
P.O. Box 670, Route 14
Penn Yan 14527
(315) 536-4616
Open Monday to Saturday, 10 a.m. to 6 p.m.; Sunday, 12 to 6 p.m.

Anthony Road Wine Co.
1225 Anthony Road
Penn Yan 14527
(315) 536-2182
Open Monday to Saturday, 10 a.m. to 5 p.m.; Sunday, 12 to 5 p.m.

Prejean Winery
2634 Route 14
Penn Yan 14527
(315) 536-7524
Open Monday to Saturday, 10 a.m. to 5 p.m.; Sunday, 12 to 5 p.m.

Earle Estates Meadery
3586 State Route 14
Himrod 14842
(607) 243-9011
Open daily except for Tuesdays and Wednesdays. Call for tour hours.

Four Chimneys Farm Winery
211 Hall Road
Himrod 14842
(607) 243-7502
Open daily. Call for tour hours.

Hermann J. Wiemer Vineyard
P.O. Box 38, Route 14
Dundee 14837
(607) 243-7971
Open Monday to Saturday, 10 a.m. to 5 p.m.; Sunday, 11 a.m. to 5 p.m.

Squaw Point Winery
Poplar-On-Seneca
Dundee 14837
(607) 243-8602

*Open April thourgh December, Monday
through Saturday 10 to 5, Sundays
12 to 5 p.m.*

Glenora Wine Cellars
5435 Route 14
Dundee 14837
(607) 243-5511
*Open daily, 10 a.m. to 6 p.m.,
September and October. (Hours change
seasonally; please call the winery for
hours during other months.)*

Fulkerson's Winery
5576 Route 14
Dundee 14837
(607) 243-7883
*Open year-round. Call ahead for tour
hours.*

Arcadian Estate Vineyards
4184 Route 14
Rock Stream 14878
(607) 535-2068
*Open year-round. Call ahead for tour
hours.*

Lakewood Vineyards
4024 State Route 14
Watkins Glen 14891
(607) 535-9252
*Open Monday to Saturday, 10 a.m. to
5:30 p.m.; Sunday, 12 to 6 p.m.*

Castel Grisch Estate Winery
3380 County Route 28
Watkins Glen 14891
(607) 535-9614
Open daily, 10 to 6 p.m.

Leidenfrost Vineyards
Route 414
Hector 14841
(607) 546-6612
Open daily. Call ahead for tour hours.

Hazlitt 1852 Vineyards
5712 Route 414
Hector 14841
(607) 546-WINE
Open daily. Call ahead for tour hours.

Standing Stone Vineyards
9934 Route 414
Valois 14888
(607) 582-6051
*Open Saturday, 10 a.m. to 6 p.m.;
Sunday, 12 to 5 p.m.*

Poplar Ridge Vineyards
9782 Route 414
Valois 14888
(607) 582-6421
Open daily. Call ahead for tour hours.

Silver Thread Vineyard
1401 Caywood Road
Caywood 14891
(607) 387-9282
*Open weekends and holidays, 12 to
5 p.m., and by appointment.*

Wagner Vineyards
9322 Route 414
Lodi 14860
(607) 582-6450
Open daily, 10 a.m. to 5 p.m.

Lamoreaux Landing Wine Cellars
9224 Route 414
Lodi 14860
(607) 582-6011
*Open Monday to Saturday, 10 a.m. to
5 p.m.; Sunday, 12 to 5 p.m.*

New Land Vineyard
577 Lerch Road
Geneva 14456
(315) 585-9844 or 585-4432
*Open Monday to Thursday, 12 to 5
p.m.; Friday to Sunday, 11 a.m. to 6
p.m. (By appointment only from January
to March).*

Reliable Producers of Wines Costing $11–$15

1. Kendall-Jackson, California, USA. . . . . Reds and Whites
2. Napa Ridge, California, USA . . . . Reds and Whites
3. Robert Mondavi, California, USA. . . . . Reds and Whites
4. Chateau St. Michelle, Washington, USA . . . . Reds and Whites
5. Cousino-Macul, Chile . . . . Reds and Whites
6. Rosemount, Australia . . . . Reds and Whites
7. Chateau Reynella, Australia . . . . Reds and Whites
8. Guigal, France . . . . Reds
9. Louis Latour, France . . . . Reds and Whites
10. Trimbach, France . . . . Whites
11. Ruffino, Italy . . . . Reds
12. Rudolph Muller, Germany . . . . Whites

Note: These producers are consistently good producers in this price range; those that
aren't large producers have an excellent reputation and their wines are sought out by
restaurants and wine shops. Wines that cost more than $15 might better be purchased on
a wine-by-wine basis rather than relying on a producer's reputation. This means you buy
it because you've either asked someone you trust for a recommendation, you've had such
a wine yourself, or you simply know wine.

Northern California Wine Tour

It's rare when a vacation spot combines all the right aspects without over-promising: peaceful serenity and world-class hospitality, dining, and of course, perfect wine. Northern California fills the order on every front. The weather on the "North Coast"—the area of the combined wine regions north of San Francisco—is gorgeous, with dry summertime temperatures ranging between 80° and 100° F. Valley-floor vineyards are matched with pine-covered mountains. Needless to say, the scenery is truly special.

Napa Valley, America's most famous wine region, stretches into a 30-mile-long valley. From San Francisco, Napa wine country is a quick hour's drive north. There are more than 200 wineries crammed into this comparatively small space; some date back more than 100 years; others are small, brand-new "boutique" producers.

Sonoma County is west of Napa Valley, and its wine growing area covers much more ground (1,600 square miles). More informal and down-home than Napa, the wines of this area continue to gain respect. In fact, the Sonoma area is actually a series of different regions, each producing different styles of wine.

Farthest north is Mendocino County, known to be rural, friendly, and unpretentious. Mendocino now has more than thirty wineries. Its producers include wineries specializing in Chardonnays, Cabernets, Zinfandels, and Pinot Noirs: In short, all the wines of Napa and Sonoma, without the crowds.

It would be impossible to feel like you've seen it all, even in a week. So keep the North Coast in mind for a series of weekend get-aways, or even day trips, when visiting San Francisco. Overnight visitors take note: These regions are no well-kept secret, and summer months can be extremely over-crowded. To assure the resort or hotel you want, make your reservations at least a month ahead of time.

THE WINERIES

The following wineries have tours and visitors' hours. Call ahead to find out the specific hours the wineries you want to visit are open to the public.

Napa Valley, California
Acacia
Las Amigas Road
Napa
(707) 226-9991

Aetna Springs Cellars
Pope Valley Road
Pope Valley
(707) 965-2675

Alatera Vineyards
Hoffman Lane
Yountville
(707) 944-2620

Altamura Winery
Wooden Valley Road
Napa
(707) 253-2000

Anderson Vineyard
Yountville Crossroad
Yountville
(707) 944-8642

Anderson's Conn Valley Vineyards
Rossi Road
Saint Helena
(707) 963-8600

Araujo Estate Wines/Eisele Vineyrad
Picket Road
Calistoga
(707) 942-6061

Arroyo Winery
Greenwood Avenue
Calistoga
(707) 942-6995

Atlas Peak Vineyards
Soda Canyon Road
Napa
(707) 252-7971

Azalea Springs
Azalea Springs Way
Calistoga
(707) 942-4811

Barnett Vineyards
Spring Mountain Road
St. Helena
(707) 963-0109

Bayview Cellars
Main Street
Napa
(707) 226-2044

Beaucanon
S. St. Helena Highway
St. Helena
(707) 967-3520

Beaulieu Vineyard
St. Helena Highway
Rutherford
(707) 967-5200

Benessere Vineyards
Big Tree Road
St. Helena
(707) 963-5853

Beringer Vineyards
Main Street
St. Helena
(707) 963-4812

Bouchaine Vineyards
Buchli Station Road
Napa
(707) 252-9065

Buehler Vineyards
Greenfield Road
St. Helena
(707) 963-2155

Burgess Cellars
Deer Park Road
St. Helena
(707) 963-4766

Cafaro Cellars
Dean York Lane
St. Helena
(707) 963- 7181

Cain Vineyard & Winery
Langtry Road
St. Helena
(707) 963-1616

Cakebread Cellars
St Helena Highway
Rutherford
(707) 963-5221

Calafia Cellars
Fulton Lane
St. Helena
(707) 963-5221

Carneros Alambic Distillery
Cuttings Wharf Road
Napa
(707) 253-9055

Carneros Creek Winery
Dealy Lane
Napa
(707) 253-9463

Casa Nuestra Winery
Silverado Trail N.
St. Helena
(707) 963-5783

Caymus Vineyards
Conn Creek Road
St. Helena
(707) 967-3010

Chappellet Vineyard
Sage Canyon Road
St. Helena
(707) 963-7136

Charles Krug Winery
St. Helena Highway N
St. Helena
(707) 963-2761

Chateau Boswell
Silverado Trail
St. Helena
(707) 963-5472

Chateau Montelena Winery
Tubbs Lane
Calistoga
(70.) 942-5105

Chateau Potelle
Mount Veeder Road
Napa
(707) 255-9440

Chateau Woltner
Silverado Trail
St. Helena
(707) 963-1744

Chiles Valley Vineyard
Lower Chiles Valley Road
St. Helena
(707) 963-7294

Chimney Rock Winery
Silverado Trail
Napa
(707) 257-2641

Clos du Val Wine Co., Ltd.
Silverado Trail
Napa
(707) 259-2220

Clos Pegase Winery
Dunaweal Lane
Calistoga
(707) 942-4981

Codorniu Napa
Henry Road
Napa
(707) 224-1668

Colgin-Schrader Cellars
St. Helena Highway
Oakville
(707) 524-4445

Conn Creek Winery
Silverado Trail
St. Helena
(707) 963-5133

Cosentino Winery
St. Helena Highway
Yountville
(707) 944-1220

Costello Vineyards Winery
Orchard Avenue
Napa
(707) 252-8483

Cuvaison Winery
Silverado Trail
Calistoga
(707) 942-6266

Dalla Valle Vineyards
Silverado Trail
Yountville
(707) 944-2676

David Arthur Vineyards
Sage Canyon Road
St. Helena
(707) 963-5190

Diamond Creek Vineyards
Diamond Mountain Road
Calistoga
(707) 942-6926

Diamond Mountain Vineyard
Diamond Mountain Road
Calistoga
(707) 942-0707

Domain Hill & Mayes
Lincoln Avenue
Napa
(707) 224-6565

Domaine Carneros by Taittinger
Duhig Road
Napa
(707) 257-0101

Domaine Chandon
California Drive
Yountville
(707) 944-2280

Domaine Charbay Winery & Distillery
Spring Mountain Road
St. Helena
(7070 963-9327

Domaine Montreax
Big Ranch Road
Napa
(707) 252-9380

Domaine Napa Winery
Mee Lane
St. Helena
(707) 963-1666

Dominus Estate
Napanook Road
Yountville
(707) 944-8954

Duckhorn Vineyards
Silverado Trail N
St. Helena
(707) 963-7108

Dunn Vineyards
White Cottage Road N
Angwin
(707) 965-3642

Dutch Henry Winery
Silverado Trail
Calistoga
(707) 942-5771

Edgewood Estates
St. Helena Highway
St. Helena
(707) 963-2335

Ehlers Grove Winery
Ehlers Lane
St. Helena
(707) 963-3200

Eisele V & L Family Estate
Lower Chiles Valley Road
St. Helena
(707) 965-2260

El Molino Winery
P.O. Box 306
St. Helena
(707) 963-3632

Elkhorn Peak Cellars
Polson Road
Napa
(707) 255-0504

Etude Wines
Big Ranch Road
Napa
(7070 257-5300

Far Niente Winery
P.O. Box 327
Oakville
(707) 944-2861

Flora Springs Wine Co.
W. Zinfandel Lane
St. Helena
(707) 963-5711

Folie a Deux
N. St. Helena Highway
St. Helena
(707) 963-1160

Forest Hill Vineyard
P.O. Box 96
St. Helena
(707) 963-7229

Franciscan Oakville Estate
Galleron Road
Rutherford
(707) 963-7111

Freemark Abbey Winery
N. St. Helena Highway
St. Helena
(707) 963-9694

Frisinger Cellars
Dry Creek Road
Napa
(707) 255-3749

Frog's Leap Winery
Conn Creek Road
Rutherford
(707) 963-4704

Girard Winery
Silverado Trail
Oakville
(707) 944-8577

Goosecross Cellars
State Lane
Yountville
(707) 944-1986

Grace Family Vineyards
Rockland Drive
St. Helena
(707) 963-0808

Graeser Winery
Petrified Forest Road
Calistoga
(707) 942-4437

Grandview Cellars
Main Street
St. Helena
(888) 472-2356

Green & Red Vineyard
Chiles Pope Valley Road
St. Helena
(707) 965-2346

Grgich Hills Cellars
St. Helena Highway
Rutherford
(707) 963-2784

Groth Vineyards & Winery
Oakville Cross Road
Oakville
(707) 944-0290

Hakusan Sake Gardens
Executive Way
Napa
(707) 258-6160

Hanson-Hsieh Vineyard
Dry Creek Road
Napa
(707) 257-2632

Harrison Vineyards
Sage Canyon Road
St. Helena
(707) 963-8271

Hartwell Vineyards
Silverado Trail
Napa
(707) 255-4269

Havens Wine Cellars
2055 Hoffman Lane
Napa
(707) 945-0921

Heitz Wine Cellars
Taplin Road
St. Helena
(707) 963-3542

Honig Cellars
Rutherford Road
Rutherford
(707) 963-5618

Jarvis Vineyards
Monticello Road
Napa
(707) 255-5280

Joseph Phelps Vineyards
Taplin Road
St. Helena
(707) 963-2745

Karl Lawrence Cellars
Monticello Road
Napa
(707) 255-2843

Kate's Vineyard
Big Ranch Road
Napa
(707) 255-2644

Lakespring Winery
Hoffman Lane
Yountville
(707) 944-2475

Livingston Wines
Cabernet Lane
St. Helena
(707) 963-2120

Los Hermanos Vineyards
Pratt Avenue
St. Helena
(707) 963-7115

Louis Corthay Winery
Galleron Road
St. Helena
(707) 963-2384

Louis M. Martini Winery
St. Helena Highway
St. Helena
(707) 963-2736

Markham Vineyards
N. St. Helena Highway
St. Helena
(707) 963-5292

Mayacamus Vineyards
Lokoya Road
Napa
(707) 224-4030

Merryvale Napa Valley
Main Street
Helena
(707) 963-7777

Milat Vineyards
S. St. Helena Highway
St. Helena
(707) 963-0758

Mont St. John Cellars
Old Sonoma Road
Napa
(707) 255-8864

Monticello Vineyards
Big Ranch Road
Napa
(707) 253-2802

Montreaux
Big Ranch Road
Napa
(707) 252-9380

Moss Creek Winery
Steele Canyon Road
Napa
(707) 252-1295

Mt. Veeder Winery & Vineyards
Mt. Veeder Road
Napa
(707) 224-4039

Mumm Napa Valley
Silverado Trail
Napa
(800) 95VINTAGE

Napa Cellars
St. Helena Highway
Yountville
(707) 944-2565

Napa Valley Port Cellars
California Boulevard
Napa
(707) 257-7777

Newlan Vineyards & Winery
Solano Avenue
Napa
(707) 257-2399

Newton Vineyard
Madrona Avenue
St. Helena
(707) 963-9000

Nichelini Winery
Sage Canyon Road
St. Helena
(707) 963-0717

One Vineyard
Saint Helena
(707) 963-1123

Opus One Winery
Saint Helena Highway
Oakville
(707) 944-9442

Paradigm Winery
Dwyer Road
Oakville
(707) 944-1683

Peju Province
St. Helena Highway
Rutherford
(707) 963-3600

Philip Togni Vineyard
Spring Mountain Road
St. Helena
(707) 963-3731

Pine Ridge Winery
Silverado Trail
Napa
(707) 252-9777

Plam Vineyards
Washington Street
Yountville
(707) 944-1102

Pope Valley Cellars
Pope Valley Road
Pope Valley
(707) 965-1438

Prager Winery & Port Works
Lewelling Lane
St. Helena
(707) 963-7678

Pride Mountain Vineyards
Spring Mountain Road
St. Helena
(707) 963-4949

Quail Ridge Cellars & Vineyards
St. Helena Highway
Rutherford
(707) 257-1712

Raymond Vineyard & Cellar
Zinfandel Lane
St. Helena
(707) 963-3141

Ritchie Creek Vineyard
Spring Mountain Road
St. Helena
(707) 963-4661

Robert Keenan Winery
Spring Mountain Road
St. Helena
(707) 963-9177

Robert Mondavi Winery
St. Helena Highway
Oakville
(707) 226-1335

Robert Pecota Winery
P.O. Box 303
Calistoga
(707) 942-6625

Robert Pepi Winery
St. Helena Highway
Yountville
(707) 944-2807

Robert Sinskey Vineyards
Silverado Trail
Yountville
(707) 944-9090

Rombauer Vineyards
Silverado Trail
St. Helena
(707) 967-5120

Round Hill Vineyards
Silverado Trail
St. Helena
(707) 963-9503

Rustridge Winery
Lower Chiles Valley Road
St. Helena
(707) 965-2871

Rutherford Hill Winery
Rutherford Hill Road
Rutherford
(707) 963-7194

Saintsbury
Los Carneros Avenue
Napa
(707) 252-0592

Sattui Winery
St. Helena Highway
St. Helena
(707) 963-7774

Schramsberg Vineyards
Schramsberg Road
Calistoga
(707) 942-4558

Sequoia Grove Vineyards
S. St. Helena Highway
Rutherford
(707) 944-2945

Shafer Vineyards
Silverado Trail
Napa
(707) 944-2877

Signorello Vineyards
Silverado Trail
Napa
(707) 255-5990

Silver Oak Cellars
Oakville Cross Road
Oakville
(707) 944-8808

Silverado Hill Cellars
Silverado Trail
Napa
(707) 253-9306

Silverado Vineyards
Silverado Trail
Napa
(707) 257-1770

Smith-Madrone Vineyards
Spring Mountain Road
St. Helena
(707) 963-2283

Spottswoode Winery
Madrona Avenue
St. Helena
(707) 963-0134

Spring Mountain Vineyard
Spring Mountain Road
St. Helena
(707) 967-4188

St. Andrews Winery
Silverado Trail
Napa
(707) 259-2200

St. Clement Vineyards
St. Helena Highway
St. Helena
(707) 963-7221

**St. Supéry Wine Discovery Center
& Winery**
St. Helena Highway
Rutherford
(707) 963-4507

Staglin Family Vineyard
P.O. Box 680
Rutherford
(707) 963-1749

Stag's Leap Wine Cellars
Silverado Trail
Napa
(707) 944-2020

Stag's Leap Winery
Silverado Trail
Napa
(707) 944-1303

Star Hill Winery
Shadybrook Lane
Napa
(707) 255-1957

Sterling Vineyards
Dunaweal Lane
Calistoga
(800) 95VINTAGE

Stonegate Winery
Dunaweal Lane
Calistoga
(707) 942-6500

Stony Hill Vineyard
N. St. Helena Highway
Napa
(707) 963-2636

Storybook Mountain Winery
Highway 128
Calistoga
(707) 942-5310

Strack Vineyard
St. Helena Highway
Napa
(707) 224-5100

Stratford Winery
Railroad Avenue
St. Helena
(707) 963-3200

Sutter Home Winery
St. Helena Highway
St. Helena
(707) 963-3104

Swanson Winery
Manley Lane
Rutherford
(707) 944-1642

The Hess Collection
Redwood Road
Napa
(707) 255-1144

Tongi Philip Vineyard
Spring Mountain Road
St. Helena
(707) 963-3731

Traulsen Vineyards
Lake County Highway
Calistoga
(707) 942-0283

Trefethen Vineyards
Oak Knoll Avenue
Napa
(707) 255-7700

Truchard Vineyards
Old Sonoma Road
Napa
(707) 253-7153

Tudal Winery
Big Tree Road
St. Helena
(707) 963-3947

Tulocay Winery
Coombsville Road
Napa
(707) 255-4064

Turley Wine Cellars
St. Helena Highway
St. Helena
(707) 963-0940

Turnbull Wine Cellars
St. Helena Highway
Oakville
(800) 887-6285

Van der Heyden Vineyards & Winery
Silverado Trail
Napa
(707) 257-0130 or (800) 948-WINE(9463)

Venge Vineyards
Money Road
Oakville
(707) 944-1305

Viader Vineyards
Deer Park Road
Deer Park
(707) 963-3816

Vichon Winery
Oakville Grade
Oakville
(707) 944-2811

Vigil Vineyard
B Street, Suite 219 & map 221
Santa Rosa
(707) 576-8280

Villa Helena Winery
Inglewood Avenue
St. Helena
(707) 963-4334

Vine Cliff Winery
Silverado Trail
Yountville
(707) 944-1364

Volker Eisele Family Estate
Lower Chiles Valley Road
St. Helena
(707) 965-2260

von Strasser Winery
Diamond Mountain Road
Calistoga
(707) 942-0930

Wermuth Winery
Silverado Trail
Calistoga
(707) 942-5924

Whitehall Lane Winery
S. St. Helena Highway
St. Helena
(707) 963-9454

Whitford Cellars
East 3rd Avenue
Napa
(707) 257-7065

William Hill Winery
Atlas Peak Road
Napa
(707) 224-4477

Woltner Estates Winery
White Cottage Road South
Angwin
(707) 965-2445

Yverdon Vineyards
Spring Mountain Road
St. Helena
(707) 963-4270

ZD Wines
Silverado Trail
Napa
(707) 963-5188

Sonoma County, California
Adler Fels
5325 Corrick Lane
(707) 539-3123

Alderbrook Winery
2306 Magnolia Drive
Healdsburg
(707) 433-9154

Alexander Johnson's Valley Wines
8333 Highway 128
Healdsburg
(707) 433-2319

Alexander Valley Vineyards
5110 Highway 128
Geyserville
(707) 433-7209

Annapolis Winery
26055 Soda Springs Road
Annapolis
(707) 886-5460

Armida Winery
2201 Westside Road
Healdsburg
(707) 433-2222

Arrowood Vineyards & Winery
14347 Sonoma Highway
Glen Ellen
(707) 938-5170

B R CohnWinery
15140 Sonoma Highway
Glen Ellen
(707) 938-4064

Balverne Winery & Vineyard
10810 Hillview Road
Windsor
(707) 433-6913

Bandiera Winery
155 Cherry Creek Road
Cloverdale
(707) 894-4295

Bararen Pauli Winery
1613 Spring Hill Road
Petaluma
(707) 778-0721

Bartholomew Park Winery
1000 Vineyard Land
Sonoma
(707) 935-9511

Bellerose Vineyard
435 W Dry Creek Road
Healdsburg
(707) 433-1637

Belvedere Wine Company
1440 Grove
Healdsburg
(707) 433-8236

Benziger Family Winery
1883 London Ranch Road
Glen Ellen
(707) 935-3000

Buena Vista Winery
18000 Old Winery Road
Sonoma
(707) 938-1266

Canyon Road Cellars
19550 Geyserville Avenue
Geyserville
(707) 857-3417

Carmenet Vineyards
1700 Moon Mountain Drive
Sonoma
(707) 996-5870

Caswell Vineyards
13207 Dupont Road
Sebastopol
(707) 874-2517

Cecchetti Sebastiani Cellar
450 1st Street East
Sonoma
(707) 996-8463

Chalk Hill Winery
10300 Chalk Hill Road
Healdsburg
(707) 838-4306

Chandelle Of Sonoma
14301 Arnold Drive
Glen Ellen
(707) 938-5862

Chateau De Baun
5007 Fulton Road
(707) 571-7500

Chateau Diana Winery
6195 Dry Creek Road
Healdsburg
(707) 433-6992

Chateau St. Jean Winery
8555 Sonoma Highway
Kenwood
(707) 833-4134

Cherry Ridge Winery
10541 Cherry Ridge Road
Sebastopol
(707) 823-9463

Christopher Creek Winery
641 Limerick Lane
Healdsburg
(707) 433-2001

Cline Cellars
24737 Arnold Drive
Sonoma
(707) 935-4310

Clos Du Bois Wines
19410 Geyserville Avenue
Geyserville
(800) 222-3189

Custom Brands Of Sonoma
1440 Grove
Healdsburg
(707) 431-8003

Davis Bynum Winery
8075 Westside Road
Healdsburg
(707) 433-5852

de Lorimier Winery
2001 Highway 128
Geyserville
(707) 857-2000

Dehlinger Winery
6300 Guerneville Road
Sebastopol
(707) 823-2378

DeLoach Vineyards
1791 Olivet Road
(707) 526-9111

DeNatale Vineyards
11020 Eastside Road
Healdsburg
(707) 431-8460

Deux Amis Wines
602 Limerick Lane
Healdsburg
(707) 431-7945

Domaine St. George Winery & Vineyard
1141 Grant Avenue
Healdsburg
(707) 433-5508

Dry Creek Vineyard
3770 Lambert Bridge Road
Healdsburg
(707) 433-1000

Teldeschi Winery
3555 Dry Creek Road
Healdsburg
(707) 433-6626

Fallenleaf Vineyards
3370 White Alder
Sonoma
(707) 996-0308

Family Wine Group
331 Healdsburg Avenue
Healdsburg
(707) 431-7677

Ferrari-Carano Winery
8761 Dry Creek Road
Healdsburg
(707) 433-6700

Field Stone Winery & Vineyard
10075 Highway 128
Healdsburg
(707) 433-7266

Fountain Grove Vineyard
2191 Laguna Road
(707) 823-2404

Frei Bros.
3387 Dry Creek Road
Healdsburg
(707) 433-4849

G Parducci
777 Madrone Road
Glen Ellen
(707) 935-0731

Gauer Estate Vineyards
5496 Red Winery Road
Healdsburg
(707) 431-2382

Geyser Peak Winery
22281 Chianti Road
Geyserville
(707) 857-9463

Glen Ellen Winery
1403 Arnold Drive
Glen Ellen
(707) 939-6277

Gloria Ferrer Champagne Caves
23555 Highway 121
Sonoma
(707) 996-7256

Golden Creek Vineyard
4480 Wallace Road
(707) 538-2350

Gundlach-Bundschu Winery
3775 Thornsberry Road
Sonoma
(707) 938-5277

H Coturri & Sons Winery
6725 Enterprise Road
Glen Ellen
(707) 525-9126

Hacienda Wine Cellars
20580 8th Street East
Sonoma
(707) 938-3220

Hambrecht & Peterson Vineyards
1040 Lytton Springs Road
Healdsburg
(707) 431-7568

Hanna Winery
5353 Occidental Road
(707) 575-3330

Hanzell Vineyards
18596 Lomita Avenue
Sonoma
(707) 996-3860

Homewood Winery
23120 Burndale Road
Vineburg
(707) 996-6353

Hop Kiln Winery
6050 Westside Road
Healdsburg
(707) 433-6491

J Fritz Winery
24691 Dutcher Creek Road
Cloverdale
(707) 894-3389

J Pedroncelli Winery
1220 Canyon Road
Geyserville
(707) 857-3531

J Rochioli Vineyards & Winery
6192 Westside Road
Healdsburg
(707) 433-2305

J Stonestreet & Sons Winery
4611 Thomas Road
Healdsburg
(707) 433-9463

Joseph Swan Vineyards
2916 Laguna Road
Forestville
(707) 573-3747

Kendall Jackson Winery
421 Aviation Boulevard
(707) 544-4000

Kenwood Vineyard Winery
9592 Sonoma Highway
Kenwood
(707) 833-5891

Kistler Vineyards
4707 Vine Hill
Sebastopol CA
(707) 823-5603

L Foppiano Wine Co
12707 Old Redwood
Highway
Healdsburg
(707) 433-7272

Lake Sonoma Winery
9990 Dry Creek-Road
Geyserville
(707) 431-1550 or (800) 750-9463

Lambert Bridge Winery
4085 W. Dry Creek Road
Healdsburg
(707) 431-9600

Landmark Vineyards
101 Adobe Canyon Road
Kenwood
(707) 833-0053

Limerick Lane Vineyards
1023 Limerick Lane
Healdsburg
(707) 433-9211

Lytton Springs Winery
650 Lytton Springs Road
Healdsburg
(707) 433-7721

Maacama Creek
15001 Chalk Hill Road
Healdsburg
(707) 433-4774 or (800) 773-4774

MacRostie Winery
17246 Woodland Avenue
Sonoma
(707) 996-4480

Marimar Torres Estate
11400 Graton Road
Sebastapol CA 95472
(707) 823-4365

Martinelli Winery & Vineyards
3360 River Road
Windsor
(707) 525-0570

Matanzas Creek Winery
6097 Valley Road
Santa Rosa CA
(707) 571-0156

Mazzocco Vineyards
1400 Lytton Springs Road
Healdsburg
(707) 433-9035

Meeker Vintners, The
9711 W Dry Creek Road
Healdsburg
(707) 431-2148

Merry Vintners, The
3339 Hartman Road
(707) 526-4441

Michel-Schlumberger Fine Wine Estate
4155 Wine Creek Road
Healdsburg
(707) 433-7427

Mietz Cellars
602 Limerick Lane.
Healdsburg
(707) 431-7671

Mill Creek Vineyards & Winery
1401 Westside Road
Healdsburg
(707) 433-5098

Mueller Robt Cellars
120 Foss Creek Circle
Healdsburg
(707) 431-1353

Murphy-Goode Winery
4001 Highway 128
Geyserville
(707) 431-7644

Old Town Winery
99 6th
(707) 573-8027

One World Winery
2948 Piner Road
(707) 525-0390

Optima Wine Cellars
498 Moore Lane
Healdsburg
(707) 431-8222

Paradise Ridge Winery
4545 Thomas Lake Harris Drive
(707) 528-9463

Pastori Winery
23189 Geyserville Avenue
Cloverdale
(707) 857-3418

Pezzi-King Vineyards
3225 W Dry Creek Road
Healdsburg
(707) 433-8785

Piper Sonoma
11447 Old Redwood Highway
Healdsburg
(707) 433-8843

Pommeraie Winery
10541 Cherry Ridge Road
Sebastopol
(707) 823-9463

Porter Creek Vineyards
8735 Westside Road
Healdsburg
(707) 433-6321

Preston Vineyards & Winery
9206 W Dry Creek Road
Healdsburg
(707) 433-3372

Quivira Vineyards
4900 W Dry Creek Road
Healdsburg
(707) 431-8333

Rabbit Ridge Vineyards
3291 Westside Road
Healdsburg
(707) 431-7128

Rafanelli Winery
4685 W Dry Creek Road
Healdsburg
(707) 433-1385

Ravenswood Winery
18701 Gehricke Road
Sonoma
707-938-1960

Richards's Grove
3575 Slusser Road
(707) 578-9607

River Road Cellars
2040 Barlow Lane
Sebastopol
(707) 829-9214

Robert Stemmier Winery
3805 Lambert Bridge Road
Healdsburg
(707) 433-6334

Roche Winery
28700 Arnold Drive
Sonoma
(707) 935-7115

Rodney Strong Vineyards
11455 Old Redwood Highway
Healdsburg
(707) 431-1533

Russian River Vineyards at Topolos
5700 Gravenstein Highway North
Forestville
(707) 887-1575

Ryecroft Australian Winery
583 1st Street West
Sonoma
(707) 996-4584

Sausal Winery
7370 Highway 128
Healdsburg
(707) 433-2285

Schug Carneros Estate Winery
602 Bonneau Road
Sonoma
(707) 939-9363

Sea Ridge Winery
13404 Dupont Road
Occidental
(707) 874-1707

Sebastiani Vineyards
389 4th Street East
Sonoma
(707) 938-5532

Seghesio Winery
14730 Grove
Healdsburg
(707) 433-3579

Silver Oak Cellars
24625 Chianti Road
Geyserville
(707) 857-3562

Simi Vineyards
16275 Healdsburg Avenue
Healdsburg
(707) 433-6981

Smothers Winery
9575 Sonoma Highway
Kenwood
(707) 833-1010

Solitude Wines
3241 Oak Farm Lane
Santa Rosa 94501
(707) 838-9750

**Sonoma County Wine &
Visitors Center**
5000 Roberts Lake Road
Rohnert Park
(707) 586-3795

**Sonoma County Wineries
Association**
5000 Roberts Lake Road
Rohnert Park
(707) 586-3795

Sonoma Creek Winery
23355 Millerick Road
Sonoma
(707) 938-3031

Sonoma Valley Cellars
15655 Arnold Drive
Sonoma
(707) 996-3056

Sonoma-Cutrer Vineyards
4401 Slusser Road
Windsor
(707) 528-1181

Stanley Vineyards & Winery
208 Haydon
Healdsburg
(707) 431-1291

Taft Street Inc.
2030 Barlow Lane
Sebastopol
(707) 823-2049

Toad Hollow Vineyards
2257 Meyers Drive
(707) 525-9838

**Topolos At Russian River
Vineyards**
5700 Gravenstein Highway North
Forestville
(707) 887-1575

Trentadue Winery
19170 Geyserville Avenue
Geyserville
(707) 433-3104

Twisted Vines-Fine Wines
29 Petaluma Boulevard North
Petaluma
(707) 766-8162

Valley of the Moon Winery
777 Madrone Road
Glen Ellen
(707) 996-6941

Viader Vineyard & Winery
1120 Deer Park Road
Deer Park
(707) 963-3816

Viansa Winery
25200 Arnold Drive
Sonoma
(707) 935-4700

Vigil Vineyards
7304 Foothill Ranch Road
(707) 537-3700

Vina Vista Vineyard & Winery
24401 Redwood Highway North
Geyserville
(707) 857-3722

Vinewood Cellars
18700 Geyserville Avenue
Geyserville
(707) 433-4474

Wattle Creek Winery
25510 River Road
Cloverdale
(707) 894-2950

Weinstock Vineyards
308 Center
Healdsburg
(707) 433-3186

Wellington Vineyards
11600 Dunbar Road
Glen Ellen
(707) 939-0708

White Oak Vineyards
208 Haydon
Healdsburg
(707) 433-8429

William Selyem
6575 Westside Road
Healdsburg
(707) 433-6425

Windsor Vineyards
239A Center Street
Healdsburg
(707) 433-2822

Z Moore Winery
3364 River Road
(707) 544-3555

Mendocino County, California
Blanc Vineyards
10200 West Road
Redwood Valley 95470
(707) 485-7352

Brutacao Cellars
2300 Highway 175
Hopland 95449
(707) 744-1320

Channing Rudd Cellars
21960 St. Helena Creek Road
Middletown 95461
(707) 987-2209

Christine Woods
3155 Highway 128
Philo 95446
(707) 895-2115

Domain Karakesh
4001 Spring Mountain Road
St. Helena
(707) 963-9327

Domaine St. Gregory
4921 Eastside Road
Ukiah 95482

Fetzer Vineyards
13500 F. Highway 101
Hopland 95449
(707) 744-1737

Frey Vineyards
14000 Tomki Road
Redwood Valley 95470
(707) 485-5177

Greewood Ridge Vineyards
24555 Greenwood Road
Philo 95466
(707) 877-3262

Guenoc Winery
21000 Butts Road
Middletown 95461
(707) 987-2385

Handley Cellars
3151 Highway 128
Philo 95446
(707) 895-2190

Hidden Cellars
1500 Ruddick-Cunningham Road
Ukiah 95482
(707) 462-0301

Husch Vineyards
4400 Highway 128
Philo 95446
(707) 895-3216

Jepson Vineyards
10400 S. Highway 101
Ukiah 95482
(707) 486-8936

Kendall-Jackson
600 Matthews Road
Lakeport 95453
(707) 263-9333

Konocti Winery
Thomas Drive at Highway 29
Kelseyville 95451
(707) 279-8861

Konrad Estate
3620 Road B
Redwood Valley 95470
(707) 485-0323

Lazy Creek Vineyards
4610 Highway 128
Philo 95446
(707) 895-3623

McDowell Valley Vineyards
3811 Highway 175
Hopland 95449
(707) 744-1053

Mendocino Vineyards
2399 N. State Street
Ukiah 95482
(707) 462-2985

Milano Winery
14594 S. Highway 101
Hopland 95449
(707) 744-1396

Navarro Vineyards
5601 Highway 128
Philo 95446
(707) 895-3686

Obester Winery
9200 Highway 128
Philo 95446
(707) 895-3814

Parducci Wine Cellars
501 Parducci Road
Ukiah 95482
(707) 462-3828

Pepperwood Springs Winery
1200 Holmes Ranch Road
Philo 95466
(707) 895-2920

Roederer Estate
4501 Highway 128
Philo 95446
(707) 652-4900

Scharffenberger Cellars
8501 Highway 128
Philo 95446
(707) 895-2065

Steele Wines
4793 Cole Creek Road
Kelseyville 95451
(707) 279-0213

Tijsseling-Tyland
2150 McNab Ranch Road
Ukiah 95482
(707) 462-1810

Weibel Vineyards
7051 N. State Street
Redwood Valley 95470
(707) 485-0321

Whaler Vineyards
2600 Eastside Road
Ukiah 95482
(707) 462-6355

Wildhurst Winery
11171 Highway 29
Lower Lake
(707) 994-6525

Northern Michigan Wine Tour

As you might expect, Northern Michigan is not exactly a hotbed of American wine production. However, it is a remarkably pretty place to visit, and the wine grapes that have been cultivated here are worth the trip. If you find yourself in and around Traverse City for the Cherry Festival, or another summer event, take a tour through the following wineries. As much as we liked them, we would not recommend visiting in the winter!

THE WINERIES

The following wineries were unable to provide information concerning their tour and visitors, hours. Please call ahead to make sure the wineries you want to visit are open to the public when you want to visit them.

Boskydel Vineyard
2881 South Lake Leelanau Drive
Lake Leelanau 49653

Good Harbor Vineyards
Route 1, P.O. Box 888
Lake Leelanau 49653
(616) 256-7165

Mawby Vineyards
4519 South Elm Valley Road
Suttons Bay 49682
(616) 271-3522

Leelanau Wine Cellars
12693 E. Tatch Road
Omena 49674
(616) 386-5201

Chateau Chantal
15900 Rue de Vin
Traverse City 49684
(616) 223-4110

Some Other U.S. Wineries
Worth Investigating

Concert Vineyards, Lakeview, Arkansas

Colorado Cellars, Palisade, Colorado

Stonington Vineyards, Stonington, Connecticut

Chateau Elan, Braselton, Georgia

Tedeschi Vineyards, Kula, Hawaii

Galena Cellars Winery, Galena, Illinois

Oliver Winery, Bloomington, Indiana

Boordy Vineyard, Hydes, Maryland

Nashoba Valley Winery, Bolton, Massachusetts

Anderson Valley Vineyards, Albuquerque, New Mexico

Las Nutrias Vineyard & Winery, Corrales, New Mexico

Alexis Bailly, South Hastings, Minnesota

Mount Pleasant Valley, Augusta, Missouri

Stone Hill Winery, Herman, Missouri

Poor Richard's Winery, Frenchtown, New Jersey

Unionville Vineyards, Ringoes, New Jersey

Palmer Vineyards, Aquebogue, New York

Westbend Vineyards, Louisville, North Carolina

Chalet DeBonné, Geneva, Ohio

Markko Vineyards, West Conneaut, Ohio

Buckingham Valley Vineyards, Buckingham, Pennsylvania

Chadds Ford Winery, Chadds Ford, Pennsylvania

Sakonnet Vineyards, Compton, Rhode Island

Tennessee Valley Winery, East Loudon, Tennessee

Mountain Valley Vineyards, Pigeon Forge, Tennessee

Bell Mountain, Willow City, Texas

Llano Estacado Winery, Lubbock, Texas

Shenandoah Vineyards, Edinburg, Virginia

Linden Vineyards, Linden, Virginia

Sweedenburg Winery, Middleburg, Virginia

Cedar Creek, Winery Cedarburg, Wisconsin

Wollersheim, Sauk City, Wisconsin

Afterword

THE HANGOVER: TOO MUCH OF A GOOD THING

You're having dinner out and the waiter keeps refilling your wine glass. You're at a party and the host insists on refreshing your drink . . . again. Who's counting? Your stomach, your head, and those tiny red blood cells that rush alcohol to the rest of your body. They're ringing the hangover bell, but you aren't listening. Unfortunately, you hear it in the morning when it's clanging right between your eyes.

Too much alcohol causes a hangover, but no one knows exactly why. Everyone has their own personal barometer; the quantity that brings on the symptoms is personal (age, weight, and sex

count) and so are the circumstances. One prevailing theory is that dehydration is the culprit because, as the body processes liquor, it uses up a great deal of water. Another hypothesis describes a hangover as a minor withdrawal episode from an addictive substance. How minor are a great thirst, a nauseous stomach, a pounding head, and an all around feeling of anxiety? That may depend on whether you can wrap yourself around your favorite pillow and go back to sleep. A nap is as good a remedy as any.

If wakefulness is required, you will probably have to face the fact that there is no cure, only helpful possibilities. Drinking lots of water helps, and starting before bed is even better. A nonaspirin painkiller may be good for your head and kinder to your stomach than aspirin. Anyone that mentions pickles or bacon fat is talking about remedies that are peculiar to them, or just plain peculiar.

RESPONSIBLE DRINKING: MORE DOES NOT MAKE IT BETTER

The thirst-quenching embrace of a cold white wine on a hot day, the mellowness of a good port after dinner— these are near perfect sensory experiences. Link them with good friends, lovers, and favorite places and they capture life's truly satisfying moments. Alcohol enhances our lives.

But alcohol is a drug, pure and simple, and it is foolish not to be aware of its dangers. It affects our bodies and brains, our judgment, coordination, and perception. The amount of alcohol that brings on these impairments is entirely individual, depending on size and weight, metabolism and age, even on the variables of a single day.

The greater tragedy is that most traffic fatalities are not confined to the drinker. Drunk drivers are involved in nearly half of all American traffic fatalities and the innocent are often the victims. Over 20,000 people are killed in the United States each year because of drunk driving-related accidents. Awareness and responsibility are the only factors that will make a difference.

Enter law enforcement. The laws vary from state to state, but police are working hard to get drunk drivers off the road. Their primary weapon is the Breathalyzer, which can count your BAC, blood alcohol content—the percentage of alcohol in your blood. A BAC percentage as low as .05 has been found to increase the normal risk of accident by two to three times. So while you may not feel that your reflexes or judgment are impaired, if you are drinking you should not be driving. Period.

In most states a .10 BAC is considered evidence of driving under the influence of alcohol (DWI). In some states, the level is .08. The penalties range from a suspension of your driver's license for as little as a few days up to a year. Convictions include fines ranging from $100 to $500 and brief imprisonment—for the first offense. Punishment increases with repeated offenses. The BAC and the penalties are changing all the time, so check the laws of your state.

"Responsible drinking" is not an oxymoron. Moderation is the key to most pleasures. It is our responsibility as hosts, friends, and even citizens to keep people from driving drunk. In many states, it is our *legal* responsibility to do so.

To drink in moderation is not to have less fun, but to savor the drink we do have. We raise our glasses for so many joyous and solemn occasions—to the bride and groom, to the job well done, to the friend we have lost, and to the pure pleasure of the drink itself.

EVERYTHING

GLOSSARY

BOTTLED BY ADAMS MEDIA

NET CONTENTS: EIGHTEEN PAGES

PRODUCT OF USA

AC/AOC: An abbreviation for apellation d'origine contrôlée; the set of French wine laws that has established winemaking standards for quality French wines. AC is the top level of quality; VDQS is a set of laws with slightly lower standards; vin de pays is the lowest set of standards.

ACETIC: Vinegary taste or smell that develops when a wine is overexposed to air and acquires a trace (or more) of acetic acid.

ACID: One of the taste components of wine. Acidic wine is sometimes described as sour or tart. The taste buds for sensing acidity are found on the sides of the tongue and mouth.

ACIDITY: All wines naturally contain acids that should be in proper balance with fruit and other components. Sufficient acidity gives wine liveliness and crispness, is critical for wines to age, and gives wine thirst-quenching qualities.

AERATING: Letting wine breathe. Aeration occurs upon opening a bottle, by exposing wine to air that can help it develop and mellow, especially red wine.

AFTERTASTE: The aroma and taste that linger at the back of the throat and nose after the wine has been swallowed.

ALCOHOLIC FERMENTATION: Natural, chemical process that turns the sugars of grapes, and any added sugars, into alcohol through the action of yeast. The better sparkling wines undergo a second fermentation in the bottle. This happens because developing bubbles are trapped when the carbon dioxide produced during the fermentation process has nowhere to go.

ALOXE-CORTON (Ah-LOHSS Cor-TAWN): A village in the Côte d'Or in Burgundy, France.

ALSACE: Major wine range in France, noted for its white wines. Alsace borders Germany.

AMONTILLADO: A style of Sherry, amber in color and fairly dry.

APÉRITIF: A before-dinner drink. In theory, it stimulates the appetite (and conversation).

APPELLATION: A specific geographic area. For instance, a California wine may be labeled as California or by a progressively more specific area, if applicable—Napa Valley, Napa Valley–Stag's Leap District, or even a single vineyard. (*See* A.V.A.)

AROMA: The smell of a wine. Aroma seems to generate a surprising number of adjectives among wine people discussing a beverage made from grape juice.

ASTRINGENCY: A lip-puckering sensation caused by sharp acidity and tannin. A wine's astringent quality often diminishes as the wine ages.

ATTACK: The first impression a wine makes on the palate.

AUSLESE: German white wines made from very ripe grape bunches. These wines tend to be sweet.

AUSTERE: Wine that has very little fruity flavor and high acidity. Some very good wines—French Chablis and Italian Gavi—may be described as austere.

A.V.A.: An abbreviation for the American Viticultural Area. A.V.A.'s are officially recognized names that are used to indicate the area from which a wine comes. (*See* APPELLATION.)

BACO NOIR: A French hybrid grape variety resulting from a cross between a European variety and a domesticated native American variety. Popular in Canada, Baco Noir is very hardy, capable of withstanding very cold winters.

BALANCE: Harmony among the wine's components—fruit, acidity, tannins, alcohol.

BARBARESCO (bar-bar-ESS-coh): A full-bodied DOCG red wine from Piedmont, Italy, made from the Nebbiolo grape. This type of wine can be a great one. Barolo and Barbaresco are the top two Nebbiolo-based wines from Piedmont, Italy.

BARBERA (bar-BEAR-ah): A red grape grown in the Piedmont region. Wines from this grape are rarely exported to North America. Growing in popularity, these wines are good, cheap pizza wines. Barbera was once widely planted in California, but many of the vines have been pulled up and replaced by more popular grapes. Barbera grapes are often part of the mix in California red jug wines.

BAROLO (bar-OH-lo): A full-bodied DOCG red wine from Piedmont, Italy, made from the Nebbiolo grape. Barolo and Barbaresco are the top two Nebbiolo-based wines from Piedmont, Italy.

BEAUJOLAIS (bo-zho-LAY): A light, fruity red Burgundy wine from the region of Beaujolais, France, made from the Gamay grape.

BEAUJOLAIS NOUVEAU (bo-zho-LAY new-VOH): The "new" Beaujolais that comes out the third week of November.

BIG: Powerful in aroma and flavor; full-bodied wine. Such wines are also said to be chewy.

BLACK MUSCAT: A wine grape used to make funky, raisiny, dark red wine. These wines are usually somewhat sweet.

BODY: The weight and texture of a wine. Glycerine is the component of wine most responsible for body.

BORDEAUX: The most important wine region in France, if not the world. The reds from this region are usually blends of Cabernet Sauvignon, Cabernet Franc and Merlot. White wines are primarily blends of Sauvignon Blanc and Semillon.

BOTRYTIS CINEREA: An affliction that occurs in white wines. It helps make them into dessert wines by concentrating juices and sugars in rotting grapes that have lost some of their water. Also known as "noble rot."

BOTTLE AGING: Process of aging a wine in the bottle to help refine its flavors.

BOTTLE FERMENTED: While *méthode champenoise* sparkling wines could be called "bottle fermented," this term is only used to pass off transfer-method sparkling wine as being something special. The term "naturally fermented in the bottle" is also used—for which "the bottle" doesn't mean "this bottle." *Méthode champenoise* is the way superior sparkling wines are made.

BOUQUET: The collection of different aromas from a wine is called its bouquet. It is also called its "nose."

BOURGOGNE: The French name for what we call Burgundy, the famous wine region of France, known for its Pinot Noir and Chardonnay.

BREATHE: Exposing wine to air to allow it complete its evolution before drinking. The wine drinker's term for "aerating."

BRILLIANT: Describes a wine that has a bright, clean appearance, with luminous reflections. To impress your friends, hold your glass up to the light and say, "Brilliant," without smiling.

BRIX: Term used to measure the sugar content of grapes prior to harvest.

BRUT: Term for dry Champagne or sparkling wine. In the Champagne region of France, this term implies added sugar, up to 1.5 percent by volume.

BULK METHOD: (*See* CHARMAT METHOD.)

BURGUNDY: The anglicized name of Bourgogne, a major wine region of France. This region is noted for its Chardonnays and Pinot Noirs. It is also a generic name for some red jug wines made in the United States.

BUTTERY: An adjective used to describe wines with a lot of flavor and a smooth texture, referencing the oiliness and flavor of butter. This term more often refers to oak-aged white wines than reds; many Chardonnays and white Burgundies are said to have buttery aromas and flavors. "Almondy" is another adjective that is often used in the same sentence as buttery. The malolactic fermentation is largely responsible for this favor.

BYOB: Bring your own bottle. This term may be used by a restaurant that does not have a liquor license.

CAB: Nickname for Cabernet Sauvignon.

CABERNET: Longer nickname for Cabernet Sauvignon.

CABERNET FRANC: Red-wine grape used primarily as a blending grape. It is popular in France, where it is blended with Cabernet Sauvignon. Château Cheval Blanc, considered by many to be the finest wine from the Saint-Emilion region of France, is 66 percent Cabernet Franc and 34 percent Merlot.

CABERNET SAUVIGNON: The most noble of red-wine grapes. Cabernet Sauvignon makes big, complex, and powerful red wines, the greatest of which are very expensive.

CACHET VALUE: The pleasure you get from drinking a trendy or famous wine. Restaurants experience cachet value by having such wines on their menus. The quality aspect of the wine is not part of its cachet value. Dom Pérignon Champagne has a lot of cachet value in many social circles. Cachet value may be defined as the pleasure you get from drinking a wine when you know what it is *minus* the pleasure you would get if you drank it without knowing what it is.

CARAMELY: Used to describe wines, usually white, that have been aged for a long time and have a rich, burnt-sugar flavor. Oak also contributes to this flavor.

CARBONATED WINE: Sparkling wines of inferior quality that have been injected with carbon dioxide, like soda.

CARBONIC MACERATION: Special technique for fermenting young red wines to make them drinkable. Widely used for Beaujolais, this process involves crushing the grapes in a carbon dioxide environment, thus preventing oxidation.

CASK: A wooden cask is used to age wine. Casks are bigger than barrels.

CAVA: Spanish sparkling wine made using the Champagne method, undergoing its second fermentation in the same bottle in which it's sold.

CHABLIS (shah-BLEE): Chardonnay-based, somewhat austere white wine from the Chablis district of France.

CHAMPAGNE: A major region of France known for its sparkling wines of the same name. In most countries (but not the United States) this word is not allowed to appear on any bottle of sparkling wine not made in Champagne, France. The Champagne method, or *méthode champenoise*, was invented in this region.

CHAMPAGNE METHOD: English for *méthode champenoise*, this is the labor-intensive process by which carbonation is added to still wine. This is the superior way to make sparkling wine.

CHAPTALIZATION: The adding of sugar to wine in order to achieve the right alcohol level. Wine grapes grown in cooler climates often don't achieve enough ripeness, thus they lack sufficient sugars to be converted into alcohol.

CHARACTER: The combination of a wine's features that make it distinguishable from other wines. It is a term usually used as a compliment.

CHARDONNAY: The most popular of all white-wine grapes, and the primary white grape of France's Burgundy region.

CHARMAT METHOD: An inexpensive process for producing huge amounts of sparkling wine. It is also called the "bulk method." Unlike the Champagne method, the second fermentation takes place in a vat, and the resulting product is filtered under pressure into bottles. Serving charmat-method sparkling wines is an excellent way to avoid impressing people.

CHÂTEAU: A piece of land. For instance, Château Latour is a specific plot of vines in Pauillac, France. This term means the same thing as "domaine." "Domaine" is more frequently used in Burgundy, and "château" is more frequently used in Bordeaux.

CHÂTEAUNEUF-DU-PAPE (shah-toe-NUFF doo PAHP): The name comes from the period of the Babylonian captivity (1300's) when French popes summered in the "new castle" near Avignon. It is a district in the southern Rhône region of France where quality red wine is produced. These wines may be made from up to thirteen different grapes, but Syrah and Grenache are the primary two.

CHEWY: A term used to describe red wines with unusual thickness of texture or tannins.

CHIANTI (K'YAHN-tee): A famous red wine made in the Tuscany region of Italy from primarily Sangiovese grapes.

CHIANTI CLASSICO: The core subdistrict of Chianti in Tuscany. There are other subdistricts, the best known of which is Ruffina.

CINSAULT: A minor red-wine grape, often used as a blending grape in the Rhône region of France.

CLARET: Medium-light red wine. In Britain, "claret" is also used to mean red wines from Bordeaux.

CLOSED: Young, undeveloped red wines that do not yet reveal their positive qualities and are sometimes harsh. Breathing can help, but oftentimes the wine is ruined by being opened, and nothing can really help.

COMPLEX: A wine with a lot of different flavor and aroma components. Complexity is good.

COOKED: Burnt-fruit flavors resembling raisin. This quality is often found in wines from very hot growing regions.

CORK: Two definitions: (1) the cork that is used to seal the bottle, or (2) an unpleasant smell and/or taste given to a wine by a bad cork (also known as "corked" or "corky").

CORKAGE FEE: If you go to a restaurant that serves wine but allows you to bring your own special wine, the restaurant will often charge an additional fee for bringing your own. This fee is called the corkage fee. It covers having the staff uncork and serve you your wine in the restaurant's wine glasses, which will be cleaned later by restaurant personnel. It also covers some or all of the profits not made on the wine you might have bought had you not brought your own.

CÔTE: A French word for slope, as in the slopes of a river valley. Many vineyards in France are on slopes.

CÔTE D'OR (coat dor): Literally means "golden slope." A French region that includes the most important Burgundy vineyards.

COUNTRY WINES: France, Italy, and Germany, whose top-quality wines are tightly regulated by their countries' wine laws, also produce light, simple, and inexpensive "country wines." These are known as *vin de pays* in France, *vino da tavola* in Italy, and *Tafelwein* in Germany.

COUPAGE: The adding of one wine to another to improve or enhance its qualities.

CRISP: Fresh, brisk character, usually associated with the acidity of white wine.

CRU: French for growth. In French usage the word means a vineyard of high quality, usually considered worthy of independent recognition under the laws of classification. An officially classified vineyard is *cru classé*.

DECANTING: Pouring a mature wine from its bottle into another bottle or container. This allows the wine to breathe. It is also the best way to separate wine from its sediment.

DELICATE: A wine that is light in texture with subtle flavors. Such wines are easily overwhelmed by powerfully flavored foods.

DEMI-SEC: A term used to indicate moderately sweet to medium-sweet sparkling wines. It is also used to indicate off-dry versions of Vouvray.

DEVELOPED: Wine that has undergone positive changes during its years of aging. Wines can also develop after a bottle has been opened.

DISTINCTIVE: Elegant, refined character that sets the wine apart.

DOCG/DOC: The abbreviations of *denominazione di origine controllata (e* *garantita*). Of the three tiers of government-regulated Italian wines, DOCG wines are the top rated, and DOC wines make up the second tier. VdT, *vino da tavola*, is the lowest rating for wines shipped abroad.

DOMAINE: A specific plot of land. This term means the same thing as "château." "Domaine" is more frequently used in Burgundy, and "château" is more frequently used in Bordeaux.

DOUX: The sweetest of Champagnes.

DRY: Opposite of sweet. By definition, this means the wine has little or no residual sugar left following the fermentation process or processes.

DULL: Lacking flavor and/or enough acidity. Sometimes wines go through a dull phase in their evolution process and may emerge as a good or even great wine.

DUMB: A wine that doesn't reveal its flavors and aromas. This is because the wine is too young or being served too cold.

EARTHY: Smell or flavor reminiscent of earth. European wines are more apt to be earthy than wines from other continents.

ELEGANT: A wine with flavor, quality, and style, and that isn't heavy, tannic, or acidic. A balance of components is also implied.

EXTRA DRY: Term used on sparkling-wine labels to indicate a wine that is fairly dry, but not as dry as brut.

FAT: Full-bodied, low-acid-flavored wines are said to be fat.

FERMENTATION: Process in which yeast turns sugar into alcohol. Heat and carbon dioxide are by-products of this process.

FIGHTING VARIETAL: The cheapest class of varietal wines. This is a slang term.

FILTERING: Elimination of the deposits formed in a sparkling wine during its second fermentation in the bottle.

FINISH: Aftertaste or final impression a wine gives as it leaves your mouth for your stomach or bucket (if you are at a serious wine tasting). Long is good; short is bad.

FINO: A dry, pale style of Sherry.

FIREPLACE WINE: A wine that is as good, if not better, without food than with food. Low acidity, high glycerine content, residual sweetness, moderate-to-low tannin, and fruitiness are characteristics that make for good fireplace wine.

FIRM: This is a serious wine term. It means the elements of a wine's structure are tightly wound together, and also implies the wine has quite a bit of flavor. This is not a good word to bluff wine snobs with. "Firm tannins" might indicate a red wine that is well made and has a bright future.

FLESHY: A wine with a lot of big, ripe fruitiness. These wines are thick on the palate. Glycerine can also give a fleshy impression in the mouth.

FLINTY: A dry, mineral-like flavor component that comes from soils containing a lot of limestone. It is an interesting flavor that is a big selling point for French white wines.

FLOR: A layer of mold that forms in some, but not all barrels, during the Sherry-making process. This development is a good thing. Unfortunately, man hasn't figured out how to make it happen; its formation is still a secret of nature.

FLORAL: A term used to describe the floral scents found in some wines. Riesling is often described as floral.

FLOWERY: See FLORAL.

FLUTE: Special glass for sparkling wines. It's tall and skinny, mainly because this is the best shape to keep the carbon dioxide bubbles from vanishing too quickly.

FORTIFIED WINE: Wines with alcohol added. Port and Sherry are the best-known examples of fortified wines. Madeira and Marsala are the major types.

FORWARD: A term that has two meanings: (1) a wine that develops ahead of similar wines from the same vintage, and (2) a wine that has fruit as the flagship of its components.

FREE RUN: Fermented grape juice obtained not by pressing grapes but rather by letting the juice run freely, thus avoiding the extraction of harsh tannins.

FRESH: A white or rosé wine with a good balance between alcohol and acidity. May also be applied to young red wine.

FRUIT: One of the taste components of wine. The interaction of alcohol and organic acids results in the development of fruit esters. These compounds imitate the flavors and aromas of other fruits.

FRUITY: Refers to prominent fruit flavors and aromas in a wine. Blackberries are often referenced in the aromas of Cabernet Sauvignon and Zinfandel wines. Banana aromas are found in many Australian Chardonnays.

FULL-BODIED: A lot of flavor, alcohol, and thickness.

FUMÉ BLANC: A style of Sauvignon Blanc developed in California by Robert Mondavi with the French Pouilly Fumé in mind—dry, smoky, and rich.

GAMAY: The red-grape variety used to make Beaujolais. Not grown very much in any other region of the world.

GEWÜRZTRAMINER (geh-VURZ-tra-MEANER): In German, literally, "spicy Traminer." Grape used for white wines in Alsace, France; Germany; and California.

GLYCERINE: A complex alcohol that gives wine its thickness. This is very desirable, up to a point.

GRAND CRU: Literally means "great growth." In France's rating system of Burgundy, this is the top designation of vineyard.

GRAN RESERVA: Name given to Spanish wines that have been aged for as long as ten years in oak barrels prior to bottling.

GREEN: Term used to describe a young wine that hasn't developed enough to balance out its acidity.

GRENACHE: A workhorse grape of the southern Rhône. Known as Garnacha in Spain.

GRIP: A function of tannin. The slightly bitter and dry taste of moderate tannin seems to give the other flavors "traction" in the mouth. Young reds with a lot of tannin may have too much grip.

HALBTROCKEN: German for "half-dry." This term is sometimes found on German wine bottles.

HARD: A red wine with tannin showing more than its fruit is often said to be hard. A hard wine may soften with time.

HARMONIOUS: Wines whose elements—fruit, alcohol, acidity, and tannin—are not totally balanced but appear to blend seamlessly.

HARSH: Rough, biting character from excessive tannin and/or acid. Excessive tannin or acid may be perceived due to a lack of fruit.

HEADY: Strong, aromatic wine with a high concentration of alcohol and other components.

HERBACEOUS: Wines with herbal undertones. This is a serious wine term, and not a good one to bluff with among wine people. Mint, sage, and eucalyptus are three herbs often detected in wine.

HONEST: A relatively flawless but simple wine. It is implied that the wine sells for a fair price.

HYBRID: A cross of two grape varieties of different species. For instance, Baco Noir is a cross of a *vitis vinifera* variety and a *vitis riparia* variety.

JEREZ: The town on the coast of Spain after which Sherry is named.

JOHNSON, HUGH: One of the major wine authorities. The wine world has a few Siskels and Eberts, H. J. is one of them.

JUG WINE: Inexpensive wine sold in large containers (bottle or bag).

LANGUEDOC: A source of good, inexpensive wine (mostly red), located on the Mediterranean coast of France.

LEES: Dead yeast left by the wine after its first fermentation. Sometimes a bottle will brag that the wine was allowed to age on its lees before it was clarified and bottled.

LEGS: Traces of oiliness left in the glass by a wine with at least average amounts of alcohol, sugar, and glycerine. The more alcohol, sugar, and glycerine, the bigger the legs. Also known as tears.

LENGTH: A good wine displays its progression of flavors across the palette as you sip it. If this display seems to take a long time, the wine is said to have length.

LIGHT: Refers to a wine that is light in alcohol and/or to its texture and weight in the mouth. Sometimes lightness is desired, and sometimes it is considered a weakness; it depends on the wine. Great Pinot Noirs from Burgundy are often light; great California Cabernet Sauvignons are never light.

LIVELY: When a wine is lively, it has a clean aroma and fresh acidity. This term is also used for sparkling wines that have a good amount of carbonation without being too carbonated.

LOIRE VALLEY: One of the major regions of France, and the source of Muscadet, Vouvray, Rosé d'Anjou, Sancerre, and Pouilly Fumé.

MACERATION: The soaking, for a greater or lesser period, of the grape skins in the must that is fermenting.

MADEIRA: An island under Portuguese rule off the coast of Africa, on which the fortified wine with the same name is produced. This fortified wine is usually used in cooking, but not always.

MAGNUM: A bottle size of 1500 ml rather than the normal 750 ml.

MALBEC: A minor red grape, most often used for blending with more popular red grapes like Cabernet Sauvignon.

MALOLACTIC FERMENTATION: The second fermentation of some wines through bacterial action, whereby the malic acid is converted into lactic acid and the acidity becomes milder.

MANZANILLA: A very dry Sherry style said to have a slightly salty tang acquired during its maturation close to the sea.

MARSALA: A fortified wine produced from local white grapes on the island of Sicily. Available in dry and sweet styles, Marsala is a common ingredient in Italian cooking. Marsala is named after the Sicilian city of Marsala.

MATURE: Fully developed, ready-to-drink wine. Ideally, wines are aged until they mature. Different wines need varying amounts of time to mature. Many great estate wines are crafted to require a decade or more to mature.

MEATY: A wine with a chewy, fleshy fruit; sturdy and firm in structure. This is a wine adjective applied to big red wines such as Cabernet Sauvignon and Zinfandel.

MÉDOC: Bordeaux's largest district, home of the communes of Saint-Julien, Saint-Estéphe, Margaux, and Pauillac.

MELLOW: A wine adjective describing a low-acid wine that is smooth and soft, rather rough around the edges. Well-made Merlot tends to be a mellow red wine.

MERITAGE: A term coined by California wine producers to indicate a high-quality wine blended from premium varieties. Because U.S. law requires 75 percent or more of a single grape variety to qualify for varietal labeling, the term "Meritage" was invented to denote a quality wine that doesn't qualify for a varietal designation.

MERLOT: A red-wine grape currently in vogue. Merlot wines tend to be easy-drinking reds and are a big hit with people recently converted to drinking red wine for its health benefits.

MÉTHODE CHAMPENOISE: This translates to the "Champagne Method." The best sparkling wines undergo their second fermentation in the same bottle in which the wine is sold. This laborious process is the *méthode champenoise*.

MINTY: A desirable aroma in some wines, particularly Cabernet Sauvignon.

MISE EN BOUTEILLE AU CHATEAU: This French term translates to "bottled at the estate." This often denotes high quality, as the winemaker has a personal relationship to the grapes he or she uses in crafting a wine.

MOSEL-SAAR-RUWER: A major wine region in Germany that lies along the connected rivers of these names.

MOURVEDRE: A red blending grape from the southern Rhône area.

MUSCAT: A type of grape that yields a raisiny fruit-tasting wine. Muscat wines are almost always sweet. Black Muscat makes wines that are dark purple, whereas orange Muscat makes bronze-colored wines.

MUST: The combination of crushed grapes, skins, and pips from which red wine is drawn.

NAPA VALLEY: A highly regarded wine region in California where the top U.S. wines are produced. Only 5 percent of California wines come from Napa.

NEBBIOLO: A red grape grown primarily in the Piedmont region of Italy. This is an important red-wine grape, capable of producing great red wines. Unlike Cabernet Sauvignon, which is found on many continents, Nebbiolo is rarely found outside of Italy.

NOBLE GRAPES: Grapes that produce the world's finest wines: Cabernet Sauvignon, Pinot Noir, Merlot, Syrah, Nebbiolo, and Sangiovese are the noble red grapes. Chardonnay, Sauvignon Blanc, and Riesling are the noble white grapes. The exact set of grapes considered to be "noble" is a moving target, varying from person to person.

NOBLE ROT: This is the nickname for *botrytis cinerea*, a mold that affects certain white grapes and helps make them suitable for dessert wines by concentrating juices and sugars.

NONVINTAGE: A wine made from grapes from more than one harvest.

NOSE: The smell of the wine; it may have a "good nose" or an "off nose." It could also have a big nose.

NOUVEAU: French for "new," this term refers to young wine meant for immediate drinking, as in Beaujolais Nouveau, which may have been made only weeks ago.

NUTTY: Nutlike aromas and flavors that develop in certain wines such as Sherries or old white wines.

OAK: Smell and taste produced in a wine that's been aged in oak barrels. Oak is a very popular tool of the winemaker, and sometimes it is overused. Oak flavor is occasionally added via oak chips thrown into the vat. It adds a vanilla flavor to wine.

OENOLOGY: The study of wine.

OENOPHILE: One who loves, appreciates, and studies wine.

OFF-DRY: Wine with noticeable residual sugar, usually above 1 percent by volume.

OLOROSO: A dark Sherry that may be sweet or dry. The sweet versions are usually called "cream" or "brown" Sherry.

OXIDATION: An alteration wines undergo after exposure to oxygen. Some exposure to oxygen is good for the wine and its flavors. Eventually, however, oxygen helps turn wine into vinegar.

PALE: Used to describe wines with less color than similar-styled wines.

PALE DRY: The style in which Fino Sherry is made.

PALOMINO: The primary white grape used to make Sherry.

PARKER, ROBERT: One of the major wine authorities. The wine world has a few Siskels and Eberts; R. P. is one of them.

PEPPERY: Red wine that has a hint of black pepper flavor, such as Zinfandel, is said to be peppery.

PETITE SIRAH: Another name for the mystery grape, perhaps the Duriff grape of France that was mistakenly brought to the United States (instead of the Syrah grape).

PHYLLOXERA: A vine louse that kills grape vines.

PIEDMONT: The great red-wine region of northern Italy, famous for its Nebbiolo wines. Also denoted as "Piemonte" on wine labels.

PINOTAGE: Unique to South Africa, this grape is a cross between the Pinot Noir and Cinsault grapes.

PINOT BLANC: A reliable white-wine grape, known as Pinot Blanco in Italy. This grape is used to make simple and clean wines in Italy, Alsace, and California.

PINOT GRIGIO: White-wine grape, also known as Pinot Gris. This grape produces good white wine in Italy, Alsace, and Oregon.

PINOT NOIR: The noble red grape of Burgundy and the West Coast of the United States. This grape isn't easy to grow, but it produces wonderful light- and medium-bodied wines that go well with food.

PIPS: Grape seeds; two per grape. Pips are a source of tannin in red wine.

PORT: Fortified red wine from Portugal, where it is known as Porto. This class of wine is available in a variety of styles, including Ruby, Tawny, and Vintage.

POUILLY-FUISSÉ: (POO-yee FWEE-say) A white wine with a good reputation, made from Chardonnay grapes in the commune of Fuissé (or one of four other neighboring communes) in the Mâcon subregion of Burgundy.

PREMIER CRU: Literally meaning "first growth," this is the highest level of quality in Médoc, Bordeaux, but it is the second-highest level behind *grand cru* in Burgundy.

PRICKLE: Presence of tiny natural bubbles in some young wines.

PROVENCE: A minor wine-producing region of France, often lumped together with the neighboring Rhône region. Provence is best known for high-quality, dry rosé wines.

PUNT: The mysterious indentation in the bottom of many wine bottles. This feature was originally intended to collect sediment before effective clarification techniques came into widespread use.

QUALITÄTSWEIN BESTIMMTER ANBAUGEBIETE (QbA): The middle quality of German wine. (*See* QUALITÄTSWEIN MIT PRÄDIKAT.)

QUALITÄTSWEIN MIT PRÄDIKAT (QmP): The highest quality level of German wines. The "prädikats" are the designation of sugar content at harvest. From driest to sweetest they are Kabinett, Spätlese, Auslese, Beerenauslese, and Trockenbeerenauslese. QmP wines don't have any sugar added to them. The second level of wine is the QbA wines. *Tafelwein*, rarely exported to the United States, is the lowest level.

RAISINY: Smells reminiscent of raisin, found in wines made from very ripe or overripe grapes. Australian red wines are often raisiny. Muscat wines are inherently raisiny, irrespective of the ripeness of the harvested Muscat grapes.

REGION: A large subdivision of a wine-producing country. For instance, France has six major regions: Bordeaux, Burgundy, Rhône, Loire, Champagne, and Alsace.

RESERVA: This word on a Spanish wine label indicates that the wine has been aged in a barrel and/or a bottle longer than regular wines from the same region. *Riserva* with an "i" is the Italian equivalent.

RESERVE: This term has no legal definition in the United States. Reserve wines are implied to be aged longer than and superior to their contemporaries.

RHÔNE VALLEY: Region in France noted for big, strong reds and some interesting white wines.

RICH: An adjective used to describe a wine that has a lot of flavor, body, and aroma.

RIESLING: A white-wine grape that is more popular in Europe than North America. This grape is every bit as noble as the Chardonnay grape. The best of these wines come from Germany and Alsace, France.

RIOJA: A wine region in northern Spain where the local Tempranillo grape is often blended with a little Garnacha to make red wines bearing the name Rioja. Some white Rioja is also produced.

ROBUST: Full-bodied, full-flavored, and high in alcohol.

ROSÉ: Pink-colored wine, usually made from red-wine grapes fermented with minimal contact with grape skins, which produces a lighter color. Some rosés are made from mixing a small amount of red wine with white. White Zinfandel is a rosé made from the red Zinfandel grape.

ROSE D'ANJOU: A rosé wine from the Loire Valley in France, made from Cabernet Franc, Cabernet Sauvignon, and other red grapes.

ROUGH: Describes a wine with harsh edges and that is biting and sometimes unpleasant. Rough wines are sometimes a good match with garlic.

ROUND: Describes a wine with balance and harmony among its various components: fruitiness, acidity, alcohol, tannin, glycerine, and sweetness

SAINT-EMILION: A major subregion of Bordeaux, France.

SANGIOVESE: A red-wine grape grown primarily in Italy. It is the primary grape in Chianti.

SANGRIA: A wine drink that is served chilled. It is made from wine and fruit.

SAUTERNES: An important subregion of Bordeaux, France, famous for dessert wines bearing the name Sauternes.

SAUVIGNON BLANC: Generally a notch below Riesling and Chardonnay in terms of the high end of the wine spectrum, this white grape makes some excellent food wines. Serve with salmon if you want to become a Sauvignon Blanc convert.

SCREWPULL: The most effective and easy-to-use cork extractor available. (*See* corkscrews section in Chapter 9.)

SEC: Literally means "dry." However, in terms of Champagne it actually means noticeably sweet.

SECOND-LABEL WINE: Many top producers in France and California maintain the quality of their flagship wines by using slightly lesser grapes in their notch below top wines, known as second-label wines. In bad years, these producers may not make their first-label wines.

SEDIMENT: The stuff found at the bottom of a bottle of red wine, which comes from the wine itself.

SEMILLON: A white-wine grape often used in France as a blending grape with Sauvignon Blanc, and in Australia with Chardonnay. It is also used quite a bit for making dessert wines.

SHARP: A wine with high acidity level is said to be sharp. Sharp wines can "cut through" rich, creamy sauces.

SHERRY: A type of fortified wine from Spain. Sherries can be sweet or not, heavy or light in body, and dark or light in color.

SHIRAZ: The Iranian town where the red-wine grape Syrah supposedly originated. Australia and South Africa refer to the Syrah as Shiraz. This grape makes some interesting and affordable red wines.

SHORT: Refers to when the finish, or aftertaste, ends abruptly.

SILKY: An adjective describing wines with a smooth texture and finish. Glycerine is the component most closely related to silkiness. "Silky" is not very different from "velvety."

SIMPLE: Opposite of complex. Straightforward, inexpensive wines are often referred to as being simple. It is not a negative term when describing a $7 bottle of wine, but it's an insult to a $70 bottle for sure.

SMOKY: An aroma sometimes associated with Sauvignon Blanc and Pinot Noir.

SMOOTH: Describes a wine somewhat rich in glycerine and usually light in tannin and acidity, which feels good in the mouth.

SOAVE: The name of a white-wine-producing region of Italy.

SOFT: May refer to soft, gentle fruit in delicate wines, or to a lack of acidity in wines without proper structure. It is used on a label occasionally to indicate a low alcohol content.

SOLERA: System of mixing wines that consists of improving young wine with the addition of older wine (and vice versa). It is the aging system used for the Sherry wines of Jerez. *Solera* wines are bottled without a vintage year, because these are wines from multiple years.

SOMMELIER: A restaurant employee who purchases wine for the restaurant and assists customers wishing to order wine. A broad knowledge of matching food and wine is essential for this job.

SONOMA VALLEY: Much larger than Napa, this region produces wines generally a notch below Napa's best. However, the quality gap is narrowing.

SPANNA: Local name in northern Italy for Nebbiolo grapes.

SPARKLING WINE: Wines with bubbles created by trapped carbon dioxide gas, induced by a second, enclosed fermentation.

SPICY: Having the character or aroma of spices such as clove, mint, cinnamon, or pepper. Gewürztraminer and Zinfandel are noted for their spiciness.

SPUMANTE: Inexpensive, sweet sparkling wine from Italy.

STEELY: Firmly structured; taut balance tending toward high acidity.

STEMMY: Indicates a harsh, green, tannic flavor.

STRAW: Used to describe a white wine with a color like straw.

STRAWBERRY: A fruity aroma that appears in certain red or rosé wines and some Ports.

STRUCTURE: The framework of the wine, made up of its acid, alcohol, and tannin content. Great wines must have a good underlying structure to support the other flavor components such as fruitiness.

SULFITES: Both naturally occurring and added to wines, they are used as a defense against oxidation and other woes.

SUPER-TUSCAN: Usually a blend of grapes that does not conform to Italian wine law, but many such wines are of superior quality. Cabernet Sauvignon and Sangiovese are usually the components of a super-tuscan.

SWEET: Usually indicates the presence of residual sugar, retained when grape sugar is not completely converted to alcohol. Even dry wines, however, may have an aroma of sweetness, the combination of intense fruit or ripeness. It is considered a flaw if not properly balanced with acidity.

SYLVANER: A workhorse white grape of Germany, often blended with Riesling. It is often found in QbA wine such as Liebfraumilch.

SYRAH: Known as Shiraz in Australia and South Africa, this red grape is used to make some great wines and some great-value wines. The northern Rhône of France is a hotbed for good Syrah.

TANNIN: A natural component found to varying degrees in the skins, seeds, and stems of grapes. It is most prominent in red wines, where it creates a dry, puckering sensation in young reds. Tannin mellows with aging and is a major component in the structure of red wines.

TART: A sharp taste that comes from a wine's natural acidity. Not necessarily a negative term.

TARTARIC ACID: The predominant wine acid that occurs naturally in grapes.

TEARS: Traces of oiliness left in the glass by a wine with at least average amounts of alcohol, sugar, and glycerine. The more alcohol, sugar, and glycerine, the bigger the tears. Also known as legs.

TEMPRANILLO: The major red grape of Spain's Rioja wines, this grape is not widely cultivated elsewhere.

TERROIR: A French word that refers to the influence of soil and climate, rather than grape variety, on winemaking.

THIN: A negative term for a wine (usually red) with insufficient body, flavor, and/or color.

TINTO: This is Spanish for red wine.

TIRED: A wine that is past its peak of flavor development. Such a wine should have been opened at an earlier time.

TOBACCO: An aroma that is noticeable in some mature wines. This is considered to be a good thing, especially in Cabernet Sauvignon.

TROCKEN: German for "dry," this is a word to look for on German wine labels. Germany is fighting its reputation for sweet wines with this term.

TUSCANY: One of the major wine regions of Italy, it is the home of Chianti and Brunello di Montalcino.

UNCTUOUS: An adjective to describe a thick, rich, and glycerine-laden wine with an equally rich aroma.

VANILLA: A spicy aroma and flavor imparted to a wine by oak-aging.

VARIETAL: Wine that is made from one dominant grape variety and is labeled as such is a varietal wine.

VARIETAL CORRECTNESS: A wine that exhibits the signature characteristics of the grape variety with which it is labeled is considered to be varietally correct. Many cheaper varietals are not varietally correct, although they might taste good.

VARIETY: Type of grape.

VELVETY: A wine that is smooth and silky in texture is often called velvety. This is a signature characteristic of Merlot. Low acid, low tannin, and generous glycerine make for a velvety wine.

VIN: French for "wine."

VINEGAR: When a wine begins to go bad from exposure to oxygen, it turns to vinegar. Some wines have a natural vinegary quality to them—not high praise.

VINIFICATION: The process of winemaking from harvest to bottling is called vinification.

VINO: Spanish and Italian for "wine."

VINTAGE: The year in which the wine was harvested. This information should appear on the bottle.

VINTNER: The person who makes the wine.

VIOGNIER: A white grape that does well in the Rhône, with apricotlike fruit.

WHITE ZINFANDEL: A rosé made from the red-wine Zinfandel grape.

WINE ADVOCATE: Robert Parker's newsletter about wine, targeted toward wine enthusiasts. Reviews in this magazine have a powerful impact on the wine market. The *Wine Advocate* does not accept advertising and therefore presents itself as unbiased.

WINE SPECTATOR: A flashy magazine about wine, with many columnists, articles, and tasting notes. Although the *Wine Spectator* accepts advertising from wineries, its reviews are considered to be reliable.

WINE STEWARD: (*See* SOMMELIER.)

WOODY: A wine that has absorbed too much oak flavor from casks or barrels is described as woody. However, some wood is good, because it adds complexity to wine.

YEAST: Single-cell organisms found in the grape skin that facilitate the alcohol-fermentation process. Extra yeast is often added by the winemaker during the winemaking process.

YEASTY: A bready smell, sometimes detected in wines that have undergone secondary fermentation, such as Champagne. This can be used as either a positive or negative adjective.

ZINFANDEL: Red-wine grape that is very popular in California but that grows almost nowhere else. White Zinfandel is a rosé, made from the red-wine Zinfandel grape.

Index